An Uncommon Woman

Mrs. Lydia Smith.

An Uncommon Woman

The Life of
Lydia Hamilton Smith

MARK KELLEY

The Pennsylvania State University Press
University Park, Pennsylvania

LancasterHistory

KEYSTONE BOOKS

Keystone Books are intended to serve
the citizens of Pennsylvania. They are
accessible, well-researched explorations
into the history, culture, society, and
environment of the Keystone State as
part of the Middle Atlantic region.

Library of Congress Cataloging-in-Publication Data

Names: Kelley, Mark, 1949– author.
Title: An uncommon woman : the life of Lydia Hamilton Smith / Mark Kelley.
Other titles: Life of Lydia Hamilton Smith
Description: University Park, Pennsylvania : The Pennsylvania State University Press, [2023] |
    "A Keystone book." | Includes bibliographical references and index.
Summary: "A biography of Lydia Hamilton Smith (1813–1884), a prominent African American
    businesswoman in Lancaster, Pennsylvania, and the longtime housekeeper and life companion
    of the state's abolitionist congressman Thaddeus Stevens"—Provided by publisher.
Identifiers: LCCN 2023022640 | ISBN 9780271096759 (paperback)
Subjects: LCSH: Smith, Lydia Hamilton, 1813–1884. | Stevens, Thaddeus, 1792–1868. |
    African American women—Pennsylvania—Lancaster—Biography. | African American
    businesspeople—Pennsylvania—Lancaster—Biography. | Businesswomen—Pennsylvania—
    Lancaster—Biography. | Housekeepers—Pennsylvania—Lancaster—Biography. |
    Lancaster (Pa.)—Biography. | Lancaster (Pa.)—History—19th century. | LCGFT: Biographies.
Classification: LCC F159.L2 S655 2023 | DDC 974.8/150092 [B]—dc23/eng/20230524
LC record available at https://lccn.loc.gov/2023022640

10 9 8 7 6 5 4 3 2 1

The Pennsylvania State University Press is a member of the Association of University Presses.

It is the policy of The Pennsylvania State University Press to use acid-free paper. Publications on
uncoated stock satisfy the minimum requirements of American National Standard for Information
Sciences—Permanence of Paper for Printed Library Material, ANSI Z39.48–1992.

Frontispiece: carte de visite of Lydia Hamilton Smith, P. B. Marvin, Photographer, likely taken
before 1868. Inscription on back reads: "This is the picture of Lydia Smith, the housekeeper of
Thaddeus Stevens. It was given to me by Mrs. L. Kerfoot Eschbach, who knew her, and was also
thoroughly identified by Dr. R. M. Bolenius and Mrs. Bolenius." LancasterHistory, Lancaster,
Pennsylvania.

CONTENTS

LIST OF ILLUSTRATIONS

PREFACE

Although I grew up near Lancaster, Pennsylvania, I had never heard the name Lydia Hamilton Smith until the moment, in Steven Spielberg's 2012 film, *Lincoln*, when the camera zoomed out to show her (portrayed by acclaimed actress S. Epatha Merkerson) lying in bed beside Congressman Thaddeus Stevens of Lancaster (portrayed by actor Tommy Lee Jones). As I sat down to watch the film, I didn't know much about Stevens, either. The best efforts of my high school history teachers had managed to lodge only three Stevens-related facts in my memory: Thaddeus Stevens had a clubfoot, one of his custom-made boots was displayed at the Lancaster County Historical Society (now LancasterHistory), and the technical college in Lancaster was named after him. As I watched Spielberg's film, the zeal with which Stevens pursued the Thirteenth Amendment, to legally and once-and-for-all abolish slavery in the United States, and Lydia Hamilton Smith's joy at seeing slavery slain made me want to know more about both of them, especially her. Who was this woman Thaddeus Stevens returned home to when the battle to abolish slavery was won? This book is my attempt to answer that question.

Thaddeus Stevens has attracted considerable attention from biographers over the years. Some of those historians apparently did not see Lydia Hamilton Smith standing beside him as he fought for human rights and the equality of all people. She does not appear in their books. Others noted her presence but saw her only as a mixed-race housekeeper who served Stevens faithfully for many years. We will see, as this story unfolds, that she was much more than that. A few biographers explored the relationship between Stevens and Mrs. Smith in light of the virulent condemnations hurled by Stevens's enemies, who alleged that Stevens lived in sin with a beautiful young woman of color.

But most professional and amateur historians conclude that there simply is not enough evidence to convict or acquit Stevens and Mrs. Smith on those charges. A few think they were lovers who hid the truth of their relationship from a society that forbade, in their time and in many places long after their time, interracial unions. We'll examine the evidence available today and allow readers to answer the question for themselves. I will weigh in on the issue myself.

Because Lydia Hamilton Smith's life began while the evil institution of slavery still flourished in parts of the United States, we need to be sensitive to the manner in which we address her. Believing that the African Americans they owned were inferior to white people, slaveowners further insulted their slaves by giving them only a first name. The practice of addressing a person of color, regardless of age, only by a first name persisted throughout the country even after slavery had been outlawed in many Northern states. Thaddeus Stevens knew that, and he may have had that condescending informality in mind when Lydia Hamilton Smith came to work for him in Lancaster. He made it clear to his household and to his colleagues, friends, and neighbors that she was to be addressed as Mrs. Smith.

I must admit that addressing Lydia Hamilton Smith in a proper, respectful way posed a challenge for me in writing this book. As my research brought me closer to her, I came to see her as a friend, and I call my friends by their first names. In our more informal times, first names seem to have become the default mode of address, regardless of a person's age. But here, as a general rule, I will use "Lydia Hamilton Smith" and "Mrs. Smith." In describing her childhood years—or to ensure clarity when other Smith family members are discussed—I will use the less formal "Lydia."

One additional observation on Mrs. Smith's name. Some biographers insist that her full name, prior to her marriage, was Lydia O'Neill, O'Neill being her mother's last name. (I found no record of Mrs. O'Neill's first name.) But, as is explained in chapter 1, Lydia chose to use Hamilton as her last name. She added Smith to it after she married Jacob Smith, but the inscription on the marble memorial placed by her grave in 1884 identified her as Lydia Hamilton, widow of Jacob Smith. This book, then, celebrates the life and accomplishments of Lydia Hamilton Smith.

ACKNOWLEDGMENTS

This book owes its existence to three initial influences: Steven Spielberg's portrayal of Lydia Hamilton Smith near the close of his movie *Lincoln*; my wife, Marty's, unflagging encouragement to satisfy our curiosity about Lydia, aroused by the film, by writing a book about her; and a chance encounter, early one morning, with Thomas R. Ryan, LancasterHistory President and CEO, and Robin E. Sarratt, LancasterHistory Vice President, as they opened the gates of Shreiner-Concord Cemetery in Lancaster, Pennsylvania, the cemetery Thaddeus Stevens chose as his final resting place because it allowed people of color to be buried there. I was already haunting the research library at LancasterHistory in search of Lydia Hamilton Smith when I met them, but their enthusiastic response upon learning what I was up to inspired me to look even harder.

Over many hours at the LancasterHistory research library, I was guided, assisted, and informed by the LancasterHistory staff. I am indebted to them for their assistance: Heather S. Tennies, Director of Archival Services; Katie Fichtner, Archives Assistant; Nathan Pease, Director of Library Services; Kevin E. Shue, Genealogist; Marianne S. Heckles, Research Assistant and Coordinator of the Photographic Collections; Martha Abel, Library/ Archives Assistant; and Cindy Wischuck, Visitor Services Associate. They were all kind enough to stop and listen as I shared my latest discovery about Lydia Hamilton Smith.

The response was much the same at the Adams County (PA) Historical Society. Tracking Lydia's early life in Adams County was much more productive with the generous assistance provided by Timothy H. Smith, Research Historian, as well as Randy Miller, Andrew Dalton, Larry C. Bolin, and the late Charles H. Glatfelter. Their previous work in uncovering evidence of Lydia Hamilton Smith's life in Gettysburg, Harrisburg, Lancaster, and Washington was invaluable in this effort.

The dedicated professionals at the Lancaster County Archives patiently retrieved the Thaddeus Stevens Estate files daily, for weeks on end, giving me access to precious court documents related to Lydia Hamilton Smith. Those documents allowed me to tell important parts of the story in Mrs. Smith's own words and in the words of those closest to her in Lancaster. Many thanks to John F. Bennawit Jr., Archives and Digital Imaging

Manager; Brian Klinger, Clerical Specialist; Jennifer Eck, Imaging Technician/Archives Clerk; and Jessica Olley, Imaging Technician/Archives Clerk.

The trail of the portrait of Lydia Hamilton Smith, commissioned by Thaddeus Stevens, led to Franklin & Marshall College in Lancaster, where Shadek-Fackenthal Library Research and Visual Arts Librarian Anna Boutin-Cooper tracked down F&M's use of a possible "other" portrait of Lydia Hamilton Smith, and Michael Lear, Research and Collections Management Specialist, helped me find and copy the F&M publication in which a reproduction of the portrait appeared. Their efforts on behalf of this book are much appreciated. I am also indebted to Louise Stevenson, Professor of History and American Studies at F&M, for helping me gain access to newspaper accounts of Mrs. Smith's social activities. My search for portraits of Lydia Hamilton Smith also led me to the Frick Art Reference Library in New York, where Giana Ricci, Assistant Librarian for Public Services, scoured the files for a portrait of Lydia painted by Lancaster artist Jacob Eichholtz. We didn't find one, but the information Ms. Ricci provided was helpful.

Historian Tim Talbott of Petersburg, Virginia, put me on the trail of Isaac Smith's unusual military history through his well-researched blog, *Random Thoughts on History*. I appreciate the information and his interest in Lydia Hamilton Smith.

Historic Preservation Trust of Lancaster County (HPTLC) Executive Director Bob Price joined me in the search for a possible "other" Lydia Hamilton Smith portrait, and I thank him for that effort. Former HPTLC president, historian, and preservation consultant Randolph Harris provided important perspectives on Lydia Hamilton Smith and Thaddeus Stevens, as did Thaddeus Stevens Society President Ross Hetrick. A six-foot bronze statue of Stevens, commissioned by the society, was dedicated in Gettysburg on April 2, 2022. Leroy Hopkins, longtime professor of German at Millersville University (in Pennsylvania) and student of African American history whose roots in Lancaster go back at least to the nineteenth century, provided important guidance on details of Lydia Hamilton Smith's funeral and encouragement to tell her story. Betty Anne O'Brien, Administrative Assistant/Bulletin Editor at Historic St. Mary's Church in Lancaster, and Reverend Brian Wayne, Pastor of St. Mary's, provided important information and guidance related to Lydia's son William, as did Alberto Rodriguez, Archivist for the Catholic Diocese of Harrisburg, Pennsylvania.

I am deeply indebted to Dr. Faith Mitchell, whose close reading of the emerging manuscript provided important guidance on language and the sociocultural realities of the United States Lydia Hamilton Smith entered in the early nineteenth century. The history presented to me in my Pennsylvania school days failed to recognize, in any way, the tremendous importance of the vibrant communities that free people of color established in Pennsylvania while the state itself took halting steps toward granting freedom and equality to all of its residents.

I am deeply grateful to the folks at Penn State University Press for recognizing the importance of sharing Lydia Hamilton Smith's story with the world. I am especially indebted to these valiant members of their staff: Kendra Boileau, Assistant Director and Editor-in-Chief; Jennifer Norton, Associate Director and EDP Manager; Senior Copyeditor Laura Reed-Morrisson; former Acquisitions Editor Kathryn Bourque Yahner; Maddie Caso, Editorial Assistant; and Brendan Coyne, Sales and Marketing Director. Their commitment to telling the stories of important Pennsylvanians is unexcelled.

In transforming this project from an idea to a book, I also had the good fortune to work closely with Mike Abel, Editor-in-Chief of *The Journal of Lancaster County's Historical Society* and book designer extraordinaire. His patience and persistence, along with his many talents, kept me grounded in moments of uncertainty. His contributions were many and excellent.

Those who have worked to preserve the memory of Lydia Hamilton Smith over the years deserve recognition here. The fine historians at Lancaster's Bethel African Methodist Episcopal Church provided an introduction to activities that occupied Lydia and her sons, William and Isaac. I am indebted to them for their preservation of the past. Lancaster performer Darlene Colon, who has portrayed Lydia Hamilton Smith many times, was kind enough to share her research with me. The Lydia Hamilton Smith Society, formed by the Junior League of Lancaster to preserve history through education and provide a mentoring program to help girls develop social, business, research, and entrepreneurial skills, maintains a website that helped focus my research into Mrs. Smith's business accomplishments. Without the inspiration and assistance of those named above, this book would not have been completed. I am grateful to all of them.

Mark Kelley, PhD
Lancaster, Pennsylvania
April 20, 2023

Introduction

On a fateful night in 1901, the celebrated American lecturer Thomas Dixon left a stage production of *Uncle Tom's Cabin* in tears. Dixon was in good company. By the turn of the twentieth century, millions worldwide had wept over Harriet Beecher Stowe's emotional portrayal of dehumanizing slavery in the antebellum South. But Dixon wasn't sad; he was angry. A descendant of Confederate veterans and Ku Klux Klansmen, he was outraged by what he viewed as Stowe's gross misrepresentation of Southern life.[1] Tears still gleaming on his face, he vowed to tell the "true story" of slavery, the Civil War, and Northern abuse of the South during Reconstruction.[2] Less than a year later, he published *The Leopard's Spots*, a historical novel in which he distorted Stowe's characters, condemned Northern liberals and emancipated slaves as villains, and celebrated Klansmen as heroes. In 1905, a second novel, *The Clansman*, appeared, again featuring the Klan as the saviors of the South. With this book, Dixon was determined to advance the cause of racial purity and warn white Americans of the threat free African Americans, an inferior race, posed to that purity. To that end, he chose as the principal villains of his twisted tale of Reconstruction a beautiful, mixed-race Pennsylvania woman named Lydia Hamilton Smith and her longtime companion, white Lancaster congressman Thaddeus Stevens.

In the mid-nineteenth century, Lydia Hamilton Smith was one of the most widely known women in the country. Opinion about her veered from admiration and respect from those who knew her best to vicious condemnation from those who feared her and all people of color. Thomas Dixon considered himself a brilliant, creative writer, but in denigrating Stevens and Mrs. Smith, he did nothing more than parrot the scurrilously racist views some of Mrs. Smith's contemporaries threw in her face. Driven by fear and hatred of African Americans, those antagonists accused Mrs. Smith of using the innate sexual wiles she possessed as a Black woman to manipulate Congressman Stevens. Her goal, they howled, was for Stevens to use the great power he wielded after the Civil War to give newly freed people of color control over the defeated Confederacy. Was Mrs. Smith guilty of such behavior? In a word: No. We will discover, as her story unfolds, that she fervently believed in the cause of racial equality that Stevens championed. We know that she and Stevens discussed the critical issues of the day. But there is no evidence to suggest that her goal, in hiring on as Stevens's housekeeper in Lancaster, was to control his political thoughts and actions.

What she was dedicated to, long before she arrived in Lancaster in 1844, was rising above the rather humble circumstances of her birth. And in that, by the standards of her time (and ours), she was spectacularly successful. We see early evidence of her drive and ambition in the fact that she signed the deed along with her husband, Jacob, when they bought a house in Harrisburg, Pennsylvania. At the time, it was considered inappropriate, if not illegal, for any woman—Black or white—to own property. Yet Lydia Hamilton Smith managed to do it. She would continue acquiring property in the years after she left her husband and joined Thaddeus Stevens in Lancaster. When she died, her estate was valued at more than $300,000 in today's currency.

Mrs. Smith's financial success, in the face of nineteenth-century prohibitions against women in business, is sufficient reason to celebrate her among the nation's outstanding women. And her fans, especially in the Lancaster area, have long saluted those accomplishments. But Mrs. Smith's display of business savvy was not her only important contribution to American life. She is believed to have joined Thaddeus Stevens in the risky (and blatantly illegal) operation of an Underground Railroad station, created to assist African Americans fleeing enslavement in the South. In nearly twenty-five years with Stevens, she became an advocate for those seeking the famous congressman's assistance in finding justice and opportunity—especially for people of color. And in what some observers consider her most important contribution, Lydia Hamilton Smith took on the arduous task of nursing a seriously ill and declining Thaddeus Stevens as he battled to abolish slavery and secure the rights and privileges of full citizenship to newly freed African Americans after the Civil War. It was, by all accounts, exhausting work. Mrs. Smith tended to Stevens, sometimes around the clock for weeks on end, at great risk to her own health. Stevens's physicians and even Stevens himself credited her with literally keeping him alive as he labored to complete his work on behalf of people of color. Even this cursory examination of an admittedly abbreviated list of Mrs. Smith's accomplishments and contributions might move us to ask why her story hasn't been told before. The answer lies, in part, in the work of the white supremacist preacher and lecturer we've already met, Thomas Dixon.

Dixon's second novel, *The Clansman*, was a big hit with its portrayal of Lydia Hamilton Smith and Thaddeus Stevens as an evil pair intent on giving newly freed people of color control of the South. But Dixon wasn't satisfied. He hungered to reach even more Americans with his celebration of the Klan and message of white supremacy. He thought he could accomplish that through the mesmerizing new medium of film. He teamed up with innovative young filmmaker D. W. Griffith (also a descendant of Confederate veterans) to produce an epic, three-hour-long version of *The Clansman* entitled *The Birth of a Nation*. In the film, as in the book, Lydia Hamilton Smith (identified as "Lydia Brown") is presented as "savage, corrupt, and lascivious. She is portrayed as overtly sexual, and she uses her 'feminine wiles' to deceive the formerly good white man [Stevens]."[3] Dixon's cinematic Lydia is "a woman of extraordinary animal beauty and the fiery temper of a Leopardess. . . . All sorts of gossip could be heard in Washington about this woman, her jewels, her dresses, her airs, her assumption of the dignity of the presiding genius of National legislation and her domination of the old Commoner [Stevens] and his life."[4]

Critics quickly condemned the film and tried unsuccessfully to have it banned. The National Association for the Advancement of Colored People warned that its white supremacist message would incite whites to engage in more of the anti-Black violence (including lynchings) already sweeping the country in the Jim Crow era. But white audiences in both North and South, including President Woodrow Wilson (an acknowledged racist), flocked to see it. Profits reached at least $60,000,000.[5] If we combine the astounding public reception of the film with an observation from historian John Hope Franklin, we can, perhaps, explain why Lydia Hamilton Smith's story fell into neglect. Franklin suggests that Mrs. Smith, Stevens, and the true story of Reconstruction slipped from the nation's collective memory because the American public, including many American historians, embraced Dixon's vile, revisionist version of Reconstruction history so thoroughly. Dixon, Franklin wrote, "has exerted as much influence on current opinions of Reconstruction as any historian, lay or professional."[6] In brief, white Americans bought what Dixon was selling. Why would anyone waste time studying or celebrating a white man and a mixed-race woman branded by Dixon as malcontents and evildoers?

We should note that Dixon's hateful distortions forced honest twentieth-century historians to admit they had allowed much of the South's version of events surrounding the Civil War—the false, racist history Dixon foisted on the nation in print and on the screen—to stand unopposed for nearly fifty years. That realization prompted a number of historians and biographers to take another look at Thaddeus Stevens's life and work. Several noticed Lydia Hamilton Smith, but all of them more or less accepted the conclusion reached in the 1920s by Lancaster County jurist Charles I. Landis. In defending Mrs. Smith and Stevens after the film came out, Landis wrote that Mrs. Smith was "a decent and respectable woman," present at Stevens's side during the momentous events of the mid-nineteenth century but not a major character in the scenes that played out. As Landis put it, she "kept herself quite within her station" and was warmly welcomed by the leading families of Lancaster.[7] That assessment holds sway to this day. In a 2021 biography of Stevens, historian Bruce Levine erases Mrs. Smith in just two sentences, writing that "a widow of mixed-race ancestry, Lydia Hamilton Smith, came to work for Stevens as a housekeeper, and the two developed a close friendship and working relationship." Levine, like most Stevens biographers, then dismisses suggestions (raised provocatively by Steven Spielberg in the movie *Lincoln*) that Stevens and Mrs. Smith were lovers. Such an idea, Levine writes, is the work of those "hoping to tarnish Stevens's image," and, he asserts, "no firm evidence substantiates it."[8] *An Uncommon Woman* begs to differ with that assessment.

No topic has generated more heated debate in the Pennsylvania environs where Lydia Hamilton Smith and Thaddeus Stevens lived—together— than the nature of their relationship. Longtime guardians of Mrs. Smith's memory generally reject any suggestion that the two were physically intimate. They contend that Mrs. Smith, a devout Irish Catholic communicant, would never have entertained thoughts of an illicit relationship with Stevens. There is, however, a minority view that assumes there was a sexual dimension to the couple's relationship. Interestingly, that view was expressed to the author primarily by people of color. In support of their belief, they note that, historically speaking, particularly in the South, white men often engaged in sexual relations with Black women. We know Southern plantation owners had no qualms about forcing themselves on enslaved women. In his play *Blues for Mr. Charlie* (1964), Black writer James Baldwin suggests the practice continued well into the twentieth century.[9] Thomas Dixon certainly believed that Lydia Hamilton Smith and Thaddeus Stevens were involved sexually. Their relationship (as he understood it) was a central reason why he chose them as the villains of his twisted history. For him, interracial sex (with its potential to produce mixed-race children) was the greatest possible threat to the purity of the white race. He warned white men of this danger by portraying Lydia Hamilton Smith as a lascivious, hypersexual, animalistic mulatto woman who used her sexual power to dominate the virtually helpless Thaddeus Stevens. The chapters ahead will consider evidence from a wide variety of sources that speaks to the nature of the relationship between Stevens and Mrs. Smith—and will invite readers to reach their own conclusions.

In the years since Judge Landis wrote his defense of Mrs. Smith and Stevens, even the place they called home—the Lancaster community—has lost touch with them, especially Mrs. Smith. The small but hardy group mentioned above has endeavored to preserve and celebrate her memory, but as of this writing (August 2022), no one has yet put forward a full account of Mrs. Smith's life, achievements, and contributions. This book is offered in at least partial atonement for that neglect, because, in this writer's estimation, Lydia Hamilton Smith has earned a place among the leading women of American history.

There is much to know about her. As her story unfolds here, we'll discover why a child born Lydia O'Neill in Gettysburg, Pennsylvania, has a gravestone bearing the name Lydia Hamilton. We'll follow her on the journey that took her to the doorstep of an already famous lawyer named Thaddeus Stevens, a man destined to become the most influential member of Congress during and after the Civil War. Mrs. Smith walked by Stevens's side for just shy of twenty-five years. Those would be years of challenge, danger, accomplishment, delight, anguish, exhaustion, discrimination, and racism.

It is interesting to note that a Lancaster newspaper (one that Stevens and Mrs. Smith read and is still being published today) recently reported on the unveiling of a statue in Sheffield, Massachusetts. The monument honors a formerly enslaved woman named Mum Bett. Inspired by the promises of liberty enshrined in the Declaration of Independence and the Massachusetts Constitution, Mum Bett laid legal claim to freedom and won in 1781. As a free woman, she chose the name Elizabeth Freeman.[10] The belated recognition accorded Elizabeth Freeman begs the question of whether Lydia Hamilton Smith, too, should have a statue. Her partner, Thaddeus Stevens, has already been honored with several. Perhaps, after learning her story, readers will be inspired to honor Mrs. Smith in the same way. We should also note that other efforts to pay tribute to her legacy are currently underway. As this book approached completion,

LancasterHistory (formerly the Lancaster County Historical Society) was developing the Thaddeus Stevens and Lydia Hamilton Smith Center for History and Democracy. The center will make a significant contribution to honoring the two. But a statue of Lydia Hamilton Smith would be nice, too.

As we'll see in the pages that lie ahead, Lydia Hamilton Smith lived an extraordinary life in a turbulent time. She touched or was touched by momentous events in our nation's history, and she never shirked the responsibilities history thrust upon her. She sought neither the celebrity nor the malignant vitriol heaped upon her by friends and foes. Nonetheless, she endured both with grace and determination.

CHAPTER I

JAMES BUCHANAN'S FATHER SLEPT HERE

Lydia O'Neill was born into a youthful United States—a mere thirty-seven years after the Declaration of Independence, the nation's founding document, was written by Thomas Jefferson. The stirring document proclaimed that "all men are created equal, that they are endowed by their Creator with certain unalienable rights, that among these are Life, Liberty and the pursuit of Happiness." Lydia's thoughts about the Declaration of Independence or Thomas Jefferson, if she had any, are lost to history. Records do not indicate whether she ever noticed that the same document that laid claim to the equality of all men also accused the British of "exciting domestic insurrections amongst us"—a reference to England's role in fomenting uprisings by African slaves, on whose backs the South's agrarian economy was built but who had no place in Jefferson's soaring rhetoric of freedom. The great democrat owned many slaves, and his home state of Virginia raised one of the loudest voices demanding the Second Amendment to the United States Constitution, the one that reads: "A well regulated Militia, being necessary to the security of a free *State*, the right of the people to keep and bear Arms, shall not be infringed." Modern scholars suggest that Southern slaveowners considered the Second Amendment essential to maintaining armed white slave patrols deputized to beat down the uprisings of outraged slaves who had sought to throw off their chains virtually from the moment they first were dragged ashore in the New World.[1]

It's unlikely, given her lack of formal education, that Lydia knew that Thomas Jefferson, as George Washington's secretary of state, conducted the first US census in 1790. In that enumeration, he was guided by Article

I, Section 2, Clause 3 of the Constitution. That rule, cleverly negotiated by Southern slaveowners, dictated that free white people (including indentured servants) each counted as one person, but the law further directed that census takers, after counting *all* of the slaves, should add only *three-fifths* of that total to the final tally. The process gave white Southerners more representation in Washington, and thus more clout, but it provided no benefit to the enumerated slaves, who remained property and without rights for two-thirds of Lydia's life.

Lydia was only thirteen when Thomas Jefferson died, but that might have been long enough for her to hear the rumors (confirmed in the twentieth century) that, in 1788, the champion of human freedom had taken as his mistress a pretty mixed-race woman—a young woman he owned—named Sally Hemings,[2] with whom he fathered several children. Jefferson was duly condemned by political enemies for crossing the great racial divide to have children with Hemings. Nonetheless, he went on to serve the nation as secretary of state and was elected vice president and president.

Whether she ever thought about Thomas Jefferson or not, the arc of Lydia Hamilton Smith's life with Thaddeus Stevens would resemble that of Hemings and Jefferson—but with significant and unhappy differences. Like Hemings, Lydia was a mixed-race woman. Like Hemings, she would one day find herself at the side of a brilliant, immensely capable, wealthy lawyer and politician. Like Hemings, she would suffer the crass, indecent slurs of Americans possessed of primitive (albeit dominant) attitudes on race. But unlike Hemings, Lydia O'Neill was born free and willingly became the companion and confidante of a free white man. And unfair as it may seem from our vantage point in the twenty-first century, the same America that elevated Jefferson—a man who slept with an enslaved woman whom he owned—to the most prestigious posts in the land would eventually deny Stevens access to those same positions, likely because he chose as his companion a free, mixed-race woman. Such was the nation; such were the benighted attitudes of the age in which Lydia lived her life.

That life began on February 14, 1813—Valentine's Day—in Adams County, Pennsylvania. (There is some debate over the year Lydia was born. We'll examine that in a moment.) By an interesting, and some might say fateful, coincidence, Mrs. Smith died seventy-one years later on February 14, 1884. Admirers today affectionately note that the sum total of Mrs. Smith's existence, all that she was and all that she did, was bounded by a religious feast day cherished in many parts of the world as a "significant

Fig. 1   Russell Tavern, north of Gettysburg, the birthplace of Lydia Hamilton Smith (date unknown). The tavern is in the center of the photograph. Adams County Historical Society, Gettysburg, Pennsylvania.

cultural, religious, and commercial celebration of romance and romantic love."[3] Some of her modern-day fans refer to her as "a woman of great heart."

Lydia O'Neill was born at Russell Tavern, on Black's Gap Road, about four miles north of Gettysburg. Black's Gap Road, thought to be the second road built in Adams County, was constructed in 1747. It ran through South Mountain and connected York (to the east) with the Cumberland Valley (to the west).[4] Russell Tavern was built by Joshua Russell, an Irish immigrant, in 1780 on a tract of land known as the Manor of Mashe, purchased from William Morrison in 1777.[5] Lydia Hamilton Smith confirmed her birthplace in an interview with a newspaper reporter in 1883 and tacked on a bonus historical note. She told the journalist she "was born in Adams County in the very house to which James Buchanan's father first went when he landed in this country. There he found the friend of his boyhood, Joshua Russell, who had preceded him in the search for home and fortune in the new world."[6]

Mrs. Smith's upbeat account of the Buchanan family's arrival in America, shared with a newsman late in her life, suggests that she bore no ill will toward President James Buchanan, who died in 1868 shortly before her companion, Thaddeus Stevens. Her positive recounting of the Buchanan saga may be evidence that, despite her devotion to Stevens, she maintained a certain independence in her attitudes toward the people who touched their shared life. (Although Stevens and Buchanan lived near each other in Lancaster for many years, their drastically different views on human and political affairs engendered no neighborly feelings. Suffice it to say, for now, that they never became friends.)

Knowing *where* Lydia was born is helpful in establishing *who* her parents were, and it involves the Russell family tree. Joshua Russell and his wife, Jean, welcomed their only son, Samuel, in 1776. The plan was for Samuel to succeed his father in running the tavern. Samuel Russell married Jane McClure, and the couple added four daughters to the Russell clan before Samuel died in 1806 at the young age of thirty, just a year after his father died. Two years later, in 1808, Samuel's widow, Jane McClure, married another Irishman, Enoch Hamilton, who stepped in to help run the tavern.

Around the time Enoch Hamilton joined the family, the tavern employed a free, mixed-race woman named Mrs. O'Neill. We know little about her, but the fact that she was addressed as Mrs. O'Neill, and not simply by a first name, suggests that she came to the tavern as a free person. We can illustrate the point without leaving Russell Tavern. Seven enslaved people appear on the Russell family tree, but with first names only: Jean, Dinah, Sall, Betsy, Ned, Jane, and Jacob. None of them has a surname, as Mrs. O'Neill does. (She also appears on the family tree, but not as a relative.)

In 1820, Enoch Hamilton and Jane McClure had a daughter they named Harriet. Seven years prior to that, in 1813, while Mrs. O'Neill was employed as a live-in domestic servant at the tavern, she gave birth to a little girl she named Lydia O'Neill. Lydia's mixed heritage was obvious from the moment she arrived. Speculation among those closest to the history of Russell Tavern is that Enoch Hamilton was likely Lydia's father. We don't know under what circumstances, and we don't know for certain. Mrs. O'Neill was employed by Enoch Hamilton. Did she consent to sexual relations with her employer, or did Hamilton force himself on his Black housekeeper? We don't know. What we do know is that Lydia later chose to be known as Lydia Hamilton. Why? Did her mother explain to her, at some point, that Hamilton was, in fact, her father? Again, we do not know. Any official record of Lydia's birth, if one ever existed, has eluded us. Her death certificate identified her as Lydia A. [*sic*] Smith.[7]

Thanks to her diverse genetic heritage, Lydia's physical appearance frustrated attempts to fit her into the discriminatory racial pigeonholes of her time. Long after she had become one of the most talked-about women in the country, gossips and assorted biographers tried to define her. "She is said to have been comely in appearance," one wrote, "light in color."[8] Another observed, "Generally she was looked upon as a Negress, although she said she had a preponderance of Creole blood."[9] Without knowing more about Mrs. O'Neill's background, we can't reject this assertion, especially if we understand the term "Creole" as it was used in Lydia's day: "As an ethnic group, [Creole] ancestry is mainly of Louisiana French, West African, Spanish and Native American origin. . . . New Orleans in particular has retained a significant historical population of Creoles of color, a group mostly consisting of free persons of multiracial European, African, and Native American descent."[10] So at least one side of Lydia's family might well have had roots in the deep South.

Thaddeus Stevens's biographer Fawn Brodie writes of Lydia Hamilton Smith, "She was a very light mulatto, of considerable beauty, and was said to have been the daughter of a white man, a Mr. Oneill [*sic*], from Russell's Tavern."[11] Poet and Lincoln biographer Carl Sandburg, born six years before Mrs. Smith died, describes her as "a comely quadroon with Caucasian features and a skin of light-gold tint, a Roman Catholic communicant with Irish eyes, her maiden name Hamilton."[12]

Uncertainty and confusion about Mrs. Smith's ethnicity would persist throughout her life and even into the sad hours immediately following her death. The hand that completed her death certificate obviously struggled with the "race" question. The section for designating the deceased's race is six lines down on the form. The word "Color" appears against the left margin, after which someone wrote the word "Black," then crossed it out. To the right of it we see a question mark, followed by the word "White," which has also been crossed out. Such tentative markings suggest that the writer had little confidence in the answer. Perhaps the clerk was unacquainted with Mrs. Smith, or perhaps there were other individuals in the room—her family and friends—who objected to the clerk's entries.[13]

The apparent uncertainty in completing Mrs. Smith's death certificate brings us back to the question of when she was born. The certificate indicates that she was sixty-nine when she died. Some historians compute back from 1884 and conclude that she was born in 1815. If the person who filled out the form wasn't even aware of Mrs. Smith's racial heritage,

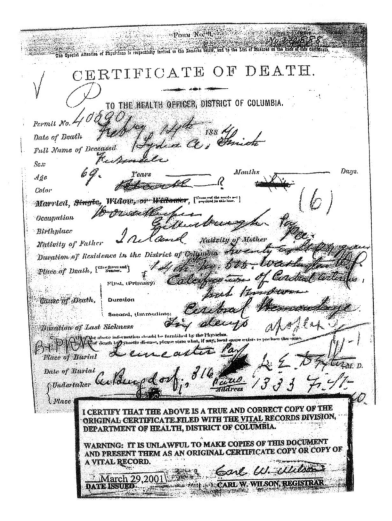

Fig. 2 Death certificate of Lydia Hamilton Smith. LancasterHistory, Lancaster, Pennsylvania.

how accurate can we expect that person to be in noting her age when she died? I have more confidence in the epitaph on her gravestone. The message carved into that stone places primary emphasis on the many years she spent by Thaddeus Stevens's side. She knew that Stevens had composed the message for his monument; might she have chosen to write the epitaph for her own memorial? If she did, she surely would have included

the year of her birth, leaving only space for insertion of the date of her death. Those favoring 1815 suggest that year had been inscribed on the stone but has simply become less legible over time. I tested that contention by making a rubbing of that portion of the inscription. The rubbing clearly revealed the year 1813. Therefore, pending discovery of more convincing evidence to the contrary, I have chosen to rely on the solid testimony of Lydia Hamilton Smith's gravestone in concluding, here, that she was born in 1813.

Mrs. Smith's death certificate does not name her parents, but it does inform us that her father was born in Ireland and her mother in Pennsylvania.[14] Other sources suggest that her mother was a mixed-race woman.[15] That fits with the other evidence we have for Lydia's origins. The fact that Lydia's mother was known as Mrs. O'Neill strongly suggests that at some point, prior to Lydia's birth, she was involved with a man of Irish descent. Marriage between white and Black people being strictly forbidden in early America (and, sadly, for many, many years afterwards), Mrs. O'Neill may have done exactly what Lydia did, claiming the surname of the man who impregnated *her* mother but assumed no legal responsibility for supporting his offspring. If this scenario is accurate, it made Lydia, in the parlance of her time, a "quadroon," that is, a person with three white grandparents and one Black grandparent. She was, by her society's ugly arithmetic, only one-quarter Black. But that 25 percent was more than enough to fuel the vitriolic voices of those who came to hate the man with whom she chose to walk through life.

That man, Thaddeus Stevens, who was born into a poor family in Vermont in 1792, turned twenty-one the year Lydia was born. Stevens's father, a noted amateur wrestler but failed farmer, had taken to drink. He abandoned his family, joined the army, and died of wounds he sustained in the War of 1812. Stevens's mother, Sarah Morrill Stevens, moved from Danville, the birthplace of her four sons, to Peacham, Vermont, where she worked as a domestic servant and nurse to earn money to send her two older boys, Joshua and Thaddeus, to school. Joshua was born with club-foot in both feet, and Thaddeus had a deformed foot as well. Biographer Fawn Brodie salutes Sarah Stevens as "a woman of great energy, strong will, and deep piety" who vowed that "her two eldest [boys] would rise above the merciless handicap of their birth."[16]

Sarah Morrill Stevens's tireless dedication put Thaddeus on a path that led through Dartmouth College to a teaching post in York, Pennsylvania, and on to what would become a very successful law practice in Gettysburg by 1816. Much has been made of Stevens's halting gait, occasioned by his clubfoot. But in his prime, after he arrived in Gettysburg, he apparently cut a fine figure. Historian Bradley R. Hoch tells us that Stevens stood five feet eleven inches tall, was solidly built but not overweight, and had a ruddy, unblemished complexion. His clubfoot was protected by a spe-cial left shoe; he did walk with a limp, and he sometimes steadied himself with a cane. In spite of his physical deformity, he was quite athletic, known to be an excellent horseman and swimmer. William M. Hall offers a sim-ilar endorsement of Stevens's athletic prowess. Stevens, he writes, was a "man of fine physical proportions . . . and excelled in manly sports. . . . He could throw the 'long bullet' further and kick a hat off a higher peg than any other man in Gettysburg."[17]

Biographers have pondered whether this clubfooted young man had any romantic interludes along the way. Some, perhaps more embarrassed by Stevens's handicap than he was, aver that he remained a confirmed bachelor all his life. But there is at least one report of a "matter of the heart" before Stevens ever left Vermont. Writer James Scovel tells us Thaddeus Stevens was "not yet of age when he became attached to the beautiful daughter of the village clergyman." Speaking for Stevens, Scovel says that his poverty

Fig. 4 Thaddeus Stevens's law office and home in Gettysburg.
Adams County Historical Society, Gettysburg, Pennsylvania.

made him feel "his unfitness for such a match," and never declared his love. Instead, young Thaddeus packed up and headed to Pennsylvania.[18]

Stevens might have kept his feelings for the young woman to himself, but he humorously confirmed his awareness of and interest in romance to his Dartmouth classmate and friend Samuel Merrill, who was already teaching in York, Pennsylvania, while Stevens finished up in New Hampshire. "This place," Stevens wrote Merrill, "is at present greatly alarmed on account of an uncommon epidemic, which it is sincerely hoped will thin the ranks of our old maids and send their withered ghosts . . . to the dominion of that old tyrant Hymen." Stevens informed Merrill that twenty "licensed copulations" had taken place so far, but he was not one of the participants.[19] Had Stevens not decided to follow Merrill to Pennsylvania, he and Lydia Hamilton Smith would not have become part of American history.

CHAPTER 2

A GIRLHOOD IN GETTYSBURG

Newspaper obituaries tell us that Lydia's mother "removed from her country home (Russell Tavern) to Gettysburg while Lydia was but a child, and remained there several years."[1] According to one account, Lydia's "girl hood was passed in and around Gettysburg."[2] And she may have had a sibling to enjoy it with, at least for a time.

In her will, Lydia Hamilton Smith bequeathed legacies to a number of relatives. The most generous gift—$500, a sizable sum in 1884—went to "Half-sister Jane Cooper (Baltimore, Md., formerly Gettysburg, who was raised in the family of Alexander Raymond [Baltimore])." Beyond the $500 for Jane, Lydia wanted to do something for Jane's children. She instructed her executors that "the interest accruing from the investment of the proceeds of the sale of houses and lots on South Water Street, Lancaster, [was] to be used for the education of her [Jane's] children—in the event of their deaths prior to Jane's, interest to her." Lydia must have cared very much for Jane to provide so amply for her in her will, but other than the will, no written or photographic record of their relationship has surfaced.[3]

The will does provide some clues about Jane. Lydia introduces Jane as her half sister, which rules out Enoch Hamilton as her father and probably means that Jane was born after Mrs. O'Neill left Russell Tavern. Mrs. Smith tells us that Jane first lived in Gettysburg, with Lydia and her mother, we presume, and then was taken or sent to Baltimore, Maryland, "to be raised in the family of Alexander Raymond." Baltimore census records for 1850 do not list an Alexander Raymond family with a little girl of color named Jane living with them (1850 was the first year census records listed women by name, regardless of color), but an Alex Reiman family does appear there, and that might be the family to which Mrs. Smith referred. (Mrs. Smith may have spelled the name *Raymond* because that's how it sounded when her mother talked about sending Jane away.) In the Reiman family, in 1850, we find thirty-five-year-old Alex, twenty-eight-year-old Elli, four-year-old Martha, two-year-old Elieth, four-month-old Isabella, and twenty-five-year-old Jane Williams. All of the Reimans are white; Jane Williams, interestingly enough, is mulatto and a servant. The Baltimore census taker estimated that Jane Williams was born in 1825. If this is Lydia's half sister, she would have been twelve years younger than Lydia and born to Mrs. O'Neill and a man named Williams.[4]

What reason might Mrs. O'Neill have to send her daughter off to be raised by a white family in Baltimore? Mrs. Smith offered no further explanation in her will; she may have been acknowledging the nineteenth-century practice of white families "acquiring Black children (enslaved or free) at a very young age and raising them within the household as domestic servants."[5] What sort of experience would that have been for a young child? Historian Crystal Lynn Webster has used the word "marginalization" to describe the status Jane Cooper and many other Black girls were thrust into: "In the antebellum North, African American children were subsumed within systems of indentured servitude that were established following gradual emancipation as a way to mediate the population's transition from enslavement to freedom. This placed northern black children somewhere between slavery and freedom, childhood and adulthood. . . . Black girls could be indentured until as old as twenty-eight."[6]

If Jane was sent to Baltimore to be trained as a domestic servant or housekeeper, the Reiman home was a good place to learn. By the mid-nineteenth century, the Reimans were among the wealthiest families in Baltimore. According to National Register of Historic Places documents for a Reiman building at 409 West Baltimore Street, "Alexander Reiman was President of the Western Maryland Railroad Company. [His brother] William J. Reiman was a dealer in provisions and commission merchandise. [Another brother] Joseph Reiman was an officer of several corporations, a member of the Committee of Five which encouraged industrial development; among his projects was the 'Reiman Block,' a mixed commercial and residential block at 617–631 West Lexington Street." Census records for 1870 show that Alexander Reiman owned real estate valued at $250,000 and had a personal estate worth $150,000—immense wealth in the nineteenth century.[7]

Baltimore census records for 1850 might hold other clues about Jane. Sometimes enumerators counted the same head twice. We know this because it happened in Lydia's own family. Her son Isaac appears in the 1870 census in two places: as a resident of her boardinghouse in Washington, DC, and as head of a household in Lancaster, Pennsylvania. Might Lydia's sister, Jane, have been counted at two locations in 1850 in Baltimore?[8]

We've already seen the 1850 entry for Jane Williams, age twenty-five, mulatto, a servant in the Alexander Reiman household in Baltimore's Eighteenth Ward. That same year, we find a mulatto woman named Jane *Cooper*, the name Lydia provides for her half sister in her will. This Jane Cooper's age is estimated as twenty-seven (nearly the same age as Jane Williams), and she's listed in a household in Baltimore's First Ward headed by a thirty-six-year-old Black "caulker" named Joseph Cooper. Five Black children are living with Joseph and Jane Cooper: eight-year-old Sarah A. Cooper, five-year-old Charles Cooper, three-year-old George Cooper, ten-month-old Lewis Cooper, and, interestingly enough, a seventeen-year-old teenager named Joseph *Williams*. No occupation is listed in the Cooper household for Jane or for Joseph Williams. By 1850, might Lydia's sister have been working as a servant across town while she and her husband began their family? It's a tantalizing prospect, but without further documentation, impossible to confirm.[9]

The Joseph Cooper family, including Jane, was still living in Baltimore's First Ward ten years later. The Cooper children enumerated in 1850 are all there in 1860, plus two new family members: eight-year-old Mary J. Cooper and five-year-old Cornelius Cooper. But in 1870, we find Jane Cooper, age forty-five (the age Jane Williams would have attained by that time), living in a household headed by thirty-six-year-old Francis Derand. Also living in the Derand household is six-year-old David Cooper. Jane's occupation is "washing & ironing." There's no mention of Joseph Cooper.[10]

In 1880, three years after Lydia wrote her will bequeathing significant sums of money to her half sister and the children, we find Jane Cooper, a widowed Black woman (probably around fifty-five, although the census taker estimated that she was thirty-six) as head of a household and working as a laundress. Living with her, according to the census record, are Hannah Cooper, a twenty-year-old single daughter who works in the laundry; a son, eighteen-year-old David Cooper, a waiter; and sixteen-year-old Mary Ann Cooper, a daughter who also works in the laundry.[11] Is this Lydia

Hamilton Smith's half sister and are these the "children" Lydia hopes to see educated? We can't know for sure, but the will tells us that Lydia managed to stay connected to Jane after she left Gettysburg, and she carried a concern for Jane and her children to the last years of her life.

By the time Lydia and her mother moved to Gettysburg around 1819, Pennsylvanians had been living under an "Act for the Gradual Abolition of Slavery" for more than thirty years. Pennsylvania was, in fact, the first state to pass such a measure. It required that "every Negro and Mulatto child born [enslaved] within the State after the passing of the Act would be free upon reaching age twenty-eight." The act was particularly opposed by German immigrants in heavily German counties, especially in southeastern Pennsylvania. The Germans had earlier been condemned as a "swarthy" threat to America by Anglo-Americans, including the distinguished Pennsylvania statesman Benjamin Franklin. Historians speculate that the Germans opposed the new law because they feared freeing African slaves would push the Germans themselves further down in the American social pecking order.[12]

But so "gradual" was the new law's movement toward abolishing slavery that human beings were still being bought and sold in Pennsylvania well after both Lydia and young Thaddeus Stevens had independently arrived in Gettysburg. By one accounting, there were seventy-one slaves in Adams County in 1810, seven of them in Gettysburg.[13] Lydia, when she learned to read (we don't know exactly when that was), and Stevens, from the moment he first rented a law office in Gettysburg, would have seen ads like this one in the *Gettysburg Centinel*, October 2, 1816: "For sale. A Negro Girl. Aged 17 years, and has to serve till 28. She is acquainted with all kinds of house work," or this one in the March 26, 1817, *Centinel*: "For sale. A Negro Girl, who has about two years and a half to serve—very stout and healthy—capable of doing all kinds of housework," or this plea for assistance from a slaver, printed in the *Centinel* on October 29, 1817: "Forty dollars Reward. Runaway from the Subscriber . . . a Negro Man, named SAM, about 22 years old, about 5 feet 10 inches high, stout-made, yellow complexion . . . is very good country miller, and a good hand at oak slips: it is thought he will make for Baltimore or Pennsylvania, and endeavor to pass as a freeman."[14] Lydia left us no record of her thoughts about such things as she was coming of age in Gettysburg, but her actions, especially after she arrived in Lancaster, Pennsylvania, serve as ample testimony to how she must have felt.

She did eventually share some memories of those years, and one of them speaks to the much-debated question of when she became acquainted with Stevens. The story, which Mrs. Smith told a newspaper reporter later in her life, concerns a young woman named Keziah (or Cassiah) Shannon. The saga began around 1819, when Lydia would have been six years old, and reached its sad ending about ten years later. It seems likely that someone, possibly her mother, repeated the story to Lydia as she was growing up, assisting her in forming a vivid memory of what happened. We are indebted to that long-ago journalist for letting us "hear" Mrs. Smith tell the story:

> It seems that a colored girl named Keziah ran off from a Mr. Shannon, of Shippensburg [Pennsylvania], made her way to Gettysburg and there got work in the hostelry kept by James McCleery, on Chambersburg Street. Presently Shannon put in an appearance and claimed Keziah as his property. McCleery hastened to consult Thaddeus Stevens, then a rising young lawyer in Gettysburg. When the case came to a hearing, Stevens arose in court and asked Shannon, "What is the age of this girl?" "Thirty-one years." "Don't you know that having reached the age of twenty-eight years, she is, under the law of 1780, a free woman?" Shannon didn't know it, but the Court did. Keziah soon followed the McCleerys to Westminster, Maryland, where she married a mulatto slave named Ephraim Wolrich, whose father, getting into financial difficulty, put his son on the auction block. Twice Keziah walked from Westminster to Gettysburg [about twenty-three miles] and begged Stevens to buy her husband. Her entreaties prevailed. Ephraim indentured himself to work for Stevens for seven years, the consideration being one hundred dollars per annum and clothing, but within a year he went to the bad. Stevens was compelled to turn him away, and this so distressed his faithful wife that she hung herself in the chimney corner on the last evening of their stay in the house of their benefactor. Here Mrs. Smith's mother found and removed the warm body and prompt measures revived the ebbing vital forces. The very next night, in their new home near the Gettysburg Poorhouse, Dr. David Horner was instrumental in again frustrating the miserable woman's design upon her own life. "Ah," remarked Mrs. Smith, "I have heard Mr. Stevens say she was the handsomest woman he had ever seen." She died a miserable death. Consumption [tuberculosis]

and a brutal husband soon brought about that which she had twice failed to accomplish.[15]

Stevens biographer Fawn Brodie offers a slightly different version of the story, which she attributes to Stevens's former law student Alexander Hood. Hood reportedly claimed that the purchase of the slave was made around 1830. Brodie's recounting has Keziah Shannon working as a housekeeper for Stevens after he freed her from slavery (the time frame is not clear). At some point, Keziah marries a mulatto slave in Maryland. She later makes the trip from Maryland to Gettysburg twice, on foot, to beg Stevens to buy her husband, who is about to be sold away by his owner. In this telling, Stevens goes to the races in Hagerstown and stops

Fig. 5 Alexander Hood, Thaddeus Stevens's law student, partner, and biographer. LancasterHistory, Lancaster, Pennsylvania.

by the slaveowner's tavern on his way home. Stevens reportedly overhears the landlord negotiating to sell the youth to a slave trader for $500. The trader counters with $400 before Stevens takes the landlord aside and "quietly" proposes to buy the young man for even less than the trader was offering and promises to free the lad after a period of indenture. Unexpectedly, the owner agrees. As Stevens makes out the bill of sale, he "slyly" asks for the slave's last name. The landlord reportedly blushes and stammers, at which point Stevens tells him, "Oh, I'll put your name in. These fellows always go by the name of their owners." According to Hood's account, Stevens had cleverly confirmed that the tavern owner was about to sell his own son. Apparently the father was relieved and pleased that his son was heading to Pennsylvania rather than into the South. This version of the story ends with Keziah's husband working for Stevens for four years, then being given money to set up in a trade.[16] There's no mention of Keziah's tragic end.

Mrs. Smith's intimate knowledge of Keziah Shannon's story may offer some support for those who argue that she knew Thaddeus Stevens long before she signed on as his housekeeper in Lancaster around 1844. Novelist Elsie Singmaster, who spent a considerable amount of time exploring Mrs. Smith's past while researching her historical novel, *I Speak for Thaddeus Stevens*, was one who reached that conclusion. Singmaster flatly dismisses the idea that Stevens and Mrs. Smith met for the first time after he bought his house in Lancaster in 1843 and hired her to work for him. "This is a mistake," Singmaster asserts in her notes. "He would doubtless have known her when she was a little girl at [Enoch] Hamilton's tavern, also in Gettysburg where she lived with her mother within a few blocks of his house. Lydia's account of Keziah proves an acquaintance."[17]

The Gettysburg of Lydia's childhood was relatively small, but it was growing. Founded in 1786 and incorporated in 1806, its location at the confluence of ten major roads attracted both travelers and settlers, and its designation as the Adams County seat of court proceedings made it attractive for young attorneys, like Thaddeus Stevens, looking to make their way in the world.[18] In 1810, Adams County's population, including 71 enslaved people, numbered 15,132. By 1820, it was 19,052, with 23 slaves. Most of those residents lived in the country and labored in agriculture, but by 1820 there were 65 merchants and more than 1,500 workers engaged in manufacturing. In 1820, Adams County's residents included 506 free people of color. And that number was growing, thanks, at least in part, to the Act for the Gradual Abolition of Slavery. Lydia Hamilton and Mrs. O'Neill were among those 506 free African Americans.[19]

Gettysburg may have been small, but that didn't spare its inhabitants, including Lydia, from witnessing their share of tragic events. And by a strange stroke of fate—or something less metaphysical, like simple coincidence—Thaddeus Stevens was often linked to them. In 1817, for example, when Lydia was five years old, a young man named James Hunter picked up a scythe and murdered Adams County farmhand James Heagy in full view of other harvesters working alongside Heagy in a field. So obvious was the likely outcome of the case against Hunter that Gettysburg's established attorneys declined to defend him. That left only one lawyer, the newest legal gun in town, Thaddeus Stevens, who agreed to take the case for the unusually high fee of $1,500 (his usual court appearance fee was $3). Stevens lost, but on the way to defeat he made history by employing the virtually unprecedented defense of temporary insanity. On the stand, Hunter testified that he "knew not at the time [of the murder] what he was doing." He said he must have been "in partial derangement produced by intoxication—together with the sudden instigation of the Devil."[20] No doubt Stevens helped the young man choose his words.

The verdict, nonetheless, was guilty, and Adams County hanged Hunter on January 3, 1818. If Lydia's mother *didn't* take her to see it, she and Lydia were among the few who passed up the opportunity to witness the county's first hanging. On January 7, the *Centinel* published a detailed word picture of the day: "Curious onlookers came to Gettysburg from miles around to see the public hanging, and a carnival atmosphere permeated the town. . . . Locals set out booths on the streets to sell gingerbread and other items. . . . [Hunter, the condemned man] was clothed in his burial shroud and bound with the hangman's rope . . . the group walked to the gallows built south of Gettysburg at the Y made by the Baltimore Pike and the Emmitsburg Road."[21]

The trial and execution reportedly had quite an effect on Thaddeus Stevens's fortunes and philosophy, for even though he lost the trial, his handling of the case earned him new respect from the community and brought paying clients to his door. Stevens later credited James Hunter's murder trial with boosting his legal career in Adams County. Historians also suggest that seeing the gruesome sentence carried out pushed Stevens to develop strong attitudes against capital punishment.[22] Years later, Stevens referred to the case in a conversation with his former law student and friend Alexander Hood. He pointed out to Hood that he had been successful in freeing all but one of the accused murderers he had defended. He added, perhaps ironically, "that every one of them deserved hanging except the one that was hanged, who was certainly insane."[23]

It would not have been unusual for five-year-old Lydia to witness a public hanging. Into the twentieth century, Americans gathered for hangings, be they court-ordered punishment or immoral and illegal lynchings (mostly of Black men) carried out by racist white vigilantes.[24] It's unlikely Lydia knew anything about Stevens's innovative defense strategy at the time, but she might well have learned about it later, from her mother or even from Stevens himself.

In 1821, while eight-year-old Lydia Hamilton was learning the domestic skills—housekeeping, cooking, sewing—that would one day qualify her to become Stevens's housekeeper in Lancaster, Stevens argued his first case before the Pennsylvania Supreme Court. It involved the liberty of a colored woman (Charity Butler) and her children (Harriet and Sofia). The court heard the case in Chambersburg, Pennsylvania, and Thaddeus

Stevens represented slaver John Delaplaine, who was seeking to reclaim Charity and her daughters and take them back to Maryland.[25] Charity's husband, Henry Butler, initiated the suit, suing Delaplaine for the "liberty" of his family. The case hinged on whether Charity, as she was passed back and forth between owners, had resided in Pennsylvania long enough (the requirement was six months) to earn her freedom under Pennsylvania law. Stevens argued that she had not.[26] Bear in mind that, up to this point, Stevens had not revealed his true convictions about slavery. He had argued successfully to free several slaves, and he had argued on behalf of slavers three times before Charity Butler's case—and lost all three. This time, he won. The Pennsylvania Supreme Court ruled for John Delaplaine, condemning Henry Butler's wife and daughters to live in slavery for the rest of their lives.[27]

This may have been the moment that crystallized Stevens's views on the evil institution. Biographer Bradley Hoch tells us that Stevens "was devastated [by the verdict]. Never before had his legal victory doomed human beings into bondage, and never again did he act on behalf of a slave's owner to keep a human being in slavery."[28] A different Stevens biographer, sympathetic to slavery, once wrote that slavery's existence was simply evidence of the "assumed inequality of men." He dismissed Stevens's evolving opposition to slavery as nothing more than the result of being "born and educated in New England, where anti-slavery sentiments first developed themselves in the United States."[29] Clearly, there was much more to it than that. Stevens may have had Charity Butler in mind at the 1823 Fourth of July celebration in Gettysburg when he offered a toast to "the next President. May he be a freeman, who never riveted fetters on a human slave."[30] That would have been a brave thing to say in a town that had mixed feelings about slavery. Adams County's free people of color must have known about Charity Butler's fate. We don't know if young Lydia knew the transformation the case had wrought in Stevens's values, but the adult Lydia Hamilton Smith almost certainly factored such values into her decision to align her fate with Stevens many years later.

An instance of violence in Gettysburg in 1824 engendered such sensationally vicious gossip about Thaddeus Stevens that even an eleven-year-old girl like Lydia could not have avoided it. The victim in this story was a young mixed-race woman named Dinah. Hoch gives us a succinct summary of the facts: "Dinah died in the quiet darkness that was just outside the Gettysburg Presbyterian Church on Thursday evening, September 23,

1824. A passerby found her body the next morning, at the edge of town, face down in a shallow well beside the church, in three or four feet of water. There was a collection of blood under the skin near her right eye. When she died, Dinah was very pregnant. Everyone in town knew that Dinah and the child had been murdered."[31]

The story on the streets of Gettysburg veered away from the facts to unfounded accusations and gossip almost immediately. Dinah had worked as a servant at George Hersh's Franklin House tavern, next to Thaddeus Stevens's law office, along with a young African American waiter named Peter Stewart, known familiarly to some as Black Peter. As soon as Dinah's body was found, Stewart volunteered that Stevens had paid him to fetch Dinah that night *and* paid him to keep quiet about it. According to Hoch, the discovery and the rumors swirling around it had people gathered on street corners all over town. Many dismissed Black Peter's street-side testimony, but Jacob Lefever, publisher of Gettysburg's *Republican Compiler* and lifelong political enemy of Thaddeus Stevens, kept the slanderous allegations alive for at least seven years before Stevens silenced him with a libel suit.

No one ever stood trial in Dinah's murder, but subsequent investigations by historians point to a possible suspect: Peter Stewart. The record shows that he had been charged with fornication and adultery two years before Dinah's murder and then acquitted. Five years after her death, he was found guilty of assault and battery on a constable named James Brown. On August 20, 1833, Jacob Lefever's paper, the *Compiler*, informed readers that "Black Peter" had died Saturday morning, August 17.[32]

If Lefever intended to pin Dinah's murder on Thaddeus Stevens, he failed. But if his intention was to smear Stevens and limit his success in the legal and political arenas, he was partially successful. By repeatedly insinuating, in print, that Stevens had a part in Dinah's death, and by publishing reputation-tarnishing articles accusing Stevens of seducing "mistress, maid and colored females," he managed to inject into public discourse a wicked image of Stevens that other detractors would expand upon and that both Stevens and Mrs. Smith would have to endure throughout their life together in Lancaster.[33]

CHAPTER 3

COMING OF AGE

If our earlier speculation is accurate, Lydia Hamilton's half sister Jane (identified in her will as Jane Cooper) was born in Gettysburg in 1825. Lydia was twelve by then—old enough, in those days, to be out working as a housekeeper or servant, although we do not know that she was. Lydia must have been excited to welcome a baby sister. She obviously developed a lifelong affection for her, even though, according to Lydia, Jane was sent away to be "raised" by what we now know was a wealthy white family in Baltimore when she was still a child. Lydia's abiding attachment to her half sister is reflected in the generous legacies she bequeathed to Jane and her children more than fifty years later. We don't know how the sisters kept in touch. If they wrote letters, those letters have been lost.

While the O'Neill-Hamilton household tended to its new arrival, Thaddeus Stevens tended to his career and his portfolio. On August 25–26, 1825, he bought 160 acres of land, the "residual" of Gettysburg founder James Gettys's farm, for $2,320. Bradley Hoch tells us Stevens "reveled in accumulating real estate"[1] and purchased more than ninety properties in Adams and surrounding counties, many of them at sheriff's sale. Historian Timothy Smith of the Adams County Historical Society told me that Stevens owned much of the land in Gettysburg—and Stevens didn't stop there. The manager of Stevens's Franklin County ironworks estimated that his ironworks property sprawled over 18,000 acres in 1868. Hoch asserts that Stevens, the man who worked so hard to put an end to slavery, was "a Northern plantation owner."[2] Owning property, as it turned out, was yet another interest Lydia Hamilton Smith and Thaddeus Stevens would share when they eventually joined forces in Lancaster.

Biographers often describe Stevens as shy and retiring, but that might not fit the Stevens we find in these years. This Stevens, we're told, lived in a "house that was the rendezvous of all the bright spirits in the country round."[3] But the son of Baptist Sarah Morrill Stevens had his limits. William Hall reports that Stevens quit drinking during his Gettysburg days out of disgust for his friends' abuse of alcohol.[4]

Opposition to slavery was growing in Pennsylvania in 1825. On April 21, in Harrisburg, thirty-five miles northeast of Gettysburg, those feelings took violent form as a Maryland slaver left the courthouse with a fugitive slave just returned to him. Historian George H. Morgan takes us to the scene: "A great number of colored people attended the investigation armed with clubs and cudgels and exhibited a menacing appearance. As a matter of precaution, the master tied the slave's hands behind his back, but as he left the Court House steps, the colored men rushed furiously upon him and attempted a rescue. A serious combat ensued in which a number of the citizens were involved and received injury. In the melee, one of the Marylanders fired a pistol after having received several blows from the colored men, one of whom he wounded in the arm."[5] According to Morgan, the armed men eventually fell back, but they mounted another attack at the inn where the slaver had locked up the fugitive. The authorities waded in and arrested some nineteen "colored men." Four were acquitted; twelve were found guilty and ordered to serve out their sentences on the treadmill, a form of hard labor brought to American shores from England.

We don't know how long the Harrisburg rioters were ordered to tread the wheel,[6] but the fact that they risked such harsh punishment to frustrate the aims of a slaver would have been noticed, with approval, in Adams County. Even though no one had attacked any slavers directly, efforts to thwart slavery were underway, and courtroom champion Thaddeus Stevens was likely part of it. In his history of the Underground Railroad, Dr. Robert Smedley mentions that "Thaddeus Stevens, as a young lawyer, first practicing his profession, rendered valuable assistance." Smedley points out that Gettysburg was the nearest Underground Railroad station to the Maryland line. He also says that "there was a very friendly feeling in Gettysburg towards the abolitionists" in the 1820s.[7] On that point, he may have been a bit too optimistic. Abolitionist preacher Jonathan Blanchard faced rough crowds when he spoke in Gettysburg a few years later. We'll see a great deal of Blanchard in the years to come. He admired Stevens tremendously and led the drive to enlist Stevens in the antislavery cause, but

Fig. 6   James Buchanan (date unknown). LancasterHistory, Lancaster, Pennsylvania.

Blanchard also carried a burden for Stevens's soul for many years. Lydia Hamilton Smith was part of the reason.

As for antislavery efforts in the 1820s, Hoch names those believed to have been conductors or stationmasters in the early Underground Railroad in Adams and Franklin Counties, and although we don't see Stevens wearing a stationmaster's cap, he's never far from the action. Hoch identifies the McAllister, Wright, and Wierman families as leaders of the Adams County Underground Railroad. We're told that William Wright and his wife, Phoebe Wierman, "aided runaway slaves as early as 1828." Sarah Wright was a witness in the 1822 "liberty" trial in which Stevens won freedom for Eunice Reed, James Snively, and Abraham Snively. And from 1835 to 1843, Stevens owned land with the Wierman family near the York Springs Underground Railroad depot.[8]

One political note before we leave the 1820s. We've already heard Lydia tell the story of James Buchanan's father landing at Russell Tavern, her birthplace, when he first came to America. In 1827, Thaddeus Stevens found himself working alongside the elder Buchanan's son, a lawyer, at a trial in York, Pennsylvania. Recognizing the impact Stevens's intellectual and rhetorical skills could have in the political arena, James Buchanan tried to recruit him to the Democratic Party. Buchanan was a staunch supporter of war hero and slaveowner President Andrew Jackson. His sympathies lay with the South and slaveowners, and Stevens knew it. He bluntly rejected Buchanan's overtures on principle. Buchanan apparently took Stevens's curt response as an insult. Stevens may have been offended, as well, that a man who defended slavery would invite him, an increasingly active abolitionist, to join the party of Jackson. The possibility of a political alliance thoroughly extinguished, the two men kept their distance from each other for nearly forty years.[9]

A more personal observation, before we move on from the 1820s, concerns Thaddeus Stevens's hair. When Lydia Hamilton first likely became aware of Stevens, perhaps in the early 1830s, he was "in the prime of his life. He was said to have been 'a remarkably fine-looking man,' six feet tall with . . . smooth skin and beautiful chestnut hair."[10] But in 1827, Stevens—and half the population of Gettysburg and many other American communities —contracted "brain fever." Like typhoid fever, brain fever was a bacterial infection, possibly spread in drinking water, that attacked the victim's entire body. The symptoms included hair loss, stupor, headache, weakness, abdominal tenderness and distention, vomiting, pneumonia, and fever. Maximum body temperatures ranged between 104.2 and 108 degrees Fahrenheit. People were laid low for an average of thirty-one days. The infection, with a mortality rate of 12 percent, was still around in the twentieth century.[11]

Besides laying him low for a month, the illness claimed Stevens's wavy brown hair. He replaced it with a series of wigs that served as a ready target of derision for his enemies in years to come. What might young Lydia have thought of her newly bald friend and his wig? Having been aware of Stevens possibly since the early 1820s, when her mother rescued Keziah Shannon, Stevens's housekeeper, from a suicide attempt, she may have taken it in stride. It's doubtful she would have teased him about it, considering that he was a man of thirty-five and she a girl of fourteen. There is no indication it gave her pause, years later, when Stevens invited her to work for him in Lancaster. She would never have guessed, in 1827, or in 1844, that one of her responsibilities in Congressman Thaddeus Stevens's household would be to prepare the wigs he wore to work on Capitol Hill.

As we've already noted, 1830 was likely the year Stevens purchased Keziah Shannon's husband, Ephraim Wolrich, from his father and owner.[12] It was also the year Gettysburg newspaper editor Jacob Lefever (of the *Compiler*) resurrected scurrilous accusations that Stevens had a hand in the murder of Dinah, the pregnant serving girl. Some observers think that Lefever wanted to discredit Stevens's involvement in the Anti-Masonic Party, which was gaining traction in Pennsylvania at the time. Whatever Lefever's motivation, by June 1831, Stevens had had enough. He sued the newspaperman and eventually won. Lefever got jail time and was ordered to pay $1,800 in damages. Stevens, hoping to put an end to the matter, offered to forego the money in exchange for the identity of the anonymous letter writer Lefever had relied on for his libelous insinuations. Lefever refused.[13] Thaddeus Stevens entered Pennsylvania politics in 1833. He was elected to the Pennsylvania Assembly as a representative from Gettysburg.

He aligned himself with the Anti-Masonic Party. As a result, he was hated by Freemasons and Democrats alike.[14] Of course, the "word around town and in the opposition newspapers claimed that Stevens and his supporters had rigged his nomination."[15]

Newspapers were *the* means of mass communication in those days, and they published a cornucopia of information. On Lydia's nineteenth birthday, February 14, 1832, the *Star and Republican Banner*, a newspaper Stevens helped finance, ran this ad: "Reward for Negro, $100. Isaac, aged 20." In late June 1832, the *Adams Sentinel* had "many columns about cholera." Two months later, devastating illness still stalked the *Sentinel's* pages. The August 28 issue reported "58 deaths in Baltimore, in a week, then 121." It appears both Lydia and Stevens avoided this epidemic.

On October 15, 1833, Jacob Lefever—the editor Stevens sued for libel—reported in his *Compiler*: "Thaddeus Stevens elected." Lefever added, "Mr. Stevens riding around the county electioneering." Stevens took his seat in the legislature in December. On November 19, 1833, the *Compiler* reported that the forge at Stevens's Caledonia ironworks had been destroyed by fire. That same day, Stevens's paper estimated the loss in the fire at Mifflin Forge to be at least $5,000. On the last day of 1833, the *Compiler* ran a real estate ad: "Russell Tavern for sale. James King the present tenant. Owned by heirs of Samuel Russell, dec'd."[16] Did twenty-year-old Lydia Hamilton see the ad? Did her mother, Mrs. O'Neill? We don't know, but given that Lydia was still telling stories about her birthplace many years later, she might have been interested to see that it was about to change hands.

We can be confident that Lydia and her mother and most of the inhabitants of Pennsylvania noticed what happened in the sky in the dark hours of November 12 through 13, 1833. Modern astronomers tell us that the Earth passed through the tail of the comet Tempel-Tuttle that November.[17] But the people of Pennsylvania didn't know that when it happened. In 1858, annalist George H. Morgan described it as the night of the "Falling Stars" and vowed that the "great meteoric shower—an exhibition of natural 'fire works'" would long be remembered. Some described it as "grand, awful and sublime." "To the ignorant and superstitious citizens and countrymen," Morgan wrote, "the phenomena was overwhelming and terrific. In the language of an observer, it 'rained stars.'"[18]

Morgan considered the sky show one of the most incredible things he'd ever seen:

Fig. 7   The Leonids meteor shower, associated with comet Tempel-Tuttle, as seen over Niagara Falls in November 1833. Alamy.

Never before or since did such a countless number of meteors fall from the empyrean in so short a space of time. Most of them were globular in shape, but many in their rapid motion left behind a luminous tail, and these the imagination of the credulous very readily transformed into so many "fiery serpents." It is almost impossible to conceive the horror of mind which seized upon some people, even when the phenomena was explained by the better informed. Many of the bold as well as timid citizens, yielding alike to apprehension, gave over all as lost, and passed the exciting period in lamentation and prayer.

At this point, Morgan observes, "It was astonishing to behold how many became suddenly devout who were never devout before, yet, generally speaking, the fit of devotion was of no longer duration than the phenomena."[19]

The display truly must have been something special. Hoch tells us, "Modern scholars estimated the rate of the 1833 meteor shower at one hundred thousand per hour." On November 18, the Gettysburg *Sentinel* reported that inquiring minds were asking whether the meteorite shower might have been the cause of the fire at Stevens's Mifflin Forge.

Eight days later, the *Star and Sentinel* informed its readers that the fire was likely the work of an arsonist.[20]

CHAPTER 4

ANOTHER NAME CHANGE

In 1834, Thaddeus Stevens struck a pensive note about matters of the heart in a letter to his brother, Abner, who was then practicing medicine in Vermont. "As to innate natural affection," he wrote, "I doubt its existence: But the influence of habitual, constant association; the concentration of all our hopes, our fears, and our designs on particular objects, create ties as strong and as painful to sunder, as those usually attributed to natural affection—these feelings must be particularly strong in mothers."[1]

It's unlikely Lydia Hamilton ever read that letter, but in 1834, she was about to test the truth of the sentiments expressed in it.

Lydia came "of age" (that is, turned twenty-one) on Valentine's Day in 1834. A few months later, Lydia Hamilton likely married a man named Jacob Smith. We have no record, in Lydia's hand or any other, of their courtship or their wedding. We can picture the blushing bride, thanks to the many descriptions left to us by biographers, but for details about Jacob Smith, the principal source of information is newspaper death notices and obituaries. Novelist Elsie Singmaster noted in her research files that Jacob was probably born in 1808, but she does not explain how she arrived at that date.[2] That would make Jacob twenty-six years old when he and Lydia were married.

In 1884, the *Lancaster Intelligencer*'s obituary for Lydia Hamilton Smith noted that she was born Lydia O'Neill and reported that she was "regarded as 'colored,' but had very little negro blood in her veins, and could anywhere have passed as a Spaniard or Cuban . . . her features being finely cut, her lips thin, her hair long and wavy and her eyes black and piercing. . . . In her younger days she was considered quite handsome, and even in her later years she retained many traces of her former beauty." The story goes on to tell us that Lydia married "at 21, upon attaining womanhood, a negro named Jacob Smith, of Harrisburg . . . a musician of some note."[3]

From the *Lancaster Weekly Examiner and Express*, we learn that Lydia "when quite young . . . [was] married to a barber and musician named Smith—in Harrisburg, a full-blooded negro."[4] Judge Charles I. Landis, a Lancaster jurist who defended the reputations of Lydia Hamilton Smith and Thaddeus Stevens long after they were gone, reported that Jacob Smith was a teamster and a musician.[5] Biographer Alphonse B. Miller tells us that Lydia's new husband was a "Negro carpenter of Gettysburg."[6] Fawn Brodie, who devotes considerable space to Lydia in her biography of Thaddeus Stevens, reports that "at approximately age 20, Lydia Hamilton Smith married a barber, Jacob Smith." Brodie adds that Jacob was "considerably darker than Lydia."[7]

But when and how did Lydia and Jacob become an item? There is evidence that Jacob Smith lived in Gettysburg for at least several years before they were married. In 1833, the *Compiler* newspaper informed readers of "an uncalled [for] letter for Jacob Smith" at the post office.[8] The Gettysburg tax rolls list a single man named Jacob Smith as early as 1829. In 1834, the year he married Lydia, the list again includes Jacob Smith; he's listed as "a single col. man with no property." We should note here that Jacob's lack of property could have been explained, in some early nineteenth-century Pennsylvania communities, by laws barring such ownership by a Black man, but that doesn't appear to have been the case in Gettysburg. A Black woman named Sydney O'Brien, once enslaved by Gettysburg founder James Gettys, won her freedom shortly after his death in 1815 and proceeded to buy a small lot along Gettysburg's South Washington Street that became the anchor for the borough's African American neighborhood.[9]

Jacob Smith appears in the tax lists for 1835 through 1837 as a barber, but his race and any property he owned are not recorded. In 1838, he's again listed as a barber with no property. By 1839, Jacob Smith vanishes from the Gettysburg tax rolls.[10] It may seem a bit unusual that Lydia does not appear on the tax rolls with Jacob after they were married. The fact is that women (perhaps with the exception of Sydney O'Brien) had few property rights in Pennsylvania in the 1830s. Those rights were still at least six years away in 1838.[11] As we'll see later, Lydia Hamilton Smith wasn't prepared to wait that long for the patriarchal society of her time to make her an equal partner in property ownership.

With Jacob supporting them, probably as a barber and, perhaps, a musician, the Smiths wasted no time starting a family. In 1835, their son William was born.[12] Two years later, in 1837, Lydia would deliver her second and last child, Isaac.[13] We don't know what sort of life the Smiths had after their sons arrived. Tax records, showing Jacob as a man with no property, suggest that they struggled. That could have been at least part of the motivation for what they did next. As we've already seen, Jacob had roots in Harrisburg. Whether to improve their situation or return to family, or for some other reason, by 1840, Jacob, Lydia, William, and Isaac Smith had moved to Harrisburg. As we'll see, their fortunes did appear to improve with the move; they would not remain "propertyless" for long.

Thaddeus Stevens spent a lot of time in Harrisburg during these years, after his election to the state legislature the year before Lydia was married. Still in his early forties, he apparently had more than politics on his mind. William Hall tells us that Stevens "paid attention to Miss Sergeant, a daughter of the great lawyer, John Sergeant, who was pleased with the idea of the marriage, and the lady was not averse, but Miss Sergeant, once, in a jeweler's store, playfully suggested to Stevens to buy her a diamond ring which she admired. His ideas of propriety were shocked, or perhaps he thought that the young lady was mercenary or ambitious rather than loving, and he took offense at this and ceased his attentions."[14] The young woman's father, John Sergeant, was a well-known political figure from Philadelphia. He served in the state legislature but had moved on to national politics (and was vice presidential candidate on the Republican ticket with Henry Clay) before Thaddeus Stevens reached the Pennsylvania House of Representatives in 1833. Unlike James Buchanan, Sergeant shared a number of Stevens's views, including opposition to slavery, which might have paved the way for Stevens's introduction to one of Sergeant's daughters—most likely the eldest, Margaretta, who would have been in her twenties at the time. She apparently rebounded well from Stevens's rejection. Margaretta later married Major General George Meade, who served as commander of the Union Army of the Potomac from the Battle of Gettysburg to the end of the Civil War. Meade was also in his twenties in 1840.

Lydia Hamilton Smith was in her mid-twenties when she arrived in Harrisburg. It may have seemed big and busy to her. Nearly six thousand people lived there, three times the number of souls in Gettysburg. In 1812, the state legislature had chosen Harrisburg to be Pennsylvania's capital and had built, on the city's north side, a grand neoclassical capitol complex that dominated the landscape. But Harrisburg wasn't an elegant city.

"The streets were dirt," according to business and labor historian Gerald Eggert, "but orderly and platted in grid pattern." During some tense political moments in the 1830s, thugs roamed the streets and threatened legislators inside the capitol, including Thaddeus Stevens. The Susquehanna River flowed along the western edge of town, with the Pennsylvania Canal, built in 1834, just east of it. Residential houses, mostly single story, crowded a few city blocks stretching southward from the capitol. Blacksmiths' shops and other businesses kept workers busy, but the factories of the industrial revolution had not yet sprung up.[15] Elsie Singmaster's research notes provide additional details about the Harrisburg of Lydia's time: "Until 15 years ago [1843] land between the Pennsylvania Railroad station & 2nd St., as far north as Raspberry Alley was a sheet of stagnant water. Also along its South edge, fronting on 2nd, a long row of rusty willows. Skating in winter. Board walks, pebbled paths. The space between the railroad station & 2nd St. held a Pagoda-like Street Arsenal."[16]

In 1840, Dauphin County census takers recorded Jacob Smith as the head of a household in Harrisburg's North Ward. No other names are listed, but the record shows three free "colored" males and three "colored" females living in the Smith house. Two of the males were under ten (William would have been five that year, and Isaac, three). Lydia was almost certainly one of two adult females in the house; we do not know the identity of the other adult female. Might she have been Lydia's mother? We also do not know the identity of the female child under the age of ten.[17]

The family's fortunes improved materially in Harrisburg. By April 1841, Jacob and Lydia were able to buy a house. Records pinpoint the location of their new property as "between Public ground on Capitol Hill, North St., the northern end boundary of Harrisburg-in range of lots laid out on Fisher Rd. (now Canal St.—1841)." The deed book indicates that John Forster and his wife, Margaret, sold the house to "Jacob Smith & his wife, Lydia Smith" for $200.[18] As far as we know, that marks the first time Lydia's name appeared in an official record; it certainly would not be the last. The home's purchase price suggests that it was modest at best. The deed book doesn't describe the house, but 1841 tax lists for the North Ward, in which we find Jacob's name (but not Lydia's), report: "Jacob Smith—Col'd—1 town lot-value $600 with log or frame house, yearly income on Persons, traders, Occupations—$534."[19] The disparity between the deed book and the tax list suggests that an overzealous, or perhaps simply incompetent, tax assessor surveyed the North Ward in 1841. Regardless, the Smiths seemed to be on their way.

Did Lydia (or Jacob) have much, if any, contact with Thaddeus Stevens while she was living in Harrisburg and he was traveling there frequently, by stagecoach, for legislative sessions? If we plot the location of Mrs. Smith's home on a map, using the description from the deed book, we find that she was living practically in the shadow of the capitol complex.[20] Chance encounters between Mrs. Smith and Stevens would seem possible, and if Stevens, who may have known Lydia from Gettysburg, had followed her fortunes even casually, he would have known that she and Jacob had moved to Harrisburg. He might even have stopped by to see how they were faring.

Novelist Elsie Singmaster was convinced that the two encountered each other in Harrisburg. She imagined how such a reunion might have gone in her novel *I Speak for Thaddeus Stevens*:

> He had gone only a short distance when, hurrying from Foster's Extension, north of the city, where she lived with her black husband, appeared Lydia O'Neill, once Hamilton by no legal right, now Mrs. Smith. She called "Mr. Stevens!" First loudly, then faintly, as though repenting her temerity. In Gettysburg, you knew Mr. Stevens was kind; in Harrisburg, you knew he was celebrated.
>
> Mr. Stevens halted instantly, and said, "Why, Lydia!" and put his hand into his pocket. "I meant to send you a present. I hope Smith'll be good to you."
>
> Her velvety eyes shining, Lydia looked up, as her mother, as Keziah Ulrich, as all Negroes and children looked at Mr. Stevens. "So do I!"
>
> "You have a fine church here."
>
> "Yes, we do. I can go to Mass every Sunday."
>
> "That's right, everything's good that helps us along. Hold out your hand."
>
> "It's too much!"
>
> Mr. Stevens waved her away. A decent little body, always neat, tidy, and respectful. He gave his head a shake and walked on.[21]

Several times in her novel, in describing interactions between Stevens and Mrs. Smith, Singmaster seems to intimate, but only obliquely, that Stevens had more than a paternal appreciation for her. She offers no concrete evidence, however. But other writers exercised none of her restraint. William Hall flatly asserts that Mrs. Smith and Stevens became lovers well before she arrived in Lancaster. After relating the story of Stevens's abandoned courtship of Margaretta Sergeant, Hall continues, "For many years Mrs. Smith, a colored woman nearly white, was his housekeeper. She was the wife of a barber. He [Stevens] first became intimate with her at Harrisburg." Hall follows that assertion with what may have constituted, for him, evidence of a special bond between Stevens and Mrs. Smith. He mentions her tender care of Stevens during the illnesses that laid him low in later years, and he points out that she left money, in her will, to keep Stevens's "grave in order."[22]

Fig. 8   William M. Hall. From *History of Bedford, Somerset, and Fulton Counties, Pennsylvania* (Chicago: Waterman, Watkins, 1884).

Numerous observers have acknowledged that Mrs. Smith's dedication to the enfeebled Stevens and her abiding concern, more than twenty years after his death, that his grave be well tended seem to exceed the thoughtfulness we might expect from a housekeeper. But does that behavior prove that she was more in Stevens's life and household than an employee? Some would say yes; others, no. Those who say no generally offer, as their trump card, the fact that Lydia Hamilton Smith was a deeply religious person, an Irish Catholic communicant, who would be very unlikely to violate her wedding vows. On the other hand, aficionados of Mrs. Smith and Stevens who answer the question in the affirmative sometimes suggest that Stevens commissioned a portrait of Mrs. Smith after she became his housekeeper in Lancaster. In arguing that Stevens and Mrs. Smith likely were more intimate than some suppose, biographer Fawn Brodie assigns great significance to the commissioning of that painting: "The act suggests something of the intensity of his [Stevens's] affection, and perhaps, too, a need to leave some kind of quiet evidence of it for the historical record."[23]

At this point, my exploration of Lydia Hamilton Smith's life inclines me to agree with Brodie and others who believe that Mrs. Smith and Stevens developed a relationship, whatever its physical nature, that exceeded the usual bond between a householder and a housekeeper. I am sympathetic to the view that Stevens's commissioning of a portrait was freighted

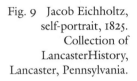

Fig. 9   Jacob Eichholtz,
self-portrait, 1825.
Collection of
LancasterHistory,
Lancaster, Pennsylvania.

with more than simple admiration for Mrs. Smith's beauty. In fact, based on my reading, I think that may not have been the first portrait of Mrs. Smith that Stevens had commissioned.

This possibility hinges on the answers to two questions. How many portraits of Lydia Hamilton Smith are there? And were Mrs. Smith, Stevens, and renowned Lancaster portrait artist Jacob Eichholtz ever in the same place at the same time? Finding the answers to these questions, and a few others, may help us better understand what happened in Jacob and Lydia Smith's household after 1840. Let's start with the portraits question.

In 1913, Pennsylvania newspaper editor and author W. U. Hensel published a paper entitled "Jacob Eichholtz, Painter." In it, he applauds the Lancaster artist's industry and artistry, and he ticks off a long list of the illustrious patrons Eichholtz painted, including Mrs. Lydia Smith. Hensel goes on to announce that *a* portrait of Lydia Smith had just surfaced in Lancaster: "Redmond Conyngham, Esq., is the owner of a recently discovered portrait of Lydia Smith, the colored woman who was Stevens's famous housekeeper during a large part of his life and who shared the bounty of his will."

Hensel is certain it was Lydia and fairly confident it was done by Jacob Eichholtz.

The identity of the picture is undoubted and its execution meritorious. It represents the subject as a comely quadroon of about twenty-five, with a pink flushed countenance. It has been supposed to be an Eichholtz.

The subject is well remembered by our older citizens as the housekeeper, nurse and business manager of Mr. Stevens from at least as early as January 1, 1845, until he died in 1868.

Hensel then writes, a bit enigmatically, "At that time [Stevens's death], she was not without the vigor to prosecute a claim against his estate." (We'll explain the origin of that last comment a bit later.) Hensel believed that the details all lined up. "The dates can be easily reconciled," he writes, "with the theory that Eichholtz painted this portrait for her or for Mr. Stevens. I incline to think he did, in view of the style of the picture and the period at which it seems to have been painted, and from the fact that Stevens was his patron."[24]

Hensel was on fairly solid ground in identifying the subject of the painting; people who knew Lydia were still around to make a positive identification. Art historians today generally agree that the portrait (still held by Redmond Conyngham's family) is, in fact, of Lydia Smith. But Hensel's suggestion that it was done by Eichholtz—after Lydia arrived in Lancaster—doesn't hold up. Lydia likely hired on as Stevens's housekeeper around 1844, and Jacob Eichholtz died in 1842. In addition, Hensel's suggestion that Lydia might have commissioned Eichholtz herself only works if she sat for it after 1844, and by then Eichholtz was no longer living.

But if Jacob Eichholtz didn't paint it, who did? The Frick Art Reference Library in New York took a close look at Redmond Conyngham's painting and photographed it for their records. Experts concluded that "the portrait resembles the work of C. B. King [Philadelphia artist Charles Bird King] more than that of Eichholtz, and is probably by that artist. . . . [Collector] Mrs. James H. Beal and [art historian] Mrs. McCook Knox agree with this attribution."[25] The Frick photo is black-and-white but the record includes a careful description of the colors used in it: "Dark red-brown eyes, black hair. White dress, pale golden yellow cloak. The background is dark greenish gray at the left and a dark brownish color at the right."

That brings us to what I believe is a second portrait of Lydia Hamilton Smith, one that was likely painted before Lydia arrived in Lancaster and

Fig. 10   C. B. King, portrait of Lydia Hamilton Smith. Courtesy of the Frick Art
Reference Library.

might be the work of Jacob Eichholtz. The Historic Preservation Trust of Lancaster County, Pennsylvania, has been credited with supplying a color photograph of this portrait to publications and websites seeking to present an image of the "real" Lydia Hamilton Smith since the early 2000s. The Lydia in this portrait looks very much like the woman in the King portrait: the eyes, nose, mouth, hairstyle, and hairline are quite similar. But the facial features in this painting are softer; Lydia looks a bit younger. In 2003, the Historic Preservation Trust gave Charles Bird King credit for this painting. But other organizations, including the Lancaster newspapers and the Thaddeus Stevens Society, based in Gettysburg, have at one time or another attributed it to Jacob Eichholtz.

If the photo is an accurate reproduction of the painting, it can't be the one examined by the Frick Art Reference Library. The color scheme and attire do not match the description the Frick provides for the King work. This Lydia is wearing what appears to be a dark brownish dress with a very high neckline, not at all like the white, shoulder-revealing dress with yellow sash King painted. In the King portrait, Lydia looks quite pale, nearly white. This Lydia has a rosy complexion and dark, reddish-brown hair. The background is a medium reddish brown, becoming very dark brown as it reaches Lydia's left shoulder.

It's interesting to note that the reddish hues in this portrait are very similar to the color scheme Eichholtz employed when he painted Thaddeus Stevens. In the Stevens portrait, the subject has a similarly ruddy complexion and the background is an almost identical reddish-brown. When did Eichholtz paint this portrait? We can pinpoint the year: Eichholtz signed his name *in* the painting, on the spine of a book Stevens's hand is resting on, and beside his name, Eichholtz added "1838."[26] Is it possible that Eichholtz painted Lydia and Stevens consecutively in the same place at the same time? If we follow the trio's travels, I believe we can construct two scenarios that would have allowed that to happen.

We start with Lydia. We've already seen, in this chapter, that the last time her husband Jacob's name appeared on the Gettysburg tax rolls was 1838. If the tax assessors made their rounds shortly after the first of the year, and the family left for Harrisburg soon afterwards, they could have been in Harrisburg as early as February 1838.

We know Thaddeus Stevens spent a great deal of time in Harrisburg in 1838. He was there on February 22. On that day, after serving as a delegate to the Pennsylvania Constitutional Convention, he refused to sign the revised document because it denied Black men the right to vote. As a state representative, Stevens would have been at his desk in the forty-eighth session of the legislature, which ran in Harrisburg from December 5, 1837, to April 17, 1838.[27]

We can track Eichholtz's travels through letters he wrote to his daughter, Catharine, and her husband, Robert Lindsay. The Lindsays lived in Philadelphia, where Eichholtz painted for many years, and they looked after Eichholtz's artistic interests there. On February 6, 1838, Eichholtz wrote his daughter that he had "received commission from Secretary of State to paint four portraits at Harrisburg."[28] On March 3, 1838, we find Eichholtz "on his way to Harrisburg."[29] On March 19, he wrote the Lindsays a chatty letter from Elizabethtown, Pennsylvania, midway between Lancaster and Harrisburg, reporting: "[rail] cars stopped by snow, painted six heads in Harrisburg. . . . Merely the heads, shall finish at home."[30]

We've managed to find Lydia Hamilton Smith, Thaddeus Stevens, and Jacob Eichholtz in Harrisburg all at the same time. Might Eichholtz have painted Mrs. Smith and Stevens while he was there in March? It's interesting to note that heading into Harrisburg, Eichholtz wrote that he had been commissioned to paint *four* portraits for Secretary of State Burrowes. While stuck in a snowstorm on his way home, he wrote that he had completed *six* "heads," which he intended to finish in his studio in Lancaster. Could Mrs. Smith and Stevens be heads five and six?

Of course, this scenario raises other questions. If Lydia was in Harrisburg during those weeks, would she have wanted to sit for a portrait with two little boys in tow? What would Jacob have thought of Stevens taking her off to have her portrait painted? Why would Stevens even want a portrait of Lydia, if she was just an attractive young woman he'd known since she was a little girl? Given the rave reviews of her beauty at the time, it's certainly possible he would have noticed her as she came of age in Gettysburg. Might there have been more to their relationship than simple friendship? Some of Stevens's critics have accused him of luring Lydia away from her husband. Did he encourage the Smiths to move to Harrisburg, where he could see more of her?

Here's a second scenario for getting Lydia, Stevens, and Eichholtz in one place at the same time so Eichholtz could paint her portrait. In this version, based on the Gettysburg tax records, we know that Jacob and Lydia Smith were still in Gettysburg as 1838 began. Stevens would have been there intermittently, when he wasn't in Harrisburg or elsewhere doing legislative and legal work. We know that Stevens "sat for his portrait while a lawyer in Gettysburg."[31] Might that year have been 1838, the year Jacob Eichholtz signed his name on the spine of a book in his portrait of Stevens? We don't know where Stevens was actually sitting when Eichholtz did his "head," but if he was in Gettysburg, then we've managed to assemble the trio in the same place at the same time again. The other questions apply here as well, starting with how Jacob Smith would have felt if Stevens had proposed having Lydia's portrait painted. Under what conditions might Lydia have agreed to such an arrangement?

Fig. 11   Thaddeus Stevens. Engraving by John Sartain from the painting by Jacob Eichholtz, ca. October 27, 1838. Original painting in the collection of Gettysburg College. Library of Congress, Washington, DC.

We don't know the answers to these questions, but the mere possibility that Thaddeus Stevens might have commissioned Jacob Eichholtz to paint Lydia's portrait—after she was married—makes me wonder what the true nature of her relation to Stevens was.

She knew he had an appreciation for attractive women. Recall that Lydia's sad story about Keziah Shannon ends with the exclamation, "I have heard Mr. Stevens say she was the handsomest woman he had ever seen."[32] Might Stevens have made this observation about Keziah in a conversation in which he extolled Mrs. Smith's beauty as well? Of course, we don't know. But I can't help wondering whether he had grown closer to Mrs. Smith than has generally been assumed even before either of them moved to Lancaster. And, if so, might it have affected Lydia's relationship with Jacob?

We don't know what Lydia was thinking in 1842 as she cared for William and Isaac in the house she and Jacob had purchased in Harrisburg the previous year. We don't know Jacob's thoughts as he sought to support his family as a barber and musician. We have a better idea of what

Thaddeus Stevens was thinking.

Stevens moved from Gettysburg to Lancaster in August of that year, hoping to improve his balance sheet, which at the time was weighted heavily to the debit side, largely thanks to his propensity for buying land. He took rooms at the Fountain Inn Hotel on South Queen Street and announced his arrival in a local newspaper: "Thaddeus Stevens, Attorney-at-law, Office opposite the Farmer's Bank, in the home formerly occupied by James Hopkins, Esq., dec'd." (His financial strategy worked; in short order, his income reached $12,000 to $15,000 a year, a princely sum at the time.)[33] But even serious debt couldn't slow Stevens's desire to buy property.

According to Judge Charles I. Landis, on April 21, 1843, Stevens bought (at sheriff's sale) a lot and two houses on the northeast corner of South Queen and Vine Streets.[34] Stevens reportedly paid $4,000 for Lot 134, but he seems to have gotten quite a bit for his money, including the Kleiss Brewery on the corner of South Queen and Vine, several smaller buildings, and a house adjacent to the brewery at 45–47 South Queen. It was common practice, in those days, for lawyers to buy up properties relatively cheaply at sheriff's (or tax) sales and then recoup their investment and earn a profit by renting them out, sometimes to former owners who had defaulted on their property taxes.[35]

That was, in fact, what Stevens did on South Queen Street. The property came up for sheriff's sale when the brewery operators (the Kleiss family) fell behind in their taxes. Mrs. George Kleiss, widow of the former proprietor of the brewery, continued to run the establishment until at least 1850, when a new tenant, Jonathan Whitlinger, took over. Stevens apparently continued to rent the houses at 45 and 47 South Queen after 1843, but we don't have the names of those tenants.[36]

Meanwhile, in Harrisburg, Lydia and Jacob Smith's marriage was unraveling. We don't know exactly why, but their obituaries offer a variety of explanations. One reported that "when quite young," Lydia had married "a barber and musician named Smith . . . a full-blooded negro, who turned out to be a worthless fellow and who ill-treated her."[37] Another wrote that "her husband with whom she lived in Harrisburg and elsewhere did not prove a congenial companion."[38] The *Republican Compiler*, after Jacob's death, seemed to take his side in the affair: "We are sorry to say that Mr. Smith was very unfortunate in his domestic relations."[39] Darlene Colon, who has researched Lydia's life and portrayed her in dramatic presentations for many years, suggests that Lydia may have wearied of Jacob's frequent

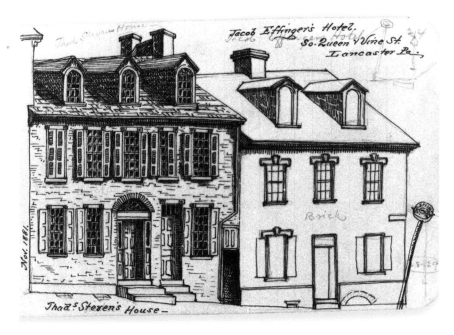

Fig. 12   David McNeely Stauffer, sketch of 45–47 South Queen Street in Lancaster. Stevens bought and rented a lot and two homes on the northeast corner of South Queen and Vine Streets in 1843. Stevens made 45 South Queen (left) his office and home, while Mrs. Smith operated the brewery and boardinghouse at 47 South Queen. This pencil sketch shows the properties as they appeared in 1881. LancasterHistory, Lancaster, Pennsylvania.

absences for musical performances.[40]

Brodie mentions an 1868 newspaper article about Stevens that relates to the idea we considered earlier—that the breakup wasn't all Jacob's fault. In the story, an editor asserts, without supporting evidence, that Stevens "separated a handsome mulatto woman from her husband . . . [and] . . . deemed it his duty to provide for her."[41] Whatever the cause, things clearly had come to a head. In 1844, "Jacob Smith and Lydia his wife" sold their house in Harrisburg to Henry Berghause for $363,[42] and Lydia left, taking nine-year-old William and seven-year-old Isaac with her. If that left them homeless for the moment, they wouldn't be for long.

Down in Lancaster, little more than thirty miles southeast of Harrisburg, Stevens had left the historic Fountain Inn Hotel for newer lodgings. Lancaster attorney and former state assemblyman Emanuel C. Reigart had built three three-story houses in 1844 on the west side of South Queen

Street, near the hotel, and Stevens had leased the middle one. Occupying one of the other new homes was Stevens's close friend Thomas H. Burrowes. Burrowes was a former Pennsylvania secretary of state and was the first Pennsylvania public school superintendent. (Stevens helped create and preserve public education in Pennsylvania.) The third house was occupied by Charles B. Penrose, a former state senator and US Treasury Department solicitor. The humble New Englander was moving in the finest social circles in Lancaster.[43]

Living in a house, rather than a hotel, meant that a man of Stevens's means needed a good housekeeper. Finding such an individual, however, was apparently not easy. One newspaper account, years later, reported that "previous to her [Lydia's] coming, he had suffered much discontent and annoyance from dishonest servants,"[44] but that was about to change. Judge Landis tells us Stevens eventually "endeavored to employ a woman by the name of Anna Sulkey, but this woman, about that time, became the wife of Dennis Martin, a 'colored' barber, who lived in this city, and she, therefore, while declining the position, recommended him to her cousin, Lydia H. Smith, then a widow with two small children. Upon this recommendation, Mr. Stevens engaged Mrs. Smith, who, shortly thereafter, came to Lancaster."[45]

Biographer Ralph Korngold thought it was a more personal process. He writes, "Stevens remembered having known Lydia in Gettysburg, before her marriage, and to have been favorably impressed. He communicated with her and engaged her." However it came to pass, Mrs. Smith was invited, she accepted, and she moved to Lancaster, setting in motion a sequence of events that would make her one of the most famous women of her time. Korngold notes that she brought her own furniture with her.[46] That detail helps us understand a provision in Stevens's will: he pointed out that Mrs. Smith would have to sort out the furniture, since his and hers had become thoroughly mixed together in his house. I can't help wondering how often that happened—how many housekeepers would have commingled their furniture with their employer's furnishings to that extent. The merging of furniture apparently didn't start in 1844. When Mrs. Smith and her sons arrived, they settled into a small "one-story frame house on the rear of Mr. Stevens' lot, fronting on South Christian Street."[47]

As Mrs. Smith shifted her focus to meeting Thaddeus Stevens's needs, her estranged husband remained focused on her. By 1844, Jacob Smith had gained quite a reputation throughout the region as a musician. The *Harrisburg Telegraph* reportedly noted that he was "for many years leader of the Harrisburg Brass Band."[48] The band seems to have ranked high in public esteem. When they were booked to perform at the inauguration of Governor William Bigler in 1851, a newspaper in Bloomsburg, Pennsylvania, told readers the "unrivaled Brass Band, of Harrisburg," would "be fully equipped . . . and take a prominent part in the Inauguration ceremonies."[49] The *Compiler* remembered Jacob's musical talents fondly after he died: "Poor Jake, he was the Prince of Barbers and an excellent Musician, and many of our lads and lasses will miss the rich music of his violin, when they meet to trip the light fantastic toe."[50] The *Lancaster New Era*, writing about the years immediately after Jacob and Lydia separated, called him "quite a proficient musician" and reported that he (and his band) had put on a very successful performance at Mechanics' Hall in Lancaster. According to the paper, that particular appearance in Lancaster had special significance for Jacob. The paper informed readers that Jacob booked the gig as an excuse to come to Lancaster "seeking reconciliation" with Lydia. The performance may have been a triumph, but his attempt to win back his beautiful wife failed.[51] There is no indication that Lydia ever entertained the thought of returning to Jacob and Harrisburg.

CHAPTER 5

Much More than a Housekeeper

Lydia Hamilton Smith was thirty-one years old when she joined Thaddeus Stevens in Lancaster, and she made a very favorable impression from the start. One newspaper described her as "a beautiful quadroon." The paper reported that "she had received no education, but by her unaided efforts had picked up a good fund of information."[1] Mrs. Smith would admit, somewhat apologetically, years later that she was never much of a reader, but she was most certainly able to read and write when she came to work for Stevens.

She also came equipped with all the knowledge and skills necessary to manage a household properly. Stevens biographer Thomas Frederick Woodley was quite impressed with her. She was, he writes, "unusually attractive, she was neat in appearance and well above average intelligence. . . . A small woman, she was light complexioned, with almost Caucasian features, and her hair was nearly straight. She gave great attention to her appearance and dress." Woodley calls her a "woman of poise and personal dignity . . . never loquacious, efficient and retiring." Stevens, he writes, "grew more and more to rely upon her."[2] The *Lancaster New Era* saluted her, many years later, as "a magnificent caterer" and reported that, "as the managing head of the Stevens household, [she] also came in contact with many of the great men of this country of whom she conversed intelligently and entertainingly." The paper noted that Mrs. Smith, having become "possessed of considerable means," "gave with [generous] hand to the deserving poor, and no one who was worthy, ever appealed to her in vain."[3] Interestingly enough, the same was often said of Stevens.

Mrs. Smith's reception in Lancaster was considerably more cordial than the one accorded her employer in 1842. She quickly earned a place in the hearts of those who became her neighbors and friends, but there was no fuss over her arrival. She was simply a free woman of color coming to Lancaster to work. Stevens, on the other hand, was something else. His legal reputation for winning big cases, his vocal opposition to slavery, and his success at winning freedom for fugitive slaves in court preceded him. He was a nineteenth-century celebrity, especially among African Americans, and "many of them came to the County-seat [Lancaster] to obtain a sight of the man of whose fame they had already heard so much."[4]

The legal community, likewise aware of Stevens's prowess as an attorney, did not welcome him to the Lancaster bar, and while "his invasion of it was regarded jealously by most of its members, he was especially antagonized by Benjamin Champneys—later [Pennsylvania] Attorney General under Governor Shunk."[5] Stevens's stance against slavery drew scorn from Southern sympathizers in the community (there were many), including famous Lancaster historian Alexander Harris. The depth of Harris's animosity was revealed when, shortly after Stevens arrived, the two men found themselves face-to-face on a "weed-grown path beside the street. One had to step aside so the other could pass, and Harris quickly resolved that he would not extend the courtesy. Walking close up to Stevens in a challenging manner, he looked squarely into the heavily-browed eyes of the Old Commoner and said defiantly, 'I never yield to a skunk.' Stevens, taken somewhat by surprise, looked at him calmly for a moment and then, stepping to the side of the path, answered: 'I always do.'"[6]

Stevens held no elected office when he arrived in Lancaster, but he was involved in politics nonetheless. His attention now focused on attaining a position on the national level. Previously, he had campaigned for presidential candidate William Henry Harrison in 1840 and believed he was a "certainty" for postmaster general (then a cabinet post). But opposition from Henry Clay and Daniel Webster snatched it away. Stevens reportedly never forgave Webster for the slight.[7] Stevens was "in the midst of his Scott-for-President movement, during the Summer of 1842 . . . when he decided to leave Gettysburg and take up his residence in Lancaster."[8] (General Winfield Scott did not win the Whig Party's presidential nod in 1842; he did head the party's ticket in 1852 but lost the election.)

Jonathan Blanchard, the abolitionist preacher Stevens had helped gain entry to Gettysburg audiences in the mid-1830s, wrote to Stevens in 1842, inviting him to speak at a meeting of the new antislavery Liberty Party in Cincinnati, Ohio. Liberty Party organizers included Salmon Chase (then a Cincinnati lawyer, later secretary of the treasury and chief justice of the US Supreme Court), Samuel Lewis (a Methodist preacher and former state schools superintendent in Ohio), and Bellamy Storer (a congressman from Ohio). Blanchard took the opportunity to remind Stevens that he was still "very anxious that [Stevens] become a Christian, for the salvation of [his] soul," but beyond that, he wanted Stevens to "employ the extraordinary powers with which God has endowed you for the furtherance of righteousness and justice on this wretched earth." The preacher confessed to Stevens that he had "an almost superstitious belief in your talents."9

Fig. 13 Jonathan Blanchard. Photo: Wikimedia Commons (from Keith Call, *Wheaton*).

It's not clear how much thought Stevens gave to the new antislavery party and Blanchard's invitation, but we know that relocating to Lancaster for financial reasons did not diminish his efforts on behalf of those trapped in the evil bondage of slavery. Dr. Robert Smedley, a chronicler of the Underground Railroad, mentions Stevens in a lengthy account of a group of "railroad" passengers who passed through Lancaster as they fled bondage in Maryland.10 One of the men in that group of freedom seekers, O. C. Gilbert, later told the story in an autobiography that was never published. In his account, Gilbert says the year was 1848 and that, at one point on their journey, he and his comrades "were directed to call at No. 45 South Queen Street [in Lancaster] and we would find a lawyer, who was a friend to the slaves."11 (Thaddeus Stevens owned that house in 1848.) Gilbert wrote that he didn't learn the lawyer's name before Stevens sent the men on to a veteran Underground Railroad conductor east of Lancaster, Daniel Gibbons. There, as Gilbert described the friendly lawyer who had sent them to Gibbons with a letter of introduction, Gibbons told the men that the lawyer was Thaddeus Stevens. He added, "Thee has no better friend in the state than the man who wrote this letter." Gilbert stayed in Pennsylvania and later toured widely with his family in a show that included his retelling the story of his flight to freedom and the worthy Underground Railroad crews, including Thaddeus Stevens, who helped him succeed.[12] Gilbert did not mention Mrs. Smith in his writing, but we know she was already working with Stevens in 1848. She might well have met Gilbert and his companions before they continued their journey east.

We'll take a closer look at Mrs. Smith's role in what became a rather elaborate and clever Underground Railroad operation in Lancaster. But, before we get to that, we need to note a couple of significant developments during her first two years in Lancaster. First, it's important to know that from the moment Lydia Hamilton Smith arrived, Thaddeus Stevens made it clear to his family and, apparently, his friends and social acquaintances that she was to be addressed as "Mrs. Smith." That may not strike us as unusual from our vantage point in the twenty-first century, but in nineteenth-century America, to call a "colored" employee by anything other than her first name was truly exceptional. We have no written record of Stevens's edict, but family and friends obviously respected his wishes and, by extension, respected Mrs. Smith. When they wrote letters to him or to her, the salutation was always "Mrs. Smith," never "Lydia."

Perhaps Stevens imposed the rule to underscore his belief that all people are equal and deserving of respect. Addressing Lydia Hamilton Smith as "Mrs. Smith" certainly sent that message to those in Lancaster who thought that this young, mixed-race housekeeper deserved no more respect than plantation owners accorded to those they enslaved. Stevens affirmed that message repeatedly over the course of his life, including in an 1838 letter to the committee organizing a new antislavery center in Philadelphia. "Interest, fashion, false religion, and tyranny may triumph for a while, and rob man of his inalienable rights," he wrote, "but the people cannot always be deceived, and will not always be oppressed."[13]

Given what we now know about the history of Lydia Hamilton Smith and Thaddeus Stevens, there might be another explanation for Stevens's insistence that Lydia be addressed as "Mrs. Smith." Perhaps it was a gesture of personal respect and affection on the part of the old bachelor. They both knew that the white-dominated America in which they lived would never countenance the marriage of a white man and a Black woman, no matter how light her complexion or how graceful her manner or how much they cared for each other. Taking her into his life as "Mrs. Smith," not simply Lydia, the serving girl, and including her in every aspect of that life, as we'll see him do, might have been as close as they could come, publicly, to telling the world how deeply involved they were. Nowhere do we read that Mrs. Smith expressed the slightest dissatisfaction over her life with Thaddeus Stevens, despite the onslaught of vicious gossip and criticism that swirled around them almost from the moment she arrived in Lancaster. And, as we saw in the introduction, the verbal assault persisted long after they were both dead and gone. Even when their life together presented challenges most bright and beautiful young women from Gettysburg would have chosen not to endure, she did not complain, and once they were together, nothing short of death ever separated them.

As Mrs. Smith focused her attention on bringing order and serenity to Stevens's home in 1846, a twenty-three-year-old attorney named Oliver Jesse Dickey came to Lancaster. O. J. Dickey, as he was known, was the son of a Beaver County, Pennsylvania, congressman. By the time he came to Lancaster, he was a graduate of Dickinson College in Carlisle, Pennsylvania, and had studied law. His purpose in Lancaster was to join Stevens's law practice; we're told that Stevens "kindly received him and proffered him the use of his office . . . [and] . . . employed him at a fixed salary to attend to a certain part of his business."[14] Alexander Harris reported that the association "led to a lifelong attachment between Dickey and Thaddeus Stevens." Stevens must have entertained quite a high opinion of Dickey's talents; he named him one of the executors of his will. As executor, Dickey would clash with Mrs. Smith. As we'll see later, it proved to be an extremely trying and ultimately disappointing experience for her.[15]

Dickey's presence in Lancaster had little impact on Mrs. Smith's life in 1846, but the arrival of two young men from Vermont, in 1847, did make a big difference. Stevens's younger brother, Dr. Abner Morrill Stevens, a fifty-three-year-old widower living in St. Johnsbury, Vermont, died that year, leaving two sons: Alanson, fourteen, and Thaddeus Jr., twelve. Morrill, as he was known, had arranged for a guardian to take the boys in the event of his own death, but the guardian's declining health made it impossible in 1847. As a result, the family decided that the boys should move to Lancaster and live under the watchful eye of their Uncle Thaddeus.[16]

Given Stevens's professional and political obligations, he had little time for parenting. Fortunately for him and for Alanson and Thaddeus Jr., they had Mrs. Smith. We can't know exactly how she felt about it, but she was now the principal caregiver for four boys: Alanson, Thad Jr., and her own sons, William, who was twelve in 1847, and Isaac, who was ten. That would have made for a busy household. And Mrs. Smith "mothered" them all.

As time went by, the Stevens boys, especially Thad Jr., came to rely on her as much as her own sons did.

Those new responsibilities would have been challenge enough for a young housekeeper, but Mrs. Smith soon had even more, equally important things to think about. As we've already seen, Stevens wasted no time getting on board with Underground Railroad activities when he relocated to Lancaster, and it is commonly believed that Mrs. Smith joined him in that critical work. We actually find support for that belief in her will.

In that document, Mrs. Smith bequeathed fifty dollars to a woman named Rhoda Goodrich (or Goodridge). Mrs. Goodridge was the widow of Glenalvin Goodridge, who made a name for himself when he established one of the nation's first photography studios in York, Pennsylvania, just twenty-five miles west of Lancaster. Glenalvin's father, William C. Goodridge, rose from slavery to become one of York's leading businessmen before the Civil War. But the primary reason the Goodridge family is celebrated today is for their involvement in the Underground Railroad. (Their story is currently on display at the Goodridge Freedom Center in York.) When she included Rhoda Goodridge in her will, Mrs. Smith connected the dots for us between the work she and Stevens were doing in Lancaster and the Goodridge family's Underground Railroad activities. Of course, it's possible the two women met through some other avenue, but it seems likely that their relationship grew, at least in part, from their mutual involvement in the Underground Railroad.[17]

We find more support for Mrs. Smith's possible Underground Railroad involvement in the official history of Lancaster's Bethel A.M.E. (African Methodist Episcopal) Church, which notes that Thaddeus Stevens and Lydia Hamilton Smith had close ties to the congregation. According to that history, the church's members were among the earliest Underground Railroad operators in Lancaster. But Mrs. Smith and Stevens were not on Bethel's membership roll; she was a devout Catholic, and he seldom darkened the doorway of any church. Their "close ties," then, must be related to the fact that "for most of their first fifty years [beginning in 1821], the people of Bethel . . . took great personal risks to assist those escaping slavery." The church's history notes that "a church women's organization known as the Tent Sisters made new clothing, distributing it to those seeking safe haven." According to the history, two African American lumber merchants, Rev. Stephen Smith and William Whipper, of Columbia, Pennsylvania, also supported the effort. The businessmen hid fugitives in false-end boxcars and forwarded them to freedom on the Philadelphia and Columbia Railroad.[18]

Bethel's official history mentions that three ministers of their church were especially involved in the Underground Railroad. One of them, Rev. Robert Boston, a barber in addition to his clerical duties, was closely allied with Stevens's efforts in the struggle. In an 1847 letter to his friend and colleague Jeremiah Brown, a former state legislator and farmer in southern Lancaster County, Stevens described recent activity and, in the process, revealed the heart of his operation. "I learn," Stevens wrote, "that the manstealers of Lancaster have taken measures to obtain authority from Maryland . . . to arrest and take into slavery two colored girls who lately lived with you and your brother. . . . Will you see that they flee to an immediate city of refuge. They should not stop short of Canada. There is a regular chain of agents and spies of slaveholders in this and all adjoining counties." Then Stevens told Brown how he was thwarting the manstealers: "I have a spy on the spies and thus ascertain the facts." The Underground Railroad was very busy, Stevens wrote. "These are the eighth set of slaves I have warned this week."[19]

Stevens was a bit modest in his letter to Brown. He actually had a network of spies, and Rev. Robert Boston of Bethel A.M.E. was one of them. The target of the spying was a "brutish slave catcher named Hughes" who rented an office on the southeast corner of Centre Square, opposite the old courthouse and directly across from "one of [Robert] Boston's salons." George Hughes, who billed himself as a private detective, was the Lancaster agent for Ridgeley, Cook & Company, a sprawling slave-catching operation headquartered in Baltimore. From his vantage point across the street, Boston could keep a close eye on comings and goings at Hughes's place. What came in, apparently rather frequently in a city so close to the Maryland border, were written messages describing runaway slaves that Hughes and his henchmen should look for.[20]

Hughes was ruthlessly dedicated to his task, but he had a serious weakness: he could not read or write. To know what the messages said and to draw up documents for arresting fugitives when he found them, Hughes was forced to rely on literate friends. One of those friends, or at least so people thought, was Edward Rauch, a deputy prothonotary whose job involved recording and filing legal papers in civil court cases. Another was twenty-six-year-old Peter Henry, a clerk in the courthouse. Rauch dutifully read the descriptions to Hughes, Henry prepared the arrest warrants, and then both of them immediately reported all the details to Stevens.[21] As Stevens alluded to in his letter to Jeremiah Brown, intelligence like Rauch's and Henry's gave the Underground Railroad conductors time to hustle fugitives away before Hughes could find them. And even though Lydia's name does not feature prominently in histories of the Underground Railroad, I think it's safe to assume she was as involved in the Railroad in Lancaster as Phoebe Wierman and Sarah Wright were in Adams County. We'll examine more evidence of this involvement later.

In 1848, as Mrs. Smith applied herself to managing Stevens's household and looking after four boys, another major challenge landed on her doorstep. Stevens's landlord and neighbor, Emanuel C. Reigart, nominated Stevens for Congress. Reigart was an influential Whig of elevated social standing in Lancaster. His endorsement would have carried significant weight. When he nominated Stevens, Reigart was not openly committed to him but knew Stevens well as a fellow attorney, former state legislator, landlord, and neighbor. Add to that the fact that Stevens had terrific name recognition in a pre-electronic era, and the outcome is not surprising. Stevens won by a nearly two-to-one margin—more than 9,500 votes to fewer than 5,500 for his opponent.[22] As they had when he was elected to the Pennsylvania legislature, Stevens's critics suggested he hadn't won fair and square. Alexander Harris, the Southern-sympathizing historian in Lancaster who never stepped aside for a "skunk," insinuated later that Stevens had bought the nomination. He used the words of Stevens's acolyte Alexander Hood to do it. Lamenting Stevens's limitless generosity to those in need, Hood had written,

> Beggars of all grades, high or low, are very quick in finding out the weak points of those on whom they intend to operate; and Mr. Stevens was always, but particularly when he was a candidate, most unmercifully fleeced. This trait was the cause of injury to the politics of this country. Before he was nominated for Congress, no one here thought of spending large sums of money in order to get votes. Now, no man, whatever his qualifications, can be nominated for any office, unless he answers all demands made upon him, and forks over a greater amount than anyone else will, for the same office. It is a most deplorable state of things, but the fact is not to be denied.[23]

Harris twisted Hood's words into an indictment, insinuating that Stevens had singlehandedly corrupted the entire American political process.

As gratifying as the victory was for Stevens, it was, at best, a mixed blessing for Mrs. Smith. The critics and political enemies who long had hounded Stevens for his advocacy on behalf of people of color expanded their field of view, now focusing some of their hatred on the mixed-race housekeeper who walked beside him. It started almost from the moment she stepped onto the streets of Lancaster. As Fawn Brodie writes, Lydia may have been an especially attractive, capable young woman in Thaddeus Stevens's eyes, but "to everyone else she was a Negro and subject to every public humiliation the white man chose to impose."[24]

It's difficult to imagine how Mrs. Smith felt as Democrats worked themselves into a racist frenzy over her presence in Stevens's life. One biographer tells us, "The whole Democratic press of Pennsylvania were in the habit of assailing Mr. Stevens on account of his association with this woman and charged that it was illicit."[25] Politics in mid-nineteenth-century America was clearly a contact sport.

During the 1848 congressional race, according to historian Milton Meltzer, Democrats suggested that Stevens's mind was as crippled as his clubfoot "and made sneering allusions to his housekeeper as though no other white employed Negro servants."[26] Those who hated Stevens and what he stood for maligned him and Mrs. Smith with abandon. Writing about Stevens and Mrs. Smith in 1970, James Jolly reports that "stories persist that Stevens and his program were informed directly or indirectly by a Negro mistress, who was ultimately buried by his side in a Negro cemetery. This erroneous rumor owes its circulation to Dixon's book [*The Clansman*] . . . he [Stevens] was accused of using his servant for pleasure, not unlike the practice of some slaveholders who Stevens deplored."[27] Judge Landis may have been thinking of how a sweet-tempered, graceful woman like Mrs. Smith would react to such hateful venom when he wrote that "if at any time she was brusque to those who addressed her in a rude and unmannerly way little blame can be made against her on that account."[28]

It's interesting to note that in 1848, while Thaddeus Stevens pursued his political ambitions and Lydia Hamilton Smith worked to rise above the difficult circumstances of her earlier life, a group of American women gathered in Seneca Falls, New York, to plead for the rights of all women to pursue their own dreams. The attendees at the first Women's Rights Convention audaciously proposed rewording the Declaration of Independence to read: "We hold these truths to be self-evident—that all men AND WOMEN are created equal." The women left Seneca Falls demanding four rights that traditionally had been denied them: the right to engage in professions, the right to own property, the right to custody of their children if they divorced, and the right to vote.

We have no written evidence that Mrs. Smith knew about Seneca Falls, but if she did, she surely would have identified with the sentiments expressed there. And she likely would have applauded the message the conventioneers sent to America: "To have the rights of drunkards, idiots, horse-racing, rum selling rowdies, ignorant foreigners and silly boys fully recognized, whilst we ourselves are thrust out from all the rights that belong to citizens—it is too grossly insulting to the dignity of woman to be longer quietly submitted to. The right [to vote] is ours, have it we must—use it we will."[29] Seventy-two years would pass before American women won the right to vote, and they are still campaigning for equal rights across the board. One of the most remarkable things about Lydia Hamilton Smith is that she found a way to secure some of those rights long before the nation granted them to its female citizens. That is a tribute to her personal ability and ambition and also to the man with whom she wisely chose to walk through life.

We can't move on from 1848 without taking note of one more event. A young man named Simon Stevens (no relation) was admitted to the bar in Lancaster. Simon was the son of a Vermont lawyer who handled legal affairs for Stevens in his home state. He had come to Lancaster some time earlier to study law with Stevens and became one of his favorite students. Fawn Brodie reports Stevens "came to treat him almost like a son . . . Thaddeus Stevens helped him financially, made him a law partner, took a personal interest in his wife and son—who was named Thaddeus in his honor—and remembered him in his will."[30] Simon Stevens was by Stevens's bedside, with Lydia Hamilton Smith and Thaddeus Stevens Jr., when Stevens died, and, as we'll see later, he remained by Mrs. Smith's side when she had an extended, unpleasant encounter with Stevens's executors after his death.

As 1848 drew to a close, it was time for Congressman Stevens to head for Washington. Historian Thomas Frederick Woodley describes his departure: "Late in November, Mrs. Smith packed her 'master's' black, broadcloth suits, several pairs of unmatched shoes, and an adequate supply of linen into the old trunk, on which was printed the legend, 'T. Stevens' and sent it by express to Washington." Thaddeus Stevens stayed in a Washington hotel, without the excellent services of Lydia Hamilton Smith, during his maiden voyage to the nation's capital.[31]

CHAPTER 6

EVERYONE'S ON THE MOVE

The America of Lydia Hamilton Smith's time imposed severe limitations on the opportunities for advancement available to a young woman, especially a woman of color. She arrived in Lancaster equipped with the domestic skills generally expected in a servant or housekeeper. But, as we've already noted, she could read and write, skills that weren't necessarily required in a household employee. Stevens biographer Fawn Brodie suggests that Lydia received more education than most young women of color in her time, and Brodie believes Thaddeus Stevens was her principal tutor. But Mrs. Smith was thirty years old when she came to Lancaster and assumed responsibility for Stevens's household and four young men, her sons and Stevens's nephews. It seems more likely that a bright, young Lydia might have taken advantage of the education offered in Gettysburg. The first (segregated) public classroom for Black children opened in 1834 (although some sources suggest that Black children attended schools in Gettysburg as early as 1824), or she might have learned to read and write in catechetical classes through the Catholic church.[1]

Lancaster attorney John A. Coyle, who attended mass at the largely Irish Catholic St. Mary's Church in Lancaster with Mrs. Smith, testified to the effectiveness of her educational process. "I recall personally," he wrote in a letter to Father George Brown, who was collecting stories of distinguished "colored" members of St. Mary's Church, "that she was as smart as a steel trap, bright, and a good conversationalist because of her many years of life with Stevens at Washington where she came in contact with the prominent people all over the United States, including those from the South who would have liked to have shot Stevens, and those of the North who felt otherwise."[2]

Those who knew her best during her years with Thaddeus Stevens would testify, many years later, that Mrs. Smith assumed many responsibilities as manager of the Stevens household, duties that kept her occupied in the house and elsewhere. With Stevens now in Washington, one of her family tasks was coordinating the activities of four boys rapidly becoming young men. For her sons, William and Isaac, it was time to learn a trade. William became a cobbler.[3] Isaac apparently gained quite a reputation as a barber and a musician. Judge Landis later wrote that "he was, like his father, musically inclined, and was the leader of the colored band."[4]

The Stevens boys followed different trajectories from those of Mrs. Smith's sons. The original family plan, apparently, was for both of them, when old enough, to study law with Stevens and possibly join his law practice. Alanson read law with his uncle for a time, but only long enough to decide that the law was not for him. He eventually headed to Franklin County, Pennsylvania, to help manage Stevens's Caledonia ironworks.[5]

Alanson's brother, Thaddeus Stevens Jr., was enrolled at John Beck's Boys Academy, a highly respected boarding school in Lititz, Pennsylvania, about eight miles north of Lancaster. Lititz was a Moravian town in 1850. Historian Simon P. Eby tells us that "the villagers were quiet, respectable tradesmen and mechanics, and their wives were tidy housekeepers and kind mothers." According to Eby, many of the wives were "educated in the [nearby] Ladies Seminary . . . and some of them, having served in it as teachers, were intelligent and refined in manners. Among these people the pupils from abroad were distributed."[6] In 1850, we find fifteen-year-old Thaddeus Stevens living with more than a dozen other teenagers in a boardinghouse presided over by Francis and Sarah Christ. Three doors away we find August Christ, identified as a "teacher," probably at John Beck's Boys Academy.[7]

If Mrs. Smith worried at all about young Thaddeus living away from home, she didn't need to. By Eby's account, John Beck ran an exceptional school. Eby tells us that Beck employed the latest pedagogical practices and techniques, and the boys seemed to thrive on it. "When school left out in the evening," Eby writes,

> the streets became alive with healthy-looking boys, who could be seen and "heard" hurrying towards their respective boarding places for their four o'clock piece. This usually consisted of a piece of good home-made bread, cut half around a big loaf, and spread with butter and molasses,

applebutter or sometimes honey. Then, munching their pieces, they would be off for an hour's exercise, until supper time, to the playground for a game of ball or shinny; perhaps for a visit to the springs, or a romp over the neighboring fields, if it was fall time, in hopes of starting a rabbit or to fly their kites if the wind was favorable.

Although Mrs. Smith monitored Thad's progress, his uncle probably made the decision to send him to Lititz. And I'd like to think Stevens, known to some as the great egalitarian, chose John Beck's Boys Academy because he appreciated the schoolmaster's philosophy of life and education. Eby informs us that Beck's "academy was emphatically a school of the people. In it was taught that which was useful in all the walks of life. And therein sat, without difference or distinction in the eyes of the master, the heir to millions by the side of the charity scholar, the humble country lad beside the sons of Governors of States, and other equally eminent citizens."[8] John Beck's academy sounds like a school Lydia Hamilton Smith's sons could have benefited from.

Thaddeus Stevens may have had little time to wonder how his nephews were faring. The Washington he descended into in late 1848 was beginning to boil, partly in reaction to the secret Underground Railroad activities Stevens and Mrs. Smith were supporting in Lancaster County. Stevens had long since established himself as a *public* defender of fugitive slaves. Historian W. U. Hensel reports that Stevens's often long, but eloquent, speeches on the subject were very much in demand around Lancaster: "These were eagerly awaited and listened to. When, too, as was frequently the case with the prominent Lancaster lawyer of his period, he and his legal colleagues visited the village taverns to try their law suits before arbitrators, he was greeted by troops of partisan admirers."[9] Hensel notes that when lawyers who disagreed with Stevens were present, the discussion sometimes got physical, and occasionally Stevens's wig was knocked off.

The atmosphere in Washington was far more hostile. Congress was in the midst of a debate over the future of slavery, especially in the new territories, that threatened to rend the young nation in two, and Stevens's thoughts on the matter were already well known. Before Stevens's first day in Congress (March 4, 1849), Senator Henry Clay of Kentucky was already formulating a plan to defuse the tension. Thirty years earlier, Clay had "helped bring an end to a sectional crisis over slavery by leading the passage of the Missouri Compromise." (That deal brought Maine into the

United States as a free state and Missouri as a slave state, and it drew a red line across the Louisiana Purchase, prohibiting slavery above 36°30′ latitude.)[10] Clay had a longstanding and ultimately unrequited desire to be president. Earlier, he had served in the House of Representatives and as secretary of state. He not only was willing to tolerate slavery but also was an advocate of the "extermination and extinction of Native Americans." At the State Department, he predicted that Native peoples would be gone in less than fifty years and said "their disappearance from the human family [would] be no great loss to the world."[11]

Before Clay could propose another slavery-salvaging compromise, Stevens took to the floor of the House to oppose slavery and any proposal that required the return of African Americans who had managed to escape their chains. He began sarcastically, protesting the pro-slavery forces' ability to suppress honest debate about slavery. "We can say anything within these walls or beyond them with impunity," he told his colleagues, "unless it be to agitate in favor of human liberty—that is aggression." He offered a novel economic argument against slavery. "The soil occupied by slavery is much less productive than a similar soil occupied by freemen," he said, using the powerful slave state of Virginia as an example. "There is scarcely a new town . . . within her whole borders. Her ancient villages wear the appearance of mournful decay . . . her fine harbors are without ships, except from other ports; and her seaport towns are without commerce." Do not let slavery spread to America's new territories, he implored; "it will render the whole body leprous and loathsome."[12]

Stevens offered another condemnation of compromises before Clay put his new plan up for a vote. In a June 1850 oration, he rejected the pro-slavery contingent's contention that the humanity-denying institution was actually a blessing, politically and morally, and that slaves, "after having tried . . . freedom, had voluntarily returned to resume [the] yoke." Before he sat down, in anticipation of the proposal he knew was coming, he swore that his constituents would never willingly assist slaveowners in reclaiming their human property. Pennsylvanians would, he said, "strictly abide by the Constitution. The slave-holder may pursue his slave among them with his own foreign myrmidons, unmolested, except by their frowning scorn. But no law that tyranny can pass will ever induce them to join the hue and cry after the trembling wretch who has escaped from unjust bondage."[13] With those words, Stevens made a promise he would be called on to keep in the very near future.

Despite protests from Stevens and others opposed to slavery, Senator Clay introduced the Compromise of 1850 in January; it passed into law in September. The compromise put the New Mexico and Utah Territories under federal oversight (while allowing states organized there to decide the slavery question for themselves). It also brought California into the Union as a free state and abolished slavery in the District of Columbia. Nine days later, Congress passed the Fugitive Slave Act, a draconian measure that preserved a slaver's right to pursue fugitive slaves into free territory and allowed slavers and their agents to dragoon the citizens of free states into assisting in the hunt.

The Fugitive Slave Act was Clay's sop to frustrated slavers who were howling about their "property" being spirited away by the Underground Railroad. Its provisions were little more than an extension of the unjust dimensions of slavery itself. The only identification a slave catcher needed was an affidavit written by the slaveowner's agent. "Negroes" were presumed slaves until proved free, but the law denied them the right to speak for themselves, and they could not demand a jury trial. Blacks caught in the Fugitive Slave Act's nets were forced to rely on the uncertain justice of the US marshals and the intervention of white friends,[14] among them Thaddeus Stevens. Newly empowered slavers took full advantage of Clay's gift. The *Anti-Slavery Bugle* soon published some startling statistics. Recordkeepers had tallied forty-six kidnappings of free people of color in 1846, but by the end of 1850, that number had tripled. Overall, many more fugitive slaves were "carried back" to the South than set free. And yet historian Hans Trefousse reports that the Compromise of 1850, "in spite of its iniquities, was popular in the country"[15]—presumably mostly with whites. It's not surprising to learn that in Lancaster County and "all across southern Pennsylvania the Negroes quietly began to arm themselves and organize for action."[16]

Evidence uncovered in Lancaster around 2004 suggests that Lydia Hamilton Smith and Thaddeus Stevens may have reacted to the new law by stepping up protections for fugitives passing through their Underground Railroad station. Developers planning a new hotel and convention center along South Queen Street in Lancaster (construction began in 2005) invited a team of archaeologists to search for artifacts in the area behind buildings still standing on the property Stevens purchased in 1843. Those structures included the double-entrance home he and Mrs. Smith shared at 45–47 South Queen Street, a three-story house Mrs. Smith built on the corner of East Vine and South Christian Streets, and the old Kleiss Brewery on the northeast corner of South Queen and East Vine

Fig. 14   Thaddeus Stevens's home and law office (left) and Lydia Hamilton Smith's brewery and boardinghouse (right) at 45–47 South Queen Street in Lancaster. Photo courtesy of Larry Lefever Photography.

Streets. As this book was being written, LancasterHistory (the Lancaster County Historical Society) was at work on a plan to develop the buildings into a museum/research complex honoring Thaddeus Stevens and Lydia Hamilton Smith.

The archaeological dig produced a treasure trove of objects linked to the period when Mrs. Smith and Stevens occupied the home at 45–47 South Queen, unearthing a cistern with a vaulted roof, a brick floor, and a "roughly square" window in the cistern's eastern wall, "just large enough for a person of medium build to fit through. Near this window, resting upright on the brick floor of the cistern . . . [was] . . . an intact, though corroded iron spittoon." Aware of Stevens's and Mrs. Smith's likely involvement in the Underground Railroad, and having deduced from the artifacts that the cistern's modifications dated to the 1850s, the researchers offered this convincing speculation: "It was possible for a person to enter the cistern from the basement of the brewery without being seen. Taken together, the penetration through the foundation, the retaining wall, the trench, and the rebuilt eastern wall of the cistern suggests that modifications were made to the Kleiss Brewery and the cistern that would have allowed a person to crawl from the basement of the building into the cistern." The archaeologists suggest that the Kleiss Brewery basement would have been an ideal place to hide fugitives, who could then have crawled into the cistern if a US marshal turned up.[17]

Considering that Stevens still owned the Kleiss Brewery building, and assuming that the widow Kleiss (who rented the establishment until 1850) and the tenant who replaced her, Jonathan Whitlinger, were amenable, it seems highly probable that Stevens established a station for fugitive slaves in the brewery basement. For the system to work, Mrs. Kleiss and then Whitlinger would have needed to pledge their support for the conspiracy, adding two more names to the Underground Railroad network in Lancaster.

Of course, it requires no great sacrifice on our part to envision fugitive slaves slipping in and out of Lancaster in their quest for freedom, but if we view the experience from their perspective, we gain a much clearer picture of the courage and fortitude those people displayed. We've already noted, for example, the fugitives riding the iron rails from Columbia to Lancaster, hidden in secret compartments built into freight cars by Stephen Smith and William Whipper. What must those cramped spaces have been like under blistering summer suns and frigid winter winds? It's been suggested that when they reached Lancaster, the fugitives "might then have been delivered, sealed into barrels, to the tavern next to Stevens' house" [i.e., the Kleiss Brewery].[18] Seeing a barrel rolled into a brewery would not have aroused any particular curiosity on the part of those passing by, but what must it have been like for the person inside the barrel?

William Still takes us "inside the barrel," as it were, in his history of the Underground Railroad. He tells the story of a twenty-one-year-old woman so desperate to be free that she allowed a companion to ship her from Baltimore, where a wealthy family owned her, to Philadelphia in a wooden box. After many, many hours of jostling and delay, including being flipped over more than once, the box arrived at 412 South Seventh Street in Philadelphia, the home of a Mrs. Myers, a woman sympathetic to fugitives, Still tells us. Knowing how long the young woman had been encased in the box, Mrs. Myers summoned her friend—and undertaker—Mrs. Ash: "The two aged women chose to be alone in that fearful moment, shuddering at the thought that a corpse might meet their gaze instead of a living creature." When the lid was lifted off, they found the young woman's seemingly lifeless body. But when they spoke to her, there were faint signs of life. The young woman was helped from the box and spent nearly two weeks recuperating before she traveled on to Canada. In the midst of her recovery,

Still tells us, the young woman "tried to describe her sufferings and fears, while in the box, but in vain. In the midst of her severest agonies, her chief fear was that she would be discovered and carried back to Slavery."[19]

The Fugitive Slave Act emboldened slavers and slave catchers and, in the process, created more work for Thaddeus Stevens. Shortly after the act was signed into law, a man named Kauffman from Cumberland County, Pennsylvania, was indicted and sued under the act for allegedly aiding a group of enslaved persons as they made their way to freedom. A slaver's widow was suing for the "full value of a lot of slaves to whom [Kauffman's] family had given food and shelter without his knowledge."[20] The slaves disappeared after their brief stop at Kauffman's home. The lawsuit, the first filed in Pennsylvania under the new law, was a celebrated one, according to historian W. U. Hensel, "because of the great public and political importance attached to the principle." Stevens, having vowed that Pennsylvanians would unite to oppose the awful provisions of the Act of 1850, defended Kauffman. After several hung juries in Pennsylvania, the case moved to federal court in Philadelphia, where the jury ruled in Kauffman's favor.

Hensel credits Stevens's skill in jury selection with having a major influence on the outcome. Although the government had what appeared to be the stronger case, Hensel writes, "Stevens excelled in the valuable professional gift of selecting a jury with excellent judgment; and a prominent citizen of his own county and a political sympathizer was on the jury. He kept his fellows out [deliberating] for six weeks and the defendant was acquitted." Hensel does not name that Lancaster County juror, but he mentions that the juror's *son* held Stevens's former seat in the House of Representatives in 1906, when he wrote his article about Stevens.[21] In 1906, Congressman John Merriman Reynolds, of Quarryville, Pennsylvania, represented Lancaster County in Washington. His father, an Irish immigrant, successful farmer, and gristmill operator—and, apparently, astute citizen juror—was Patrick Hewitt Reynolds.[22]

The Kauffman trial may have been celebrated in its time, but it was soon eclipsed in the public mind by the case Stevens took on in 1851. On September 11, 1851, a Maryland slaver named Edward Gorsuch showed up at a home near Christiana, in southeastern Lancaster County, with his son and nephew, a US marshal, and five other armed men, looking for four runaway slaves. Gorsuch and company approached the home of African American innkeeper William Parker, where, they had been informed, Gorsuch's slaves were being hidden. When Parker refused to produce the men, the marshal charged into the house. Parker met him there with a five-pointed harpoon, which he threw at the marshal, and then picked up an axe.

The marshal fled outside and stood beside Gorsuch. In the meantime, Parker's wife had sounded a horn from an upstairs window. Soon, a crowd of Black men and women, many armed with guns, scythes, clubs, and corn cutters, surrounded the house. As a standoff took shape, a white miller named Castner Hanway rode up and stopped to watch. When the marshal spotted Hanway, he ordered him to assist in making the arrests, as the Fugitive Slave Act authorized him to do. Hanway refused, in words that echoed Stevens's proclamation on the floor of the House of Representatives. He said, "I'll do nothing to help the Fugitive Slave Act or any other act." The marshal turned to two Quakers—also white men—and they, too, refused, and told the marshal to get off Parker's land. As the three white men turned away, gunfire erupted. The marshal and his men fled, but Gorsuch stood and emptied his gun at the assembled African Americans before he was tackled by four of them. "When they finally left him, bleeding and unconscious," Fawn Brodie tells us, "the women moved in with scythes and corn cutters and hacked him to pieces." Gorsuch's son and nephew were wounded but recovered.[23]

By nightfall, the fugitives Gorsuch came to retrieve, along with William Parker and his wife, had all headed for Canada. But the government wasn't finished with what officials at the time called the Christiana Riot (more recently referred to as the Christiana Resistance). Federal officials returned with a dragnet that yielded three white and thirty-eight Black suspects. The governor of Pennsylvania, on orders from Secretary of State Daniel Webster, charged them all with treason.[24]

The trial was held in federal court in Philadelphia. Thaddeus Stevens led the defense team, but, fearing his reputation might negatively influence the jury, he allowed co-counsel John M. Reed to do the talking. W. U. Hensel provides a vivid picture of the scene in the courtroom, writing that Stevens "was the central figure and dominating spirit of the scene, which was rendered especially picturesque by the two dozen accused colored men sitting in a row, all similarly attired, wearing around their necks red, white and blue scarfs, with Lucretia Mott [a well-known abolitionist] sitting at their head, calmly knitting, the frightened negroes half hopefully regarding her sidewise as their guardian angel, and the tall, stern figure of Stevens as their mighty Moses."[25]

Supreme Court Justice Robert C. Grier and US District Court Judge John K. Kane presided over the trial. Grier, in particular, was especially exercised over the events in Christiana. Hensel first informs us that Grier had a reputation as a "learned and ordinarily temperate" jurist. Then, we're told, "his shrill, piping voice hurled his anathemas at the 'male and female vagrant lecturers' of the abolition cause, 'infuriated fanatics and unprincipled demagogues' who had counseled 'bloody resistance to the laws of the land,' the necessary development of whose principles and the natural fruitage of whose seed, he declared, was this murderous tragedy."[26]

As we approach the verdict, recall that the defendants were charged not with murder but with treason. And, despite Grier's apparent disgust with Stevens, Mott, and any other abolitionists he might encounter, Hensel tells us that the justice "felt constrained to admit the accused had not been shown to have been involved in a transaction which 'rose to the dignity of treason or a levying of war.' The prisoners were acquitted."[27]

The Christiana Resistance trial is an appropriate moment to introduce Anthony Ellmaker Roberts. Roberts, a longtime friend of Thaddeus Stevens, was sworn in as the US marshal for the Eastern District of Pennsylvania about a year before the events in Christiana took place. After the suspects were arrested, Roberts, an avowed abolitionist, was responsible for their custody until trial. (Such were his sympathies that he may have served the defendants Thanksgiving dinner on November 27, 1851.) Prosecutors had given Roberts two "voluntary" detainees to hold. The authorities believed the two men had discovered Edward Gorsuch's plans and tipped off William Parker before the slaver arrived. That, the prosecutors planned to argue, was evidence of a conspiracy to resist the laws of the United States. Mysteriously, the two men escaped two weeks before they were due in court. At the time, prosecutors voiced their suspicions that Roberts had set the men free, a suspicion confirmed by Underground Railroad leader William Still two decades later.[28]

We can see in Roberts's handling of the Christiana Resistance defendants why Thaddeus Stevens might have been so fond of him. The two men appeared to be in close agreement on critical issues of their time, particularly the question of slavery. It is not surprising, then, that Stevens named Roberts one of the three executors of his will. He obviously trusted him to do things right. We can only wonder, then, whether Stevens would have approved of the way Roberts and fellow executor O. J. Dickey dealt with Lydia Hamilton Smith after his death. We'll examine that confrontation a bit later.

CHAPTER 7

THE WIDOW AND THE CONGRESSMAN

Throughout 1850 and 1851, when Stevens wasn't in court in Pennsylvania fighting to free those caught in the dark web of the Fugitive Slave Act, he was back in Washington trying to kill the act itself. According to Hans Trefousse, Stevens introduced several "petitions for the repeal of the hated measure" during the short session of 1850–51. His efforts elicited praise from Congressman Joshua Giddings of Ohio, then the leader of the anti-slavery forces in the House, who said of Stevens, "He is one of the strong men of the nation. I entertain no doubt about his entire devotion to our cause; in short, our numbers are increasing both in Congress and through-out the nation."[1] And when he wasn't battling for the proposition that "*all* men [*sic*] are created equal," Stevens relaxed, as he had done since his Gettysburg days, by gambling. Such activity might have seemed per-fectly harmless to Stevens, but in the eyes of his self-righteous enemies, it was just another strike against his moral character, which was already sul-lied by the presence of a Black "mistress" in his home. Stevens's game of choice was faro, a French card game wildly popular in nineteenth-century America. Ironically, one of his detractors, George Fort Milton, left us the most sparkling description of the places Stevens visited just down Penn-sylvania Avenue from Capitol Hill.

Milton, a Southern newspaper publisher and Democratic activist, writes that "a typical establishment, in which many of Stevens' lighter moments were spent, was fitted up in 'a magnificence which is princely . . . Negro attendants in splendid livery attended your every want with a grace and courtesy positively enchanting.'"[2] Milton also shares a story, possibly apoc-ryphal, about one of Stevens's gambling sessions. As Milton relates the

Fig. 15   Stevens sold this log house to Lydia Hamilton Smith in 1852. The house still stands at 138 West Middle Street in Gettysburg. This illustration is based on the current appearance of the building. LancasterHistory, Lancaster, Pennsylvania.

story, Stevens was exiting a DC gambling establishment when he met two ministers from Lancaster, who were raising money for a new church steeple. Stevens knew he had a dollar in one pocket and one hundred dollars in the other, but he apparently lost track of which was where when he consented to make a contribution. Reaching into his right pocket, thinking it held the dollar bill, he was a bit surprised to find himself holding the hundred-dollar bill aloft. True to his generous nature, albeit a bit chagrined, he handed over the money and quipped, "God moves in mysterious ways his wonders to perform." With that, Milton tells us, the congressman hastened up the street.[3] Milton includes Lydia Hamilton Smith in his attempts to besmirch Stevens's reputation. Noting that Stevens never married, Milton mentions a portrait of Mrs. Smith he saw in Lancaster while researching his book. He refers to her as "Miss Smith" and says, "Thad Stevens' negro mistress-'housekeeper' is the euphemistic phrase the Lancastrians sedulously employ."[4]

We don't know how Mrs. Smith felt about Stevens's recreational habits, or if she even made it her business to have an opinion. Managing Stevens's household, looking after her sons, keeping in touch with Stevens's nephews, and (likely) caring for travelers on the Underground Railroad may have been more than enough to occupy her time and her thoughts. But despite that busy schedule, she found time to launch another project in 1852—acquiring real estate.

Several of Stevens's biographers claim that Mrs. Smith bought her first property from him in 1860. Stevens did sell Mrs. Smith a plot of land that year; it was part of the parcel he purchased on South Queen Street, Lancaster, in 1843. But it wasn't her first investment. Technically, the first time Lydia Hamilton Smith's name appeared in a real estate transaction was in 1841, when she and Jacob Smith bought the little house on Harrisburg's north side for $200. They sold that house for a profit of $163 in 1844, when they separated, but we have no record of how they split the proceeds.

Adams County records reveal that Mrs. Smith's next foray into property ownership was not in 1860, either, but it did involve Thaddeus Stevens. The date of purchase, on records discovered by researchers at the Adams County Historical Society, is December 1, 1852. According to the record, "Lot T-A (Deed W-410): Adam Shoemaker Residence" was a two-story log dwelling, located on the south side of the second block of West Middle Street in Gettysburg. The ownership history indicates that Thaddeus Stevens bought the property from Andrew Little in 1837 and sold it to Lydia Hamilton Smith in December 1852, and she, in turn, sold the house to Francis Chrismer on April 1, 1856. The Adams County researchers suggest Mrs. Smith purchased the property for the same reason Stevens had purchased it, for use as an income-generating "rental property." In tax records for 1863, the house was valued at $175.

The house still stands at 138 West Middle Street in Gettysburg, identifiable by a Historic Gettysburg Adams County plaque that states: "Stevens' Log Cabin, c. 1790." A second plaque, placed by Main Street Gettysburg, describes the house as "a fine example of an 1830s house." Timothy Smith of the Adams County Historical Society has serious doubts about Stevens's ever having lived in the house, but a local newspaper did publish a story about the house in 1999, headlined "Log Home Recalls Gettysburg's Pre-Civil War History."[5] The purchase of a humble log house in Gettysburg, in 1852, marked the beginning of a real estate career that would find Lydia Hamilton Smith investing in numerous properties in Lancaster, Philadelphia, and Washington.

A reference to Lydia's sons in the official history of Lancaster's Bethel A.M.E. Church sheds light on how William and Isaac, both teenagers by now, were occupying themselves in 1852. In April 1879, arsonists set fire to the church. Two men were seen running away but were apparently not apprehended. The Shiffler Fire Company responded to the blaze "immediately," and, we learn, "the building remained structurally intact." Bethel's historian explained the incendiary assault as "an unwelcome reminder of the price of freedom for Lancaster's African community,"[6] fourteen years

Fig. 16 The last location of the Shiffler Fire Company. The building still stands on South Queen Street, minus the cupola and fire engine. LancasterHistory, Lancaster, Pennsylvania.

after the nation sacrificed hundreds of thousands of lives to end violence against people of color. The Shiffler Fire Company, the church history tells us, was once sponsored by Thaddeus Stevens, and for a time it counted both of Lydia Hamilton Smith's sons among its volunteers. In fact, William and Isaac not only worked with the Shiffler Fire Company but helped start it.

LancasterHistory archives indicate the Shiffler Fire Company, No. 7 was organized in 1852. It soon became the Independent Fire Co. and then the Fulton Fire Co. The name changed again in 1854 to the Conestoga Fire Company. The name Shiffler Fire Company was readopted in 1855 and Thaddeus Stevens was elected president in 1856.[7] Thanks to historians Franklin Ellis and Samuel Evans, we have a fairly detailed account of how the Shiffler Fire Company, No. 7 came to be.

Ellis and Evans take us back to a summer evening in 1852. They write, "The boys who made the old dirt bank at the corner of Middle and Rockland Streets their playground conceived the idea of organizing themselves into a fire company . . . membership was restricted to those who were between the ages of twelve and sixteen years." As they were getting underway, we learn, "the first apparatus was a small carriage built by a negro named Smith, upon which the boys carried a small hydrant hose. An old barn at the foot of Thaddeus Stevens' house lot served as an engine house."[8] We don't know which of Lydia's sons built the rig.

It's interesting that the boys chose the name "Shiffler" for their company. The company's namesake—George Shiffler—was an eighteen-year-old Protestant nativist shot and killed during anti-Catholic riots in Philadelphia in 1844. The riots lasted three days, during which anti-Catholic mobs burned or damaged Irish Catholic homes, schools, and churches. Shiffler was felled by rounds fired from the Hibernia Hose Company, "supposedly while defending or rescuing the American flag."[9] It's not clear why the sons of a devout Irish Catholic, as Lydia was, would choose to honor a nativist in naming their fire company. Perhaps the Smith boys were outvoted by their fellow firefighters. Ellis and Evans suggest that Lancaster's "Catholic element" was not pleased with the name and pressured the boys to change it, which they did, to Independent, and then to Fulton, and, ultimately, back to Shiffler. We don't know if Lydia voiced any displeasure over the name her sons chose, but we do know she was a faithful member of St. Mary's Church in Lancaster.

William and Isaac and their fire-fighting colleagues certainly deserve credit for providing such an essential service to Lancaster's Southeast Ward, but their sense of civic duty apparently exceeded their level of maturity. Ellis and Evans tell us that "the boisterous behavior of the boys at fires became notorious and they were regarded in the eyes of the public as a nuisance and the vigilance of the constabulary was often taxed to its utmost in restraining them from going to fires."[10] The criticism apparently doused the boys' enthusiasm. "For over a year," the historians report, "the hose carriage, a good one which had been substituted for the first, stood neglected." Eventually, the younger members of the company withdrew, older volunteers stepped up, and Thaddeus Stevens donated land on Strawberry Street for a new two-story fire house. Stevens was reportedly happy to serve as president of Shiffler Fire Company, No. 7 for the rest of his life.[11] Stevens's law associate O. J. Dickey and his nephew Thaddeus Stevens Jr. also joined the company in the mid to late 1850s.

Late December 1852 brought sad news for William and Isaac Smith. Three Gettysburg newspapers picked up a death notice from a Harrisburg newspaper. On January 3, 1853, the *Adams Sentinel* reported: "The *Harrisburg Telegraph* records the death, from dropsy, of Jacob Smith, (colored) for many years leader of the Harrisburg Brass Band, aged 35 years.—Mr. Smith formerly resided in Gettysburg, and had considerable reputation as a musician."[12] The *Star and Republican Banner* for December 31, 1852, carried the same notice. The *Gettysburg Republican Compiler* for January 3, 1853, credited the *Harrisburg Democratic Union* for its report. The *Compiler*'s version provided more details about Jacob's death and his life:

> Died, at Harrisburg, on Monday morning last [December 27, 1852], after a lingering illness, Mr. Jacob Smith, (colored) aged about 40 years. Poor Jake, he was the Prince of Barbers and an excellent musician, and many of our lads and lasses will miss the rich music of his violin, when they meet to "trip the light fantastic toe." His remains were accompanied to the tomb yesterday afternoon by a large concourse of his friends, preceded by the Brass Band of which he had been the leader. Peace to his ashes. We are sorry to say that Mr. Smith was very unfortunate in his domestic relations.[13]

Recall that the *Compiler* and its editor, Jacob Lefever, were among Thaddeus Stevens's bitterest enemies in Gettysburg. Lefever no doubt knew that Lydia had left Jacob and was, in 1852, Stevens's housekeeper in Lancaster. Might that last line of the *Compiler*'s story be Lefever or his coworkers insinuating, once again, that Stevens, with his scandalous involvement with a mixed-race woman—in Gettysburg, it was Dinah, and now it was Mrs. Smith—was responsible for the sadness that had descended on Jacob Smith's home? We don't know. We also do not know whether his sons or his estranged wife attended his funeral. All we really know is that Lydia Hamilton Smith was now a widow.

Thaddeus Stevens received some disappointing political news in 1852. The Whig Party, after backing him for two terms in the House of Representatives, did not nominate him for a third term. Having risen from the low point of his political career in 1842 to claim a place as a congressional crusader against injustice, Stevens once again found himself out of office. Some observers attribute this lull in his career to that very crusading; some Lancaster County voters may have thought Stevens was too involved in the battle against slavery, too close to the violence of the Christiana Resistance.[14] When Congress adjourned on March 3, 1853, Thaddeus Stevens returned to Lancaster. Hans Trefousse says he spent the next several years focusing on his law practice and the Underground Railroad, work we believe he shared with Mrs. Smith.[15] But, as we'll see shortly, Stevens did not forsake political thought or strategizing completely during his time away from Washington.

By the time Stevens had reestablished himself in Lancaster, his nephew Thaddeus Stevens Jr. had finished at John Beck's Boys Academy and headed to the University of Vermont, possibly in late 1852 or early 1853. He hadn't been there long before his path through higher education turned rocky. He flunked out of the University of Vermont, moved on to Dartmouth College (his uncle's alma mater), and managed to get himself expelled from Dartmouth four times before he completed his degree.

As his difficulties mounted, school officials had notified his uncle that Thad Jr. was a problem. Thad and his uncle exchanged a number of letters during that time. Uncle Thaddeus was not pleased with what he was hearing from New England. "I am greatly grieved," he wrote, "at the information which I have recd. from Vermont concerning you . . . they say you are lazy, inattentive, absent, and unprepared in your studies." Stevens then links Thad's current problems to things he had learned about his nephew before he left Lancaster. "This is afflicting news," he wrote, "but I had feared it from your habits here." And then Stevens lands on a problem that would plague young Thaddeus for the rest of his life. "I fear also you love rum, and sometimes drink it—If so, the sooner you are abandoned the better as there is no hope for one who ever tastes strong drink."[16]

We've already seen that Stevens's father succumbed to "drink," and Stevens himself had, for the most part, ceased drinking out of disgust over the behavior of his companions in Gettysburg. At this point in his life, he had very little tolerance for alcoholics. He laid full responsibility for Thad's future at the young man's feet: "It remains for you to determine whether you will alter your habits, and increase your progress or abandon College." His words were stern, but within them we can see an uncle sincerely concerned about his nephew. "I submit these remarks with pain," he wrote. "But your whole life depends on your present conduct."[17]

Knowing that he had gone a long way toward alienating his uncle, Thaddeus Jr. turned to the other "parent" in his life, Lydia Hamilton Smith, to whom he had obviously written before. His letter of March 26 (1853?) addressed to "Mrs. Smith" begins, "Dear Madam, I received your letter of the 12th today. I will go to Peacham [Vermont] and if possible be there when uncle is there so that I can see him." Thad tells Lydia he had come to Littleton, New Hampshire, about sixty miles north of Dartmouth (after his latest expulsion from college, no doubt), and "have been studying withe [*sic*] the minister of the place." He writes confidently that "I shall go back to . . . college about the first of May."[18]

In her earlier letter, Mrs. Smith must have told Thad that his uncle was ill. (Stevens battled a variety of ailments in the last two decades of his life.) Thad told her that he was sorry his uncle was not feeling well, and then he shared with Mrs. Smith his plan for getting back into his uncle's good graces. "I will try and see him," he wrote, "and let him know all of my affairs since he knows the worst part of them. I think that they have been made worse than they are. At all events, he can ascertain the truth when he comes out."[19]

Thad thanked Lydia for sharing news of his brother Alanson's life at the Caledonia ironworks. (Lydia apparently kept in touch with both nephews.) He said he'd written several times since Alanson was posted to the furnace, but had had no reply. Lydia's communication about Alanson apparently concerned him: "I do not think that he is naturally bad. I think that it is ignorance and atheism that effects [*sic*] him. I think that he will learn better. Experience is a good but severe teacher. I have found it so."[20] Such were the words of wisdom from the younger brother—who was having trouble managing his own affairs at that moment.

Thad confessed to Mrs. Smith that he had not intended to write to her or his uncle until he was back on campus. If Dartmouth had banished him forever, he said, his original intention was "not to have let you hear from me again. But as you have been so kind as to write me, I will answer your letter and will let you know from time to time how I get along." He closed on an optimistic note: "I think that there is no doubt but what I shall get back to college in May. Give my love to Uncle and write me soon again. In the meantime believe me to be truly your friend and servant, Thaddeus Stevens."[21] Thad was readmitted to Dartmouth. He completed his studies and returned to Lancaster to study law with his uncle.

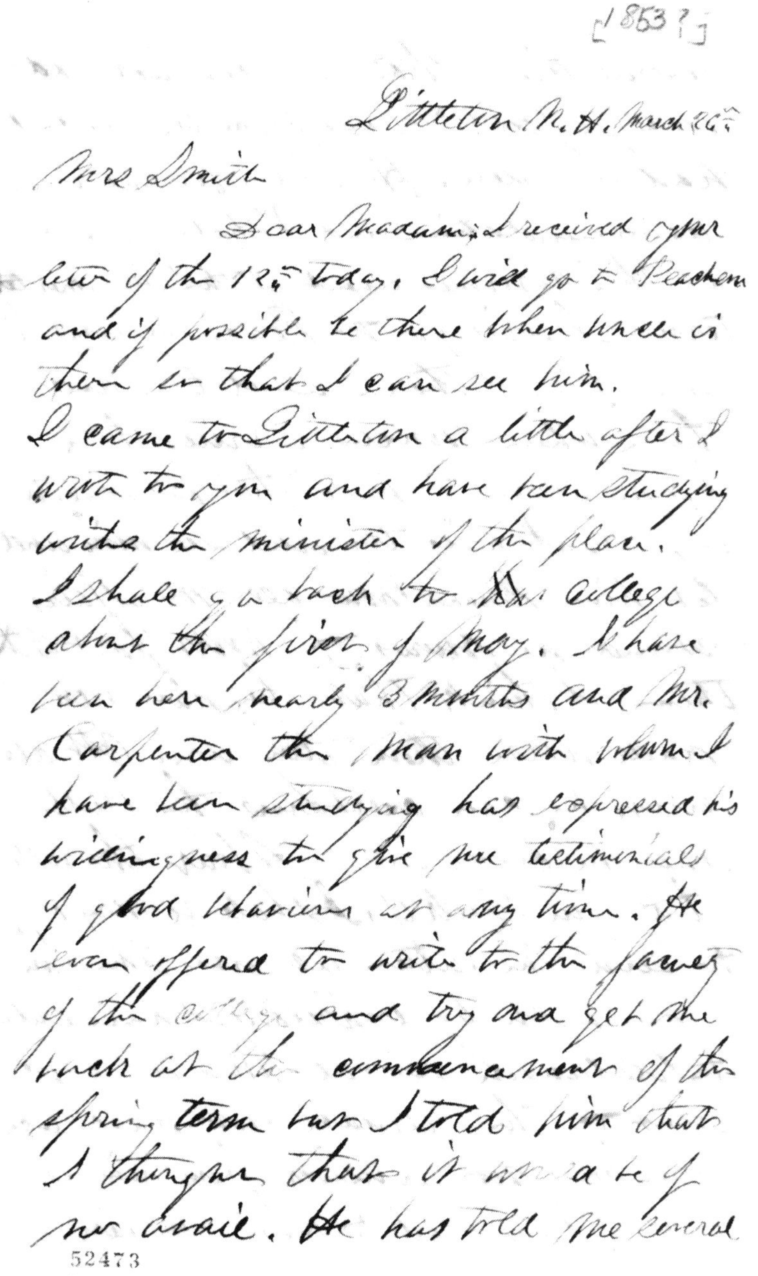

[1853?]

Littleton N. H. March 26th

Mrs Smith

Dear Madam; I received your letter of the 12th today, I will go to Peacham and if possible be there when uncle is there so that I can see him.

I came to Littleton a little after I wrote to you and have been studying with the minister of the place. I shall go back to the college about the first of May. I have been here nearly 3 months and Mr. Carpenter the man with whom I have been studying has expressed his willingness to give me testimonials of good behavior at any time. He even offered to write to the Faculty of the college and try and get me back at the commencement of the spring term but I told him that I thought that it would be of no avail. He has told me several

52473

Fig. 17 Letter from Thaddeus Stevens Jr. to Lydia Hamilton Smith, March 26 [1853?]. LancasterHistory, Lancaster, Pennsylvania.

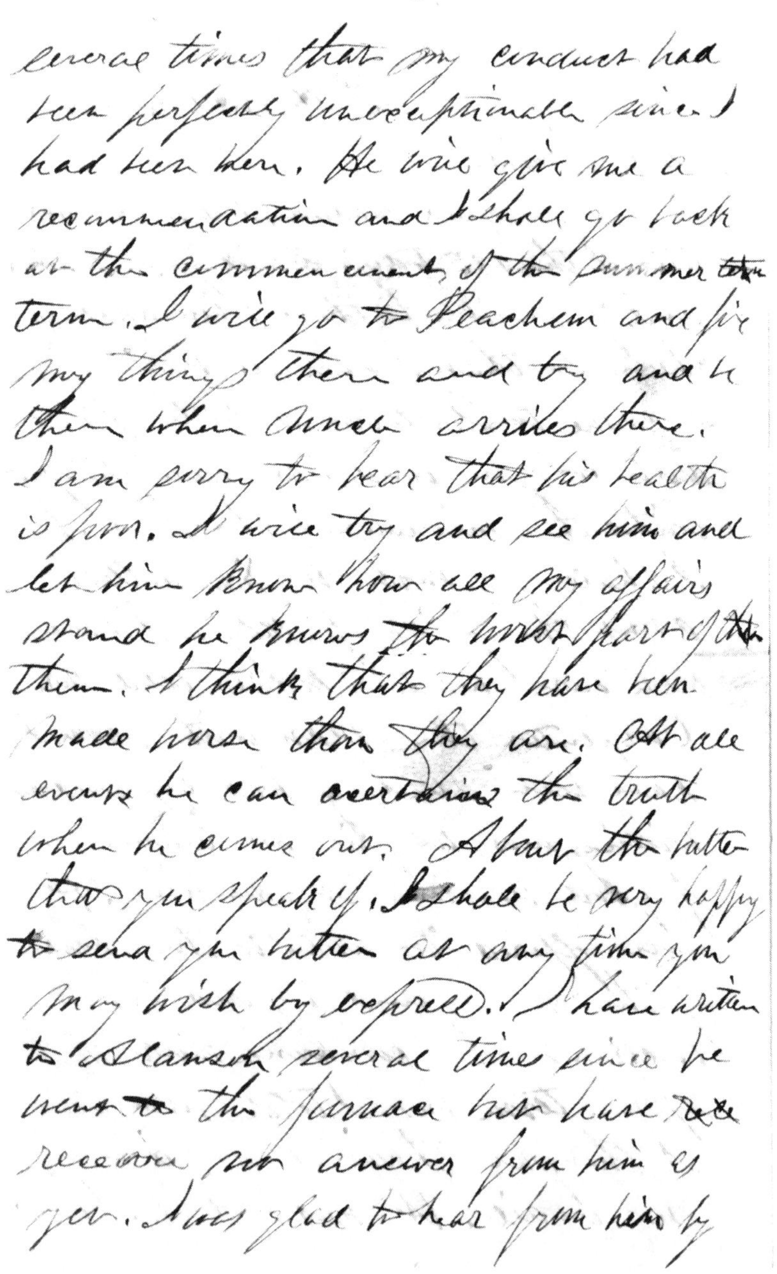

several times that my conduct had been perfectly unexceptionable since I had been there. He will give me a recommendation and I shall go back at the commencement of the summer term. I will go to Peacham and fix my things there and try and be there when Uncle arrives there. I am sorry to hear that his health is poor. I will try and see him and let him know how all my affairs stand he knows the most part of them. I think that they have been made worse than they are. At all events he can ascertain the truth when he comes out. About the letter that you speak of. I shall be very happy to send you letters at any time you may wish by express. I have written to Alanson several times since he went to the furnace but have received no answer from him as yet. I was glad to hear from him by

Fig. 17   *(continued)* Letter from Thaddeus Stevens Jr. to Lydia Hamilton Smith, March 26 [1853?], second page.

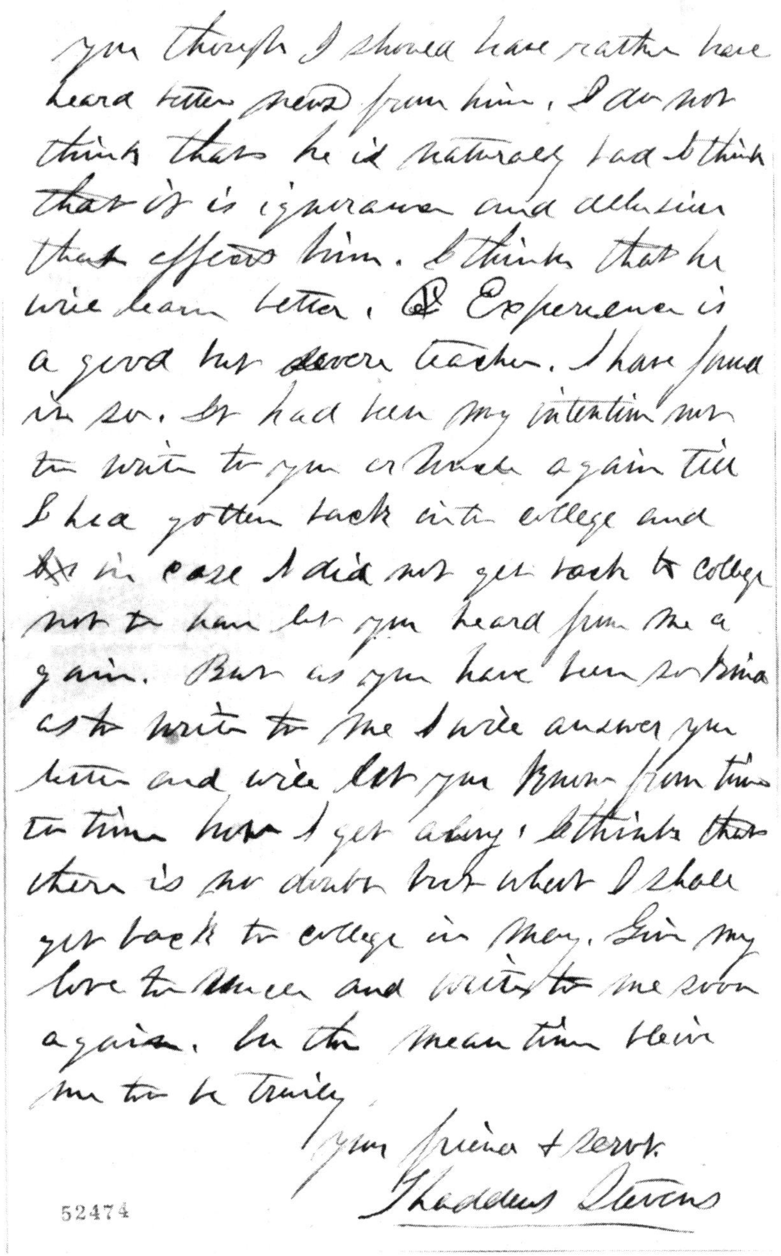

you though I should have rather here
heard better news from him, I do not
think that he is naturally bad I think
that it is ignorance and delusion
that effects him. I think that he
will learn better, & Experience is
a good but severe teacher. I have found
it so. It had been my intention not
to write to you or Wade again till
I had gotten back into college and
[...] in case I did not get back to college
not to have let you heard from me a
gain. But as you have been so kind
as to write to me I will answer your
letter and will let you know from time
to time how I get along. I think that
there is no doubt but what I shall
get back to college in May. Give my
love to Wade and write to me soon
again. In the mean time believe
me to be truly,

　　　　your friend & servt.

　　　　Thaddeus Stevens

52474

Fig. 17　*(continued)* Letter from Thaddeus Stevens Jr. to Lydia Hamilton
Smith, March 26 [1853?], final page.

CHAPTER 8

BOOZE, POLITICS, AND
THE UNDERGROUND RAILROAD

While Lydia Hamilton Smith and Thaddeus Stevens grappled with how best to support Thad Jr. in his battle with the bottle in New Hampshire, booze was threatening to derail Mrs. Smith's younger son, Isaac, back home in Lancaster. We don't know how or when it started, but her concern had obviously come to a head in the fall of 1854. On September 8, an arrest warrant signed by Lydia Hamilton Smith was issued for the arrest of one "John Jones (col) charging Deft [defendant] with having given whiskey to her son Isaac Smith on Saturday the 2nd inst." Jones was arrested and held over to face charges "of giving whiskey to a minor & making him drunk." Mrs. Smith posted $100 bond for herself and for Isaac, promising they would appear as witnesses against Jones at the next quarter session of Lancaster County Court. Unable to post bail, Jones spent at least thirty days in jail waiting for his trial. Records don't tell us whether the court imposed any additional sentence after that.[1]

The description of the alleged crime, written on the outside of the warrant, indicated that Jones had been arrested for "furnishing Liquor After Notice." That suggests he had been warned, possibly by Mrs. Smith herself, to stay away from her seventeen-year-old son. Who was this John Jones? We really don't know. The Lancaster city directory for 1843 lists a William Jones as a tavern operator at the corner of West Walnut and Mulberry Streets in Lancaster. An 1857 edition of the directory lists John Jones but identifies him as a "segarmaker, home at Manor Avenue and West King Street" in the city. Whoever he was, he may have picked the worst possible teenager to entice with alcohol. The law under which Mrs. Smith swore out her complaint had only been enacted in May 1854. Her warrant accused Jones of being "in violation of the 1st section of the Act of Assembly (passed May 8, 1854) to protect certain domestic and private rights, and prevent abuses in the sale and uses of intoxicating drinks."[2] Living with Thaddeus Stevens, one of the sharpest lawyers ever to practice in Lancaster, apparently had practical benefits. Mrs. Smith obviously learned a great deal of property law from Stevens, and her well-informed encounter with John Jones suggests that he schooled her on criminal law as well.

Mrs. Smith may have taken such drastic action against John Jones in September because she saw Isaac heading down the same ruinous road Thad Jr. was on. Five months earlier, in what appears to be Isaac's first brush with the law, on Tuesday night, April 4, 1854, Constable Philip S. Baker had arrested her younger son on a misdemeanor charge of public intoxication and indecent exposure. Baker swore that "Isaac Smith colored was drunk and exposed his person in the public streets and that he had a bottle of whiskey & refused to give it up."[3] Unable to post $50 bail (Lydia does not appear to have come to the rescue), Isaac was committed to the Lancaster County prison to await trial. We don't know what punishment the court eventually meted out. But grief over the young men in Mrs. Smith's and Stevens's life was mounting. As Thad Jr.'s trouble conjured for his uncle visions of the boy's drunken grandfather, Isaac's encounters with alcohol surely forced Lydia to recall the impact of his father's behavior, which some observers attribute to drinking.

Thaddeus Stevens had another reason to grieve in 1854. His saintly mother, Sarah Morrill Stevens, died on August 5 while tending her cows on a farm he had purchased for her in Vermont. Hans Trefousse tells us that "her passing away left a permanent void in his life, no matter how closely attached he felt to his other relatives, especially his nephews, Thad, Jr. and Alanson and niece, Lizzie."[4] Sarah Stevens had known, virtually from the moment he was born, that her son would be a force for good in the world. She worked long hours to give him the education he needed and instilled in him the rock-solid morality of her Baptist faith that would guide his thoughts and actions throughout his life.

Stevens's critics often seized on his lack of regular church attendance as proof that he was an infidel. But to those able to look past their prejudices, he affirmed his belief in the values he had learned at his mother's knee. He underscored his respect and appreciation for his mother's faith by providing a $1,000 legacy in his will to help build the first Baptist church in Lancaster. Sadly, no gesture could relieve Stevens of his self-imposed guilt over his mother's death. Later in his life, he lamented that he had ever bought a farm for his mother. "Poor woman," he said. "The very thing I did to gratify her most hastened her death. She was very proud of her dairy and fond of her cows, and one night going to look after them, she fell and injured herself, so that she died soon after."[5]

In addition to coping with the family issues Stevens and Mrs. Smith both faced in 1854, Stevens was actively involved in politics of an unexpected stripe, one that Lydia might have found difficult to accept, and his colleague A. E. Roberts was part of the plan. Recall that Congressman Stevens lost out in his bid for renomination by the Whig Party in 1852, partly because his more conservative colleagues thought he had stood too close to the violent defense African Americans mounted in the Christiana Resistance. His former student and partner Alexander Hood later wrote that from 1853 to 1858, Stevens was busy practicing law and helping form the Republican Party.[6] But Hood glossed over some interesting and perplexing developments during that time.

A new paper hit the streets of Lancaster in August 1854—the *Inland Weekly*—and some observers thought Stevens was behind it. Its editorial stance, however, was far from the antislavery ideology Stevens had espoused so vigorously. On September 16, the *Inland Weekly* ran a banner headline reading "KNOW-NOTHINGS." The Know-Nothings had first surfaced in 1852 with a nativist take on political affairs in the United States. Staunchly anti-immigrant and anti-Catholic, Know-Nothings (known as the American Party in some places) sprang up in opposition to Irish immigrants arriving in the United States in large numbers and the Catholic Church's expanding influence on education and other aspects of public life.

Adherents came to be known as Know-Nothings when they consistently responded to inquiries about their rituals and mysteries with: "I know nothing about it." A document from the Newburg, Pennsylvania, chapter (about eighty miles west of Lancaster) underscores their secretive nature. It reveals that candidates for membership were forced to "swear upon that sacred and Holy emblem before Almighty God, and these witnesses, that you will not divulge or make known to any person whatever, the nature of the questions I may ask you here, the names of the persons you may see here or that you know that such an organization is going on as such, whether you become a member or not!" Know-Nothings had

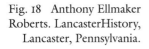

Fig. 18   Anthony Ellmaker
Roberts. LancasterHistory,
Lancaster, Pennsylvania.

considerable success in the 1850s, electing governors in Massachusetts and
Delaware and pushing Millard Fillmore onto the presidential ballot in 1856.[7]

The nine-point Know-Nothing platform spelled out in Lancaster's
Inland Weekly included: (1) require twenty years of residence, rather than
the current five, for US citizenship; (2) impose more restrictive immigra-
tion laws (no foreign paupers or convicts allowed); and (3) oppose the
political power of the Catholic Church. The *Inland Weekly* reported that
Know-Nothing lodges were forming around the region, and the *Lancaster Examiner* informed Lancastrians that the Honorable Thaddeus
Stevens himself had been inducted. Stevens successfully steered the Know-
Nothing congressional nomination to none other than former US marshal A. E. Roberts.[8]

As you may recall, Roberts, an avowed abolitionist, drew criticism
from federal prosecutors for the sympathy he showed defendants in the
Christiana Resistance trial. He was still drawing fire in 1854. A nativist
paper in Lancaster—the *Public Register and American Citizen*, published
by supporters of Congressman Isaac E. Hiester—laid into him. Hiester,
who had won Stevens's Ninth District seat in 1852, lived in New Holland,

about twelve miles east of Lancaster. A. E. Roberts also lived there. On September 20, 1854, the *Public Register and American Citizen* had this to say about the Know-Nothings' nominee: "No man in the county of Lancaster has done so much to introduce foreign paupers within its borders as Anthony E. Roberts. He has established quite a colony in or near New Holland."[9] The *Lancaster Examiner* joined in the *Public Register*'s attempt to paint Roberts as a fraudulent Know-Nothing and to expose Stevens as the man behind the curtain. The paper editorialized about Roberts, "Inconsistent in everything else, he is consistent only in his blind obedience to Thaddeus Stevens. If he is elected, we shall be represented by the shadow of Mr. Stevens without his brains."[10] Roberts won and served two terms in Congress.

Much of the credit for Roberts's success must go to Thaddeus Stevens, who cleverly manipulated the nativist Know-Nothing party to elect an abolitionist to Congress in a district where political and racial sentiments were more in line with Isaac Hiester than A. E. Roberts. In retrospect, it looks like a classic ends-justify-the-means scenario, but would Lydia Hamilton Smith agree with that? The Know-Nothings set an impossibly high bar to citizenship and sought to keep future immigrants out of the country, and they condemned the Catholic Church's "power" in American society. We have no indication of Mrs. Smith's reaction to Stevens's involvement in this political gamesmanship—or if she even had an opinion. Others did react. One historian considers the maneuver one of the lowest points in Stevens's career: "That he could ride the waves of bigotry to power is a blot on Stevens' character, especially since he himself was not a bigot."[11]

Thaddeus Stevens's nephew Alanson turned twenty-one in 1854. He was by then assistant manager at Stevens's Caledonia ironworks in Franklin County. We know, from Thad Jr.'s letter to Lydia, that Alanson shared some of his thoughts and feelings with her and his uncle. But he didn't tell them everything about his life at Caledonia. For instance, he told no one in his family, in 1854, that he'd made a young friend in Franklin County, a little girl named Mary Primm, the child of a Caledonia Furnace worker. Mary reckoned later that she was nine years old in 1854. She remembered the year and how old she was, she said, because her mother died that year, and Alanson attended the funeral. They were already friends, she said: "He used to carry me on his shoulders when I was a little girl." At the funeral, she remembered, "he lifted me in the carriage."[12] In a few short years, Mary Primm would become much more than Alanson Stevens's friend, a fact that would be met by his uncle, his brother, and his surrogate mother with chagrin.

The Underground Railroad stations that Stevens had supported in Adams and Franklin Counties remained very active during Alanson's years at Caledonia, and an important changing of the guard took place in 1854. Matthew Dobbin, a schoolteacher whose family farm would later become the stage for the Battle of Gettysburg, decided he was too old to carry on as an Underground Railroad conductor (a post he had held since 1837), so he appointed Hiram E. Wertz of Franklin County to succeed him. Dobbin died a year later.[13] Hiram Wertz now had responsibility for Underground Railroad activity stretching from Quincy in Franklin County to Africa, just west of South Mountain. In a *Compiler* story featuring Wertz, we learn that "Africa was a small settlement [20 to 25 families] located one mile south of Greenwood, and was peopled by African Americans who were employed by Thaddeus Stevens to dig iron ore for his Caledonia furnace."[14]

It seems likely Alanson knew all about the Railroad activity, given that several of his uncle's properties served as depots for fugitives on their way to freedom. Bradley Hoch tells us that "locals remembered the furnace master's house at Maria Furnace [in Fairfield, Pennsylvania] that had a second exit from the attic, and a house located between Fairfield and South Mountain whose basement had a false wall." According to Hoch, people thought "such properties" helped many fugitive slaves on the journey north.[15] These are reassuring details; they illustrate that despite Stevens's calculated swerve into the bigoted ranks of the Know-Nothings in 1854, he and Mrs. Smith and their partners in subverting the Fugitive Slave Act remained steadfast in their opposition to slavery and their support for the Underground Railroad.

By 1855, Lydia Hamilton Smith had been managing the house Thaddeus Stevens rented from Emanuel Reigart, on the west side of South Queen Street in Lancaster, for over a decade, but her lodgings and his were about to change. Reigart's daughter, Susan, announced her engagement to William P. Brinton. The plan was for the Brintons to move into the house Stevens was renting from Susan's father. That meant Stevens needed to find another place to live.[16]

His solution was to exercise an option he'd acquired back in 1843. He hired contractors to renovate the house he'd bought on the east side of South Queen Street, and he moved in when Susan and William were wed in 1856. Stevens's improvements to the structure included adding "a considerable ell extending from the eastern elevation of the house, and a contiguous extension to the south, physically connecting the . . . house and Kleiss Brewery with a storefront which served as his law office."[17] The renovations turned the unassuming one-and-a-half-story home into a full three-story mansion.

Biographer Richard Nelson Current provides this description: "It was a double house, with two doors in front, beside one of which [the one farthest south] was a brass plate reading, 'Office, Thaddeus Stevens, Attorney at Law.'" Current thought the "interior of the living quarters was so plainly furnished as to be almost ugly. A marble-topped table in one corner, several un-upholstered chairs scattered around, a large mirror and a few portraits on the walls . . . such were the bare furnishings of a parlor that could have been made cozy and attractive, looking as it did upon a small garden in the rear." Current had a higher opinion of the second floor. It was more livable, he wrote, with the "library . . . adjoining Stevens' bedroom and ministering conveniently to his habit of reading in bed." The walls of Stevens's new law office, installed in two rooms downstairs, were lined with legal books that Stevens was more than willing to lend to interested readers.[18]

Mrs. Smith quickly transferred her management skills to the newly renovated home at 45–47 South Queen Street. It's likely she moved into Stevens's house around this time, along with the household staff she supervised. The original living arrangement, Thomas Frederick Woodley tells us, was for her to occupy the small house behind 45–47 until her sons were old enough to look after themselves. William was twenty-one in 1856; Isaac was nineteen. Each of them had learned a trade: William was a shoemaker, Isaac a barber and a musician. Alanson and Thad Jr. were on their own in Franklin County and Vermont, respectively; surely Isaac and William were ready to try their wings in Lancaster. We've already seen two of them stumble on their way to independence. All four of them would face more challenges in the years to come.

Moving into Stevens's house would have made Mrs. Smith's job easier. And, contrary to Current's assessment, it seems likely that she made Stevens's remodeled house feel like a home. Woodley gives her high marks for her housekeeping. "She conducted it quietly," he writes, "and efficiently, kept it immaculately clean and supervised the other servants. She prepared the food he liked, surrounded him with domestic comforts, and

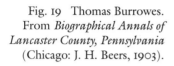

Fig. 19 Thomas Burrowes. From *Biographical Annals of Lancaster County, Pennsylvania* (Chicago: J. H. Beers, 1903).

when business called him out of town, packed his suitcase or trunk. . . . When he did entertain, she served the food and refreshment personally."[19]

Woodley's observations about Mrs. Smith align him with other biographers who reject the idea that her relationship with Thaddeus Stevens ever went beyond that of householder and housekeeper. I think that perspective might say more about them and the racial attitudes of the period in which they were writing than it does about the actual bond between Mrs. Smith and Stevens. Those who knew them well and socialized with them certainly suspected there was more to it than employment. Current notes that "many of his neighbors came to look upon her as more than a housekeeper, and some went so far as to speak of her, though never in his presence, as Mrs. Stevens." Of course, she lived in a society that, especially in slaveholding states, tacitly accepted informal relationships between white men and nonwhite women but would never have countenanced a Black "Mrs. Stevens." Current's speculation leads him to the conclusion we've already considered: "With Mrs. Smith almost as materfamilias in all but name, Stevens had become a kind of paterfamilias of the household on South Queen Street. In the place of children of his own were two of his nephews, Thaddeus and Alanson."[20] Add Mrs. Smith's sons, William and Isaac, and we have what looks very much like a nuclear family.

As to their relationship, Mrs. Smith lived beyond the role of a typical housekeeper. She not only planned and catered social functions on South Queen Street but also wrote the invitations and socialized with the guests when they arrived. As we've already seen, she was a vivacious presence at any gathering. The guests, many of them neighbors, were distinguished people, highly respected throughout Pennsylvania and beyond. Mrs. Smith grew especially close to those who lived in Lancaster, including the families of Dr. Henry Carpenter, a leading physician of the day, and the Honorable Thomas H. Burrowes, former Pennsylvania secretary of state and the first superintendent of the Keystone State's public schools. Judge Landis, who once wrote that Lydia "kept herself quite within her station," nonetheless reports that "Mrs. Smith was often at the houses of those gentlemen [Burrowes and Carpenter] and of others of like social position in the city, and she was on terms of intimacy with their families." So close was Mrs. Smith to the friends and neighbors with whom she and Stevens socialized that she left legacies for many of them in her will.[21] Again, not the sort of behavior we might expect from the hired help. Did these white friends with whom she spent so much time treat Mrs. Smith like Stevens's "wife," or simply as Thaddeus Stevens's vivacious domestic servant? Judge Landis seems to imply the latter when he writes that, in his view, she "kept herself quite within her station." But her close relationship with so many of them suggests that they, at least, accepted her as Stevens's companion. And as we'll see later, many of them maintained both personal and financial relationships with her long after Stevens's death.

Lydia Hamilton Smith touched many lives in many places with her friendship and her generosity, but Lancaster attorney John A. Coyle, her fellow communicant at St. Mary's Church in Lancaster, thinks that her crowning achievement was turning Stevens toward religion. Stevens talked about religion in his later years and allowed himself to be baptized by a Catholic nun. But in his Lancaster days, Coyle considered Stevens to be an atheist and a bigoted Know-Nothing.

To support the atheism claim, Coyle cited what he was told by a member of the bar examination committee in Lancaster. "Years ago," Coyle wrote in a letter to Father George Brown at St. Mary's Church, "it was customary for the students when passed successfully to provide refreshments for the committee. At one of these meetings, after examination of the young men, he [Stevens] proposed a toast, 'Here's to the man they call Christ.'" That was all the proof Coyle needed. Referring no doubt to

Stevens's deathbed baptism, Coyle gave all of the credit to Lydia. "At any rate," he wrote, "I am satisfied that Eliza [Coyle's name for Lydia] had much to do with the change in Stevens' religious attitude."[22]

Mrs. Smith's faithful attendance at mass at St. Mary's Church may have had some impact on the fact that Stevens struck up a friendship, of sorts, with her priest, Father Bernard Keenan. Coyle reported that "Father Keenan of St. Mary's was seen many times coming out of Stevens' office," but, Coyle wrote, the good priest wasn't smiling. He was "in a state of great excitement. They were good friends," Coyle contended, "but Stevens probably often offended him in remarks about, or discussion concerning religion." Stevens, Coyle wrote, "had a nasty tongue." It's not clear, from Coyle's letter, exactly what he thought of Thaddeus Stevens. He closed, enigmatically, with "I have a personal recollection of Stevens with which, however, I won't burden this communication."[23] How disappointing.

Mrs. Smith would have turned left out her front door as she headed to St. Mary's Church in the first block of West Vine Street. If she turned right, a few short steps would have taken her to the front door of Christopher Dice's grocery store at 43 South Queen Street. No doubt she appreciated having a grocery store near at hand, but being a grocer wasn't the role that tied Dice closest to her and Stevens. In a talk before the Lancaster County Historical Society in the early 1930s, W. Frank Gorrecht, former publisher of the *Lancaster Examiner*, told Dice's story with the assistance of Dice's daughter, Barbara Dice Bush. That story brings us back to a name we've heard before—Edward Rauch.

Gorrecht told the audience that Christopher Dice was "Stevens' most intimate and confidential friend." Dice and Edward Rauch, he said, were part of the inner circle of the Underground Railroad network in Lancaster.[24] As we know, having anything to do with the Underground Railroad was risky business, especially after passage of the Fugitive Slave Act. Despite that danger, both men put themselves on the line against slavery, time and time again.

We met Rauch earlier acting as a double agent, seeming to help slave catchers but actually reporting their plans directly to Stevens (and Mrs. Smith) so fugitives could get away before slavers and their minions showed up. Rauch must have been pretty convincing as a slave catcher. Gorrecht said that when the Fugitive Slave Act went into effect, Rauch became "the worst hated and the most despised man in the community."[25] In one encounter, Rauch was walking near Lancaster's Centre Square when a group of citizens, already upset over the kidnapping of a free Black woman by slave catchers, recognized him. Someone in the crowd shouted, "'Here comes one of the slave catchers, get a rope, hang him, hang him.' Rauch was seized and roughly handled. A rope was thrown across the arms of the lamp post, and had not Stevens appeared and persuaded the enraged citizens to desist, there is every reason to believe the affair would have ended in the death of Rauch."[26]

Gorrecht said he learned the story after another newspaperman, angry because Rauch wouldn't admit he was wrong in an argument, had exclaimed, "You were too stubborn to tell the truth when they strung you up to the lamp post in Centre Square, and so why should we expect anything better of you now?" Rauch's response underscored his deep devotion to the Underground Railroad and Thaddeus Stevens: "Well, they could have hanged me until I was dead before I would have betrayed Stevens."[27]

Christopher Dice's daughter, Barbara Dice Bush, explained the connection between Edward Rauch and her father. As you read this, bear in mind that this was all taking place within a few hundred feet of Centre Square, not far from slave catcher George Hughes's office and a couple of yards from Thaddeus Stevens's front door. Mrs. Bush said she knew Edward Rauch well: "He came to our place very often. Rauch could not call on Stevens without danger of being detected, but he could go to the grocery store of Mr. Dice a dozen times a day without creating suspicion, give his information to the groceryman, and the latter pass it on to Stevens."[28] This, it is true, is purely a matter of presumption, but it is logical, and there is indirect corroboration in the fact that Mrs. Bush was kept in total ignorance of the reasons for Rauch's visits. Gorrecht also underscored the financial cost—thousands of dollars—that Thaddeus Stevens absorbed to keep the Underground Railroad running across southern Pennsylvania.

The Shiffler Fire Company, the one William and Isaac Smith helped create, was on the move in May 1856. A substantial two-story brick firehouse was finished and ready for occupancy on Strawberry Street, near South Queen Street, on land donated by Thaddeus Stevens.[29] William and Isaac don't appear in the company's minutes that year, but O. J. Dickey was elected treasurer. Dickey was also elected Lancaster County's district attorney that same year. In 1857, he gave up his quarters at Stevens's law office "when he found it necessary, from the press of business, to open an office" of his own.[30]

We must note one more bit of sadness that darkened the lives of Lydia Hamilton Smith and Thaddeus Stevens in 1857. A young man arrived unexpectedly at 45 South Queen Street. When Mrs. Smith opened the door, she found herself face-to-face with Keziah Shannon Wolrich's son, Bill. (Recall that Keziah was the young mixed-race housekeeper who tried to hang herself in Stevens's house in Gettysburg. She was discovered in her first attempt by Lydia's mother.) Bill said he had come to Mrs. Smith and Stevens hoping they could help him find a job. He had come to the right place.

Stevens landed Bill a position as a waiter on the SS *Central America*, a steamship that plied the East Coast, hauling passengers and cargo between the Isthmus of Panama and New York City. With Bill on board, the ship sailed to Panama, where it took on passengers and a cargo of 400 million dollars in gold bars and coins. On its way to New York, the ship sailed into a hurricane and sank, taking 425 passengers and crew, including Bill Wolrich, and all the gold to the bottom of the sea. Along with the towering grief the accident caused for families of the victims, the lost gold helped trigger the financial panic of 1857.[31]

CHAPTER 9

LIFE, DEATH, AND MARRIAGE

In 1858, the recently formed antislavery Republican Party put Thaddeus Stevens's name forward to succeed his friend (and now fellow Republican) A. E. Roberts as the congressman from Pennsylvania's Ninth District. It was a risky move. Southern-sympathizing Democrats still dominated politics in Lancaster, and they didn't like Stevens and what he stood for. The *Lancaster Intelligencer* greeted the news with an obscene racial slur in an all-caps headline. The accompanying article accused Stevens of being "the very head and font of abolitionism." But with support from wealthy farmers and religious sects like the Mennonites, Stevens won easily.[1] Historian Andrew Robertson notes the irony of Stevens winning in Lancaster County. He writes that "voters [in 1858] made the President of the United States, their adopted son, James Buchanan [a staunch Democrat], a constituent of his mortal enemy, Thaddeus Stevens."[2] By 1858, there had been no lessening of the animosity that sprang up between the two Lancastrians many years earlier in Gettysburg.

The 36th Congress of the United States convened on March 4, 1859. Thaddeus Stevens was there but no longer lodging in a Washington hotel. This time he rented a three-story brick house behind the Capitol at 279 South B Street, and he asked Mrs. Smith to join him there as his housekeeper. She accepted and quickly settled into what was, in effect, an expanded role in Stevens's household.[3] As we saw earlier, Judge Landis emphasized that, in Lancaster, Mrs. Smith knew her place—as housekeeper—and always stayed "within her station." He illustrated his point by telling us what she *didn't* do. "Owing to [Stevens] having no female relatives in his home," he wrote, "at one of these parties his friend and neighbor, Mrs. [Susan]

Brinton, received for him, at another, Mrs. Oliver J. Dickey performed the same service."[4] (Mrs. Smith would have planned, sent invitations for, and catered these parties.) In Washington, with Stevens's blessing, Mrs. Smith's role grew significantly. As Current describes it, she did everything a *wife* would do: "Lydia Smith would bustle about, setting up the table for the [card] players, adjusting the lamps, bringing refreshments, and attending to other details in wifely fashion." Current reports that people couldn't help noticing that the housekeeper at 279 South B Street was not ordinary, but they were "not so brash as to inquire into the domestic affairs of their host." "Nevertheless," Current tells us, "the guests . . . assumed that his [Stevens's] regard for the mulatto woman was not entirely platonic."[5]

In a sense, this was a role Lydia Hamilton Smith had spent her whole life preparing for. The observations from John A. Coyle, her acquaintance from St. Mary's Church in Lancaster, bear repeating here. Coyle summed up the qualities that made Lydia so impressive as she stood by Stevens's side in Washington, DC: "She was as smart as a steel trap, bright, and a good conversationalist because of her many years of life with Stevens at Washington where she came in contact with the prominent people all over the United States, including those from the South who would have liked to have shot Stevens, and those of the North who felt otherwise."[6]

Coyle alluded to the negative side of Mrs. Smith's presence in Washington. In Lancaster, most of the ugliness she and Stevens faced about their relationship came from local Pennsylvanians—Democrats, Southern sympathizers, racist riff-raff. In Washington, this mixed-race couple was visible to the entire nation. And those who didn't go so far as to accuse them of violating God's supposed prohibition on interracial coupling still thought Mrs. Smith explained a lot about Thaddeus Stevens. "A frequent visitor during the winter of 1865–66," Current tells us, "believed that the influence of this colored mistress was largely the cause of Stevens' bitter animosity to Southern whites."[7]

Was that opinion based on comments the "visitor" heard Mrs. Smith make in Washington? Perhaps. But accepting the visitor's contention as true would mean ignoring the views on slavery and racial equality that Stevens had formed before he left Gettysburg. Lydia was in Gettysburg in those days and likely knew Stevens, but she was then a child. It seems unlikely that she was in a position to influence his thinking. Did she influence Stevens's attitudes and actions on racial matters after she came to Lancaster? Of course she did. But trying to write off Stevens's animosity toward those who engaged in enslaving human beings as the ventings of a white man doing the bidding of his Black "mistress" simply exposed the huge chasm between those who knew slavery was evil and those who chose to continue benefitting from it. As we'll see, Lydia Hamilton Smith and Thaddeus Stevens were clearly, if not officially, committed partners as they strode through their moment in history.

As Stevens and Mrs. Smith headed into their new life in Washington in 1859, there were a number of significant family-related developments in Pennsylvania. In a letter to his nephew Thaddeus Morrill Stevens (a doctor in Indianapolis), Stevens informed him that his cousin Thad Jr. had joined the family law firm in Lancaster. (Family friend Simon Stevens was also added to the practice that year.) Stevens told the doctor that Thad Jr.'s brother, Alanson, was "assisting to manage my Iron Works. "[8] But, as we will see, Alanson was engaged in much more than iron making. And Lydia's son William, now a twenty-four-year-old shoemaker, was involved in much more than making shoes. We don't know whether Stevens and Lydia knew what the young men were up to in 1859. Stevens would discover Alanson's situation soon enough; we have no written evidence that Lydia was aware of what was happening in William's life, but she must have known something about it.

What we know about William's ultimately tragic fate comes from court records and newspaper accounts. From the auditor's report filed in connection with Mrs. Smith's estate after she died, we hear testimony from Lydia's cousin Anna Sulkey Martin. (By some accounts, it was Anna who recommended Mrs. Smith to Thaddeus Stevens in 1844, when he needed a housekeeper.) She told the court she was "well-acquainted with Lydia Smith and her whole family." She said she had known William "from his childhood up until the time of his death."[9]

Anna told the court that, in 1861, William was "engaged to Sarah Clark. They both said so." Anna said Sarah Clark was her niece, her sister's daughter, and her father was Herman Clark of Highspire, Pennsylvania, near Harrisburg. Then Anna's testimony turned dark. She said, "I was present at his death. He shot himself."[10] Why would he do that? The *Lancaster Examiner and Herald* took note of the shooting but offered no explanation: "Dead.—The young negro Smith, who shot himself with a pistol a short time since [April 2, 1861] died from the effects of his wounds on Tuesday morning." The *Lancaster Daily Evening Express* offered more details about what it called a "ghastly" pistol accident. Longtime Lancaster newspaperman Jack Brubaker republished highlights of the *Express*'s story in 2013, informing modern-day readers that "Wm. Smith, a young colored man, [shot himself] while handling a pistol in the presence of his mother and one of the servants at the Hon. Thaddeus Stevens, South Queen Street" home. The *Express* reported that William accidentally shot himself "directly over the heart," inflicting a wound that proved fatal. The newspaper treated the tragedy as a morality tale: "Here is another painful warning of the careless handling of firearms."[11] William was the first member of Lydia's family to be buried in St. Mary's Cemetery on New Holland Avenue in Lancaster, in a plot she either already owned or purchased at the time of his death. But we can't let the unfortunate William rest in peace just yet. We have substantial indications that his death may have been more than a tragic firearms accident.

In Anna Martin's deposition, we learn that William "could not speak after he had shot himself." Anna confirmed the newspaper's sad report that Lydia was present when her son died. Then she adds a detail absent from the newspaper stories. After William shot himself, she said, "a letter was found on his person from Sarah Clark in which she refused to marry him." Was William so distraught over his fiancée's rejection that he resorted to desperate measures? Or was there more to it than that? Court records suggest there was.[12]

One complicating factor enters the picture in the form of Charles Christopher Smith, who filed a claim as an heir to part of Lydia's estate. In his deposition, Charles Smith told the court he was born on March 1, 1859, in Lancaster. He said, "Charlotte Smith or Charlotte Foster was my mother." He further testified, "They say William Smith was my father, but I cannot tell about that part. I was a small boy when I left Lancaster, Pa. I do not remember anything about my father. . . . My mother always said that I looked like him." Charles said his mother never said much about his father, but his grandmother, who helped raise him in Philadelphia and New York, "used to say why don't you save up your money and go to Washington to see your grandmother, Lydia Smith." Charles said he never heard from Lydia Smith and didn't know what communication, if any, the rest of his family had with her.[13]

Charles directed Lydia's executors to his second cousin, Drucilla Waters, in Philadelphia, for further details. Drucilla said that she lived in Lancaster during the Civil War and "knew Lydia Smith well and Isaac and William Smith her sons. I was present immediately after Charlotte Foster gave birth to Charles Smith," she said. "Charlotte told us who the father of the boy was. She said it was William Smith. She said she was to be married to William Smith. But they did not get married. They met with an accident and did not get married. She was never married. I heard her speak about their not getting married. They were to be married the week William shot himself. He shot himself and died from lock jaw from the effects."[14]

Drucilla said the arrival of Charlotte's baby was very upsetting to her family. "The fact of her having this boy without her being married," she told the court, "made a great talk and sensation amongst her relatives. Her family and folks were very much out done at her conduct. They were surprised. They did not expect it of her." Drucilla shared what she knew of Charlotte and William's relationship. "William courted her and made love to her and this happened, but they never got married. When Charles was born all the family were very sorry and put-out about it. She was well raised." Drucilla said Charlotte Foster "never had anything to do with Lydia Smith. Mrs. Smith and Mrs. Foster did not associate, nor have much to do with each other." She ended her testimony with an endorsement of her cousin's claim. "I have kept track of Charles Smith since his birth," she said. "She [Charlotte Foster] said in my presence it was the child of William Smith. That is what Charles Smith was—the child of William Smith by her."[15]

What are we to make of this testimony and William's death by gunshot from our vantage point more than 150 years after the event? Jack Brubaker put the question to Lydia Hamilton Smith scholar and interpreter Darlene Colon in 2013. Her speculation about the shooting was that William may have been among the African American men who were rejected when they offered to fight for the Union in April 1861 as the Civil War began. A volunteer regiment from Bethel A.M.E. Church in Lancaster was sent away by officials who refused to arm them. Perhaps William marched to the courthouse with them. Darlene Colon had an idea about how he reacted. "I envision him as being very angry when the gun went off," she said. "There's no way to know."[16]

Anna Martin's testimony about the letter in William's pocket and Charles Smith's claim that William was his father seem to point us in a different direction. Did Sarah Clark send the letter to William to break off their engagement because she had discovered William's involvement with Charlotte Foster? If so, William may have been despondent rather than angry when he shot himself in the chest. It's interesting, and perhaps significant, that the bullet lodged just above his heart. The *Lancaster Intelligencer* must have had some evidence related to the case in 1884, given its flat assertion, in Lydia's obituary, that "William . . . committed suicide several years ago."[17]

If it was suicide, that would have raised some red flags when his mother sought to bury William in St. Mary's Cemetery. In the nineteenth century, the Catholic Church routinely denied suicide victims a funeral mass and burial. (St. Mary's wouldn't have been an exception in opposing burial. Even Shreiner's Cemetery, the cemetery Thaddeus Stevens chose for his grave site because it did not discriminate on the basis of race, banned suicide victims when it first opened.) Early in the twentieth century, Pope Pius X reminded the faithful that "in the Fifth Commandment God forbids suicide, because man is not the master of his own life no more than of the life of another. Hence the Church punishes suicide by deprivation of Christian burial." The Church has adopted a more sympathetic policy today, but even in William's time, the rules could be stretched. Sometimes people who took their own lives were buried at the far edges of the cemetery, away from most of the other graves. That might be how Father Keenan at St. Mary's dealt with William's death. If you visit the cemetery today, you will notice two things: Lydia's plot is on the back section of the cemetery, not entirely isolated, but at some distance from the center of the graveyard. William's grave, beside Lydia's, is marked by a very modest memorial, so badly worn now that it is virtually unreadable. Even when first mounted, it would not have drawn attention to the person laid to rest there. And if you examine the tombstones around Lydia's plot, you'll notice that no one else was buried near William for at least twenty years; most of the gravestones behind Lydia's plot were placed there forty years after William died. And after 150 years, no one has been laid to rest on the other side of William's grave. In the midst of her grief, did Lydia have to negotiate her son's final resting place with her beloved priest, Father Keenan?[18] If so, it is hard to imagine how difficult that conversation must have been. Archivists for the Harrisburg, Pennsylvania, diocese of the Roman Catholic Church have not found any record of a funeral mass for William Smith.

Alanson Stevens's experience in Franklin County, in 1859, would prove equally tragic. When Thaddeus Stevens told his nephew Thaddeus Morrill Stevens that Alanson was assistant manager at the ironworks, he left out the most important development for Alanson that year, probably because he was unaware of it. There is no evidence that Mrs. Smith knew about it, either. In the years after he arrived at the ironworks, Alanson's friendship with Mary Primm, the furnace worker's little girl, had grown into much more than rides on his shoulders. Years later, Mary pursued a claim against Thaddeus Stevens's estate, and the first words of her deposition were, "I am the widow of Alanson J. Stevens. I was married to Alanson J. Stevens on the 21st of October 1859 at the Jones House, Harrisburg, Room No. 13." Mary was fourteen years old in 1859. Alanson was twenty-six. After the ceremony, Mary said, "we went to Washington from Harrisburg on a wedding trip and from there to Caledonia Furnace to housekeeping."[19] Bear in mind, as we examine her story, that Mary was in her forties when she testified in court, retrieving memories stored, originally, in the mind of a fourteen-year-old girl. I leave it to the reader to decide whether the stories she tells are accurate.

If Alanson and Mary visited Washington that October, Thaddeus Stevens and Lydia Hamilton Smith likely were not there. The special session of the 36th Congress had adjourned on March 10, and the first regular session would not convene until December 5. In any event, it doesn't sound like the newlyweds had much of a honeymoon. Mary testified that "we remained about one week, we stopped in Washington at a hotel, but I don't remember the name. We did not visit any of the public buildings. I was taken sick. Alanson did not take me up to see his uncle, I don't know whether he was in Washington at the time or not. He did not point out the house in which his uncle lived. He brought me to Harrisburg on our return, but I was too sick to go further, and he left me there at the United States Hotel."[20]

Were Alanson Stevens and Mary Jane Primm married? That, of course, was the crux of the legal wrangling over her claim, as Alanson's widow, on Stevens's estate. Mary swore in court, "I got a marriage certificate when we were married. I had it. It was burned in Chambersburg in McRea's house. I took it there in a box with other things for safe keeping. That house burned down and all the contents including the certificate."[21]

Some people who knew the couple in those days swore they did marry; others were just as certain they didn't. Jacob and Mary Tuckey, who took Mary in after her mother died and her father moved away, testified that Alanson and Mary were at their house when they rode off to get married. According to Jacob Tuckey, Alanson returned, without Mary, less than a week later. Tuckey said he and Alanson were sitting on the porch the next night, when "Lance" said, "Now we are married, and it is nobody's damned business."[22]

Tuckey testified that Alanson and Mary lived with his family for a time after they returned to the ironworks. He thought they sounded like husband and wife. "In addressing her, Alanson often called her his 'wife' or 'Mollie,' I have heard him call her Mrs. Stevens," he said. As for Mary, "she always spoke to me of Alanson as her husband." But John Sweeney, manager at the ironworks from 1858 to 1868, swore that "no person ever supposed she was ever married. He never introduced her to me or spoke of her to me other than as Mary Primm. She never said to me in her life that she was married to Alanson J. Stevens."[23]

Married or not, Alanson and Mary moved into one of the houses Thaddeus Stevens provided for Caledonia Furnace workers in May or June 1860, according to John Sweeney. Two weeks later, Stevens paid a visit to his ironworks. Sweeney said, as they toured the grounds, that Stevens noticed smoke rising from the chimney of what he thought was an unoccupied worker's house, and asked, "Who's living there?" Sweeney testified, "I told him Alanson and Mary were keeping house." Sweeney said Stevens's curt response was, "It was very bad behavior on the place—that was all that was said on that subject and Mr. Stevens remarked as we parted, 'Charge him with what ever he gets.'"[24] Stevens left without confronting his nephew; he would convey his strong displeasure later. Two months after Stevens's visit, and ten months after they reportedly got hitched, Alanson and Mary welcomed their first child, Andrew Curtin Stevens, on August 18, 1860. But their joy over their new arrival was cut short. The baby lived just nine weeks. Many years later, the details of the tragedy were still vivid in Mary's mind. She told the court that Andrew was born in the house where she and Alanson were living. She said, "Alanson sent for the physician [a Dr. Byers] at the time of the birth of the first child, and at the time of its last illness." Mary said Alanson was there for all of it. "Alanson was present at the death of the child," Mary testified. "I think it died on his lap."[25]

Mary said Alanson did his duty as father of the child: "He accompanied me to the grave. There were several carriages. I had his arm from the house to the carriage, and from the carriage to the grave. There were other persons at the funeral and at the grave." Mary said she and Alanson used their own modest transportation to get to the graveyard. "It was our buggy," she said, "that could hold but two persons." The Tuckeys witnessed Andrew's funeral and Alanson's reaction to his death: Alanson "recognized *them* [a second child was born in 1862] in the family as their children," Jacob Tuckey said, and "when the little boy died, he took it very hard." We have no evidence that Stevens and Lydia knew about the child's death or attended the funeral. With their firstborn child dead and buried, Mary told the court that Alanson put her in school, first in Mechanicsburg, then in Chambersburg. But she spent relatively little time in classes. When the Civil War began, she said, Alanson moved her to Taylor's Hotel in Chambersburg. Her husband "was then in the three months service."[26]

In 1861, after Confederate troops fired on Fort Sumter in South Carolina and threatened to attack Washington, DC, President Lincoln issued a call for a 75,000-man volunteer militia to help put down the insurrection. Lincoln's call went out on April 15, and Alanson signed up as a private in Company A of the 2nd Regiment, Pennsylvania Volunteers, in Chambersburg, Pennsylvania, on April 20. Thad Jr. left his uncle's law practice and joined up the same day, in Lancaster, as a private with Company F of the 1st Regiment, Pennsylvania Volunteers.[27] Lydia's son Isaac enlisted two years later, when African American men were finally allowed to carry a gun in defense of the Union.

CHAPTER 10

THE WAR YEARS

By 1860, Lydia Hamilton Smith had been managing Thaddeus Stevens's household for sixteen years. We've seen her life grow increasingly complex and stressful, but there's never any indication during these years that she ever doubted her ability to handle it. Her partner, Thaddeus Stevens, won reelection as Lancaster's congressman by a landslide: 12,065 votes for Stevens, 470 for his opponent.[1] Stevens's political and professional success drew the pair into the very heart of the social worlds of Washington and Lancaster. In his defense of Mrs. Smith and Stevens years later, Judge Landis noted that Stevens cared little for "social life" but "gave large parties that many prominent people of this city [Lancaster] attended."[2] We know Mrs. Smith planned and oversaw every detail of those events, down to the invitations. One of those invitations, most likely in Mrs. Smith's own hand, reads: "Lancaster, Aug. 21st, 1860, Mr. Thaddeus Stevens requests the company of Mr. and Mrs. Wm. Wright on the evening of Friday, the 24th inst."[3]

Managing the routine activities of Stevens's house and office at 45–47 South Queen Street had become a significant task by 1860, aside from the frills of parties and gatherings. For one thing, a lot of people lived there. Census taker William Lowry counted them in 1860; he was a little off on his estimate of their ages, but the rest of the data seems accurate. He probably didn't talk with Lydia Hamilton Smith or Thaddeus Stevens. Lowry came knocking on June 15. Congress didn't adjourn in Washington until ten days later.

Lowry lists eight inhabitants of Stevens's house: Thaddeus Stevens, attorney, seventy-six (he was sixty-eight); Lydia Smith, forty-four (she was forty-seven); Hester Hoover, forty-four; Sam'l Hoover, nineteen; Francis Hoover, sixteen; John Hoover, thirteen; Mary Frecht, eighteen; and Martha Swint, sixteen. Mrs. Smith is the only member of the household identified by race, as Lowry put her down as "mulatto." We don't learn the occupation of anyone other than Thaddeus Stevens. We do discover that by 1860, Stevens owned real estate worth a total of $150,000, a princely sum in the mid-nineteenth century, and $2,000 worth of personal property (furniture and other possessions). It appears that none of the Hoovers in the house owned any real estate. Nor did Mary Frecht or Martha Swint. But Lydia did—$1,800 worth.[4] Despite an unfortunate marriage, increasing concerns about her sons, vicious criticism of her relationship to Thaddeus Stevens, heartache over Thad Jr.'s drinking problem, the risk of arrest for running a station on the Underground Railroad, and greater and greater responsibility for Stevens's *two* households, Lydia Hamilton Smith had managed to launch a business career the majority of men *and* women of her time, Black or white, would envy and respect.

According to the records, 1860 was the year Thaddeus Stevens sold Lydia Smith a "piece of land on the NW corner of Vine St. and a 14 foot wide public alley in Lancaster between South Queen St. and Duke Street on which the said Lydia Smith has erected a brick dwelling house on the south by Vine, on the east by public alley and parallel lines on the other two sides—33 feet on Vine, 31 feet on alley, other land of Thaddeus Stevens on North and West."[5] In essence, this was the southeast corner of the property Thaddeus Stevens bought at sheriff's sale back in 1843.

Mrs. Smith was on her way to becoming "one of only three women of color to own property in Lancaster County during the middle of the nineteenth century."[6] I don't think it takes anything away from her achievements to admit that Stevens helped her along the way. His regard for her was likely so great by this time that he was more than happy to do it. After so many years together, he knew Lydia Hamilton Smith better than anyone else. He definitely knew she intended to rise above her humble beginnings. In his last days, when Stevens was conversing with his good friend and law partner Simon Stevens, he touched on her inclinations. In testimony years later, Simon Stevens said, "On the last occasion when I rode out with him which was about ten days before his death, he spoke of Mrs. Smith's acquisitiveness and said, 'No matter what her love of money is, she has never neglected me or my household—whether we were in health or in sickness.'"[7] This is a tremendously informative bit of testimony. It gives us a glimpse into Stevens's tremendous appreciation for all the ways Mrs. Smith had served him over a quarter of a century. We hear a man who rose from poverty to wealth, a man who did everything in his power to help Mrs. Smith reach her goals, sound almost proud of her material success.

But the most revealing part of Stevens's reflection is the very last clause. Lydia had never stinted in her care for him and his household "whether we were in health or in sickness." A man as articulate as Thaddeus Stevens didn't absent-mindedly use language that echoed traditional wedding vows. In that moment, it seems to me, in the presence of a man he could trust, Stevens claimed Lydia Hamilton Smith as his wife, regardless of the fact that the church and the state had forever withheld their blessing. We need to bear Stevens's words in mind as we see how Mrs. Smith was treated, later, by others in Stevens's orbit.

The surprising thing about Mrs. Smith's transaction with Stevens in 1860 was that the land she bought (for $500) already had a house on it, "which the said Lydia Smith has erected."[8] It has been suggested that Lydia built the house for herself and her sons, and it's possible William and Isaac may have lived there at some point, but it's doubtful that their mother did. More likely, Mrs. Smith moved into Stevens's newly renovated house at 45–47 South Queen Street in 1856, and, perhaps with Stevens's encouragement, built the house on East Vine Street as an investment. Architecture scholars Sally McMurry and Nancy Van Dolsen report that Mrs. Smith followed the example of Philadelphia builders who began, in the mid-nineteenth century, erecting two- and three-story brick rowhouses—purpose-built tenements—to meet a critical shortage of rental housing for the working class. Traditional one-story homes were still the norm in Lancaster in the early 1850s. Adopting the Philadelphia style made Lydia Hamilton Smith a trendsetter. A walk down almost any residential street in Lancaster today demonstrates convincingly how well that trend caught on. Mrs. Smith went three full stories with her house. Inside, "the main block of the first floor originally consisted of a single room and entry containing the stairs. Cooking and other domestic work was conducted in a cellar kitchen, complete with hearth, dry sink, storage cupboards and dresser. The upper stories contained chambers for sleeping."[9] If we take a moment to revisit the $1,800 worth of real estate credited to Mrs. Smith in the 1860 census, it seems likely we're looking at the value of the house on East Vine Street. Mrs. Smith owned it for the rest of her life; her executors sold it in 1886. I believe progressive businesswoman Lydia Hamilton

Smith's intention, from the laying of the first brick, was to erect an income-generating rental property, and that's exactly what she did.

Lydia Hamilton Smith and Thaddeus Stevens were both in Lancaster as the nation careened toward war in early 1861. They were there on April 2, when William Smith shot himself above the heart, and a week later when he died. We have no record of William's funeral and burial, but we have to assume his grieving mother was there. And we hope, although we don't know, that Stevens was there to support her.

They were there on April 12, when rebel forces fired on Fort Sumter in South Carolina and ignited the Civil War, which would bring even more tragedy to the Stevens-Smith household. Stevens had been tending to his law practice since the special session of the 36th Congress adjourned on March 28. We don't have written testimony of it, but surely he dropped everything and joined Mrs. Smith and others in Lancaster in sending Thad Jr. and the other members of Company F of the 1st Regiment, Pennsylvania Volunteers, off to defend the Union. We do have a written record of Alanson's departure.

William Camp, a Caledonia Furnace employee who had become acquainted with Stevens when he settled Camp's father's estate, wrote to Stevens to tell him of Alanson's departure and the general mood at the ironworks. "I have just bid Alanson Good bye," he said. "He has gone to fight the battle of his country. The mildest state of excitement reigns here our best men have tendered their services. And everybody left back is anxious to go business in this place is entirely suspended—stores all shut up. $6000 was raised yesterday to support the families of the soldiers during their absence." Camp closed with a profession of his great desire to follow Alanson to war: "If it would be policy to stop operations at Caledonia, our force to a man will go, & I will go with them."[10]

Thaddeus Stevens returned to Washington for the start of the 37th Congress on the Fourth of July, 1861, but in a departure from their usual custom, Mrs. Smith stayed behind in Lancaster. Perhaps she was still mourning William's tragic and untimely death, or she might have been attending to business interests, hers or Stevens's. Stevens reached out to her in a letter dated July 24. Some historians point to the tone and content of the letter (the only one discovered so far from Stevens to Mrs. Smith) as further evidence that their relationship rose well above that of householder and housekeeper. In the letter, Stevens appears to be responding to news he'd received about her from someone else, or perhaps from her own hand.

"Dear Madam," he wrote, "I am glad to hear that you are well—I am no worse than usual." (Stevens's once-robust health had been in decline for several years by this time.)

He continued, "We have had a bloody battle and a bad defeat—But men are not discouraged." Stevens was referring to the First Battle of Bull Run, fought just north of Manassas, Virginia, about twenty-five miles from the Capitol, on July 21. It was, indeed, a "bloody battle," with more than 2,700 Union soldiers wounded, slain, or missing in action and nearly 2,000 Confederate troops dead, wounded, or missing.[11] Stevens was among the most ardent advocates of mounting a punishing response to the Southern rebellion. This early setback obviously did not dampen his ardor for a total victory against the Confederacy.

Stevens's next sentences seem designed to ease Mrs. Smith's (a wife's?) worry on behalf of all the Stevens men in her life. "I think Congress will adjourn next week," he told her, "and I shall be home the week after—Thaddeus and Alanson were not in the battle; I suppose they will soon go home—Give my respects to Mrs. Erb and all the friends, [Yours] Thaddeus Stevens."[12] He was home by early August. Alanson and Thad Jr. came home, too, after completing their three months' service, but with the war very far from won, they would not be home for long. Thad Jr. returned to Lancaster near the end of July 1861,[13] but by then Mrs. Smith and his uncle had returned to Washington. He likely kept busy looking after Stevens's law practice, as he had before his three months' service. But he apparently wasn't keeping in touch with his uncle, and Lydia was not pleased. Two days before Christmas, she wrote a letter entreating him to pay a visit to Washington. "Dear Sir," she wrote, "The winter is here and you have not come to visit your uncel yet. He has been expecting you—try and come on soon and see Washington. In those war times there is quite a throng here. Washington never was as great a bizness a place as it is now—and your second cousins are hear. Lerch[?] is the name of the young men wright me and tell me when you will come Alanson Stevens is in Kentucky he is a lutenant your uncle is not well. Yours with regard, Lydia Smith."[14]

Mrs. Smith's simple message to Thad—"your uncel is not well"—masks the serious concern she had for Stevens's health in 1861. Dr. Henry Carpenter, Stevens's physician (and close friend) in Lancaster, testifying in Mrs. Smith's legal pursuit of back wages Stevens had promised her, said that "during the last years of his life his health was feeble." Carpenter said Stevens suffered from a bowel disorder that made him prone to frequent bouts of diarrhea that laid him low and could only be relieved through daily doses of morphine and strychnine. Testifying in those same proceedings, Stevens's Washington physician, Dr. Noble Young, added to the list of ailments. He said Stevens "had a valvular disease of the heart."[15] We don't know if Thad Jr. responded to Lydia's plea, but she had long since taken up the post at Stevens's side that she would not abandon until his death.

Alanson Stevens completed his three months' service and returned to the Caledonia Furnace and Mary Primm by the end of July 1861, but his stay was brief. On August 11, he and several other men from the Franklin County area, including Mary's brother, John H. Primm,[16] reenlisted, this time for three years. Alanson went in as a lieutenant with Independent Battery B of the Pennsylvania Volunteers and was promoted to captain in January 1863. He and his battery were part of the 2nd Army Corps, Army of the Ohio, stationed in Kentucky.[17]

Mary Primm would testify, later, that before Alanson left for the second time, he gave her a note signifying that they were married. Caledonia manager John Sweeney admitted to seeing it. "I saw the paper," he said. "Mary showed it to me it was soon after he went into the Western Army. The paper was about six or seven inches long, it read, 'I here acknowledge Mary Primm to be my lawful wife, as I go forth to battle. Signed A. J. Stevens,' I had that paper in my hand, and I recognized it as his handwriting. I handed the paper back to her and I have not seen it since."[18] About five months after Alanson returned to war, Mary gave birth to their second child, Alanson Jane (Jennie) Stevens, born January 21, 1862, according to Mary. Alanson appeared to welcome the news. Mary's sister, Martha Primm Myers, testified that she saw a letter Alanson wrote to Mary soon after the baby was born. In it, Alanson addressed Mary as his "Dear Wife," and he told her to "take good care of our daughter and when I live to get home we will raise her up right."[19]

Alanson also stayed in touch with his uncle. On November 19, Stevens wrote his nephew that he was "glad to hear that with all your hard work you are still in good health." Alanson's battery had been part of a battle in Perryville, Kentucky, in October; the Union troops prevailed. Stevens told Alanson that his brother, Thad Jr., back in uniform with the 122nd Pennsylvania Infantry, was "down near the enemy and a battle seems likely."[20]

Six months later, on May 22, 1863, Stevens wrote to Alanson from Caledonia. He informed him that the previous Sunday "some rascal fired the mountain . . . and it had burnt more than 5,000 acres of the furnace

land." He went on to recount, for Alanson, Thad Jr.'s harrowing experience at the Battle of Chancellorsville, where the Confederate Army defeated
Union troops in a terrible clash: nearly 31,000 casualties, more than 3,000
killed. "Your brother has got home safe," he wrote, "after having been in
a very severe fight—I believe he behaved well—He has managed to lose
two good horses neither of which was killed I think . . . I incline to think
he is cured of war." He told Alanson, "I could wish you were safely back."
He closed the letter with the matter of Mary Primm. "I must say to you,"
he wrote, "that if common fame (not Sweeney) be true, you are bestowing
the money you send here on a very worthless, dissolute woman—Stage,
hack drivers and others speak freely of it—This is all I intend to say as I
have made no inquiry into the subject."[21]

We don't know how or if Alanson responded to his uncle, but on June
1, perhaps spurred on by his uncle's report, Alanson wrote a lengthy letter to Mary. In it, he pledged his faithfulness to her and asked if she was
still wearing the ring he had slipped on her finger, as she slipped one on
his, the day before he left for his three months' service. "It is becoming the talk of the county," he wrote, "that you are becoming reckless
and loosing your self respect." Mary replied quickly and indignantly. She
denied the accusations and asked, "Who is that writes to you and will
you give me the means to leave this place . . . I will take Jinney [Alan-
son Jane, their daughter] and go to the poor house before I will stay
here." Then she challenged Alanson with his own transgression in the
summer of 1861, after he returned to the furnace from his three months'
service. "You and Doctor King," she wrote, "had that Girl down in the
bottom." Mary apparently continued the theme in a letter on December 4, 1862. In that letter, she told Alanson she was subject to "dishonor
and disgrace" at Caledonia. In her testimony, later, she explained, "I was
left there in a defenseless position, and persons were saying that I was
not married to Alanson Stevens, particularly Mr. Sweeney scattered the
report around broadcast, and I wrote this letter in a moment of passion,
I guess. I suppose I was irritated and angry and was left there alone with
no one to protect me."[22]

No written evidence has surfaced suggesting Alanson ever had a frank
discussion about Mary Primm and marriage with his uncle or poured out
his feelings to Mrs. Smith, as Thad Jr. had done from New Hampshire. But
we know the topic came up in Independent Battery B, as the Pennsylvania Volunteers battled the rebels in Kentucky. With those young men, in

contrast to his earnest admonishments to Mary, he didn't sound like a married man at all. Tillman Tolbert, who worked with Alanson at Caledonia, served with him in Battery B, and knew Mary, testified later that "when we first went out . . . I had a conversation with Alanson about being married. We were plaguing him about being married and he said, 'he would not marry the prettiest girl that walked in shoe leather.' He never introduced Mary Primm to you as his wife. He never spoke of her in my presence as his wife."[23]

Walter Crawford, another Franklin County man who went with Alanson to war, testified that while he and Alanson were bathing after a day of fighting, he noticed a medallion with a gold case around Alanson's neck. In the medallion was the "likeness" of Mary Primm. "Is it possible," Crawford asked Alanson, "you are married." Alanson replied vehemently, "No, by God. And never will be."[24]

The closest Alanson came to sharing his true feelings may have been in a conversation with Caledonia worker James Taylor. According to Taylor, the day Alanson recruited him for his battery, he told him, "Jim, I wish I had got killed when I was in the three month service." Taylor said, "I asked why. He said, 'I would be out of this trouble.' I asked him what trouble he had. He said, 'I have a good bit of trouble', but he did not say what trouble he had. Says I, 'It's purty hard for a man to go away and leave his wife.' He says, 'Jim, I've got no wife.' Says I, 'Ain't you married?' He says, 'No, Sir!' And he swore an oath, 'I never will be.' That's all I can tell you."[25]

While Alanson anguished over his personal problems in the midst of war, Lydia's son Isaac was wrestling with his own demons in Lancaster—in his case, with alcohol. Recall that Isaac was arrested in 1854 when he was just seventeen. Officials said he "was drunk and exposed his person in the public streets and that he had a bottle of whiskey & refused to give it up." A few months later, Lydia charged John Jones with getting Isaac drunk on whiskey. She may have ascribed Isaac's first offense to liquor from Jones.[26]

Those experiences apparently did nothing to dry up Isaac's weakness for booze. On August 13, 1862, we find Isaac and a companion, Jacob Woods, in custody, charged with drunken and disorderly conduct in Lancaster. Lydia was likely in Washington with Stevens that August, but even if she had been at home on South Queen Street, there was little she could do this time. Isaac and Jacob Woods were sentenced to thirty days' hard labor in the Lancaster County jail. And before Isaac's term was up, Mayor George Sanderson, the presiding magistrate in the case, ordered Isaac to serve an additional five days.[27] Court records don't tell us why Sanderson added the jail time. Watching Isaac fall into the same downward spiral that ruined his father can only have added to the heartache Lydia had felt since she lost William little more than a year before.

Thad Jr. checked in with the home front on December 4, 1862. The third session of the 37th Congress had convened three days earlier, which meant that Stevens and Mrs. Smith were in Washington. Thad told his uncle that his unit of the Army of the Potomac had been camped near Falmouth, Virginia, for two weeks. He complained about the lack of news about the fighting and poor mail service. He was pessimistic about how the war was going, at least where he was. "We seem to have run against a wall here," he wrote.

Many men in his regiment were sick, he said—mostly fever and rheumatism. But he was glad to learn his uncle was feeling better. As a major advocate for providing the army with everything it needed to bring the South to heel (Stevens now chaired the all-important Ways and Means Committee that controlled the purse strings), Stevens's health had become news. Thad said he "was glad to see by the papers that your health was much better. I was not aware you had been ill so long. I hope that going to Washington will prove beneficial to you." He expressed reservations about the president's ability to end slavery. "I shall be rejoiced," he told his uncle, "to see slavery abolished in sixty years and doubt it will be in six hundred." His final words suggest that he expected Mrs. Smith to read his letter or have Stevens share it with her: "I received Mrs. Smith letter and will answer soon." He said he'd already written a letter to Mrs. Smith and was sending it home with a comrade from Lancaster whose wife had died. In a postscript, he wrote, "Enclosed is a letter for Alanson—please frank it and send it to him."[28]

Thad was rapidly moving up in rank. In September 1862, he was promoted to major. By August 2, 1863, he'd made lieutenant colonel.[29] At the same time, his brother, Alanson, had Stevens lobbying his superiors to promote him to colonel or lieutenant colonel. In a June 7 letter, Stevens told Alanson "The Major" considered him more useful as captain of his battery, but he admitted "it [his captain's rank] certainly is not as profitable."[30] Perhaps Alanson wanted to earn more money to send home to Mary and his daughter.

In an August 2 letter, Thad Jr., camped near Williamsport, Maryland, reported that his soldiers were "exercised about the draft." Congress had passed the Enrollment Act on March 3, 1863, requiring every male citizen and those immigrants who had filed for citizenship, between the ages of twenty and forty-five, to serve in the army. Federal agents then set quotas for the number of draftees each congressional district was required to send. This first-of-its-kind provision sparked riots in some cities, especially New York.

In what may have been a swipe at the affluent farmers back home, Thad told his uncle, "I judge from the accounts I read that the fear of bullets is stronger in the Lancaster County heart than the love of Gold. If the Government drafts often enough it will turn a handsome penny."[31] Draftees could now buy their way out of service for the hefty sum of $300. Thad's comrades may have been upset that they couldn't cash in on that by agreeing to serve in someone else's place in exchange for some extra money. Thad's uncle had opposed the $300 exemption provision on behalf of his pacifist, Amish, Mennonite, and River Brethren constituents. They were willing to pay the exemption fee, but Stevens argued (unsuccessfully) that making them do it violated their conscientious and religious values. His efforts on the Draft Law and war funding pleased his constituents so much that they met him (and Mrs. Smith?) on Centre Square when they returned from Washington and, with the popular Fencibles Band playing, serenaded them down South Queen Street to their home, where Stevens addressed the crowd. A gang of rowdy Copperheads (Democrats who opposed the war) tried to disrupt the proceedings by egging Stevens, but he ignored them and finished his speech.[32]

Thad, all of twenty-eight by this time, noted that his young charges had done some successful fishing in the nearby Conococheague River. "A party caught over 300 the other day," he wrote. "Capt Brenneman's men on picket caught over a bushel." Then, as he had in previous letters, Thad confirmed his uncle's perception that he had had enough of war: "I hope that we shall be home soon. I do not see that we are of any further use here." His last request, as usual, was, "Give my respects to Mrs. Smith."[33] Thad would be home soon, but not because the army had no "further use" for him.

On January 1, 1863, President Lincoln issued the Emancipation Proclamation, freeing all enslaved people in territories held by Confederates. (Thaddeus Stevens had introduced an Emancipation Resolution in the House of Representatives nearly two years earlier, but it failed.) As he freed the slaves, Lincoln emphasized the importance of enlisting Black soldiers in the Union Army. The order from the War Department establishing the Bureau of Colored Troops to oversee Black enlistment wasn't issued, however, until May 22.

Between Lincoln's declaration and formal establishment of the Bureau of Colored Troops, Lydia's son Isaac had another run-in with the law. District Attorney J. B. Livingston charged Isaac and a man named John Buckley with "Hawking and Peddling." At that time, Pennsylvania's law concerning peddlers stated that "no person shall be licensed as hawker and peddler or petty chapman [itinerant merchant] within this state but such only as a citizen of the United States and who from loss of limb or other bodily infirmity shall be disabled from procuring a livelihood by labour, which disability shall be proven by certificate or certificates from two physicians of respectable character." (Basically, the law reserved hawking and peddling for persons with a physical disability so severe that they could not perform traditional labor.) Isaac and John Buckley were accused of selling oysters on the street.[34] Isaac apparently did sell oysters. He was listed as selling them in an 1863 Lancaster city directory: "Smith, Isaac, oysters, 3 E. Orange, h W King near Cross Keys."[35] We have to assume he was cited for selling oysters without a license. He obviously couldn't have had a license because, as an able-bodied man, he didn't qualify for one. It wasn't a terribly serious offense, in any case. The fine for unlicensed "Hawking and Peddling" was $50.

Isaac should have been able to handle that. By 1863, he had two principal sources of income in addition to oysters. He was widely recognized for his talents as a barber and as a musician. Around Lancaster, he was known as "Little Ike Smith," for an obvious reason. At the Lancaster County prison, where officials took a very precise measure of a man, they recorded Isaac as a "mulatto" man, with black hair and black eyes, who stood four feet eleven inches tall.[36] When he stayed away from alcohol, it seems, he was a popular guy. Judge Landis, who vigorously defended Mrs. Smith and Stevens, was especially fond of Isaac. "I very well recall Isaac Smith," the judge wrote, "who was commonly known as 'Little Ike' Smith. For some years he kept a barbershop on South Queen Street. He was, like his father, musically inclined, and was the leader of the colored band. He was small in stature and very black and it was evident from his appearance that there was not the slightest trace of Caucasian blood in his veins."[37] Here the judge appears misinformed. If the jailers knew that Isaac was a mixed-race man, why couldn't Judge Landis see it?

When the United States Bureau of Colored Troops was created in late May or early June 1863, the men from Bethel A.M.E. Church in Lancaster finally got their chance; they fought with the 54th and 55th Massachusetts Volunteer Infantry Regiments as part of a more than 178,000-man force of free Blacks and freedmen who answered the call. Twenty percent of those brave men gave their lives for the cause.[38] Isaac Smith joined Company D of the 6th US Colored Infantry in July 1863, but his military record is complicated. One of the questions we'll examine is whether he signed up voluntarily or was drafted—and if he *was* drafted, should he have been forced into uniform? That will be sorted out later.

The summer of 1863 was the high point for the secessionist forces. Confederate troops took the fight onto free soil and threatened to overwhelm the Union. The two sides met for the most significant clash of the war at the Battle of Gettysburg, which raged across Pennsylvania farmland on the western edge of Gettysburg, Pennsylvania, from July 1 to July 3. The battle still ranks as the bloodiest three-day clash in American history—56,000 casualties, thousands of soldiers killed on both sides. It ended, as most American high school students know, with Union troops just barely managing to drive General Robert E. Lee and his Confederate Army away from the corpse-strewn fields of Pennsylvania and back to Virginia.

Thaddeus Stevens's nephews had no part in the great battle—Alanson was in Kentucky, as we know, and Thad Jr. in Virginia. But Lydia Hamilton Smith did play a role there, according to newspaper accounts. On August 6, 1863, the *Gettysburg Star and Banner* published the following story under the simple headline "Generosity": "A correspondent informs us of a certain colored woman, Mrs. Lydia Smith, whose sympathy for our wounded soldiers is deserving of special notice. At her own expense she purchased a one horseload of provisions and clothing and distributed them personally in the hospitals. The rebels as well as the Union wounded received her attention. This is quite a commentary upon Gen. Lee's army of kidnappers and horse thieves who came here and fell wounded in their bold attempt to kidnap and carry off these free people of color."[39]

For the record, a different version of this story was published by a Civil War memorabilia collector named J. Howard Wert in the August 6, 1907, issue of the *Harrisburg Telegraph*. But I think Wert has taken inaccurate liberties with the original account. Wert's Lydia Smith is an impoverished woman who speaks in the colloquial language of a poorly educated person. He implies that she lived in Adams County in 1863.

Charles H. Glatfelter, of the Adams County Historical Society, had serious doubts about Wert's scholarship. He observed, "Can one accept the accuracy of embellishment such as is displayed here?"[40] The answer to that question, based on available information, is no. Lydia had been living in Lancaster for nineteen years by the time of the Battle of Gettysburg. She was quite literate and spoke and wrote in straightforward, clear language. And, by 1863, she was certainly not poor. As we saw in the 1860 census, she already owned $1,800 worth of real estate. Be it known that J. Howard Wert's acolytes continue to propagate his erroneous account and publicize what I suspect are mistakenly identified relics in his collection today. Let the reader who encounters them beware.

The Confederate invasion of Pennsylvania exacted a drastic financial cost from Thaddeus Stevens. On July 12, 1863, word reached Lancaster that the rebels had taken all of Stevens's "horses, mules, and harness; his bacon (about 4,000 pounds), molasses, and other contents of the store, and about $1,000 worth of corn in the mills. . . . Then they burned the furnace, two forges and the rolling mill" and trashed or burned any buildings still standing. The *Lancaster Intelligencer*, always antagonistic to Stevens and his antislavery views, used the destruction at Caledonia to remind readers of Stevens's speech, nearly a year earlier, at the Lancaster County Republican Convention, where he thundered, "Abolition! Yes: *abolish everything on the face of the earth* but this Union; *free every slave*—SLAY EVERY TRAITOR—BURN EVERY REBEL MANSION, if these things be necessary to preserve this temple of freedom to the world and to our posterity. *Unless we do this we cannot conquer them* [emphases in original]." The editors reminded Stevens that "curses, like chickens, come home to roost . . . and Mr. Stevens has had it verified in his own experience . . . in the entire destruction of his Iron Works . . . a loss, it is said, of from $30,000 to $100,000." The *Lancaster Examiner and Herald* took the opposite view. "To us," the editors wrote, "Thaddeus Stevens wears a crown which will forever dazzle and glitter. . . . By the lowly, the poor, the oppressed, or wherever the heel of the strong and powerful is felt, Thaddeus Stevens will be loved and revered."[41] Stevens knew why the Southerners targeted his property. Few members of Congress had been so outspoken in their opposition to slavery or so ardent in their support of crushing the Confederacy. He was not surprised that they singled him out for special punishment.

Despite his staggering financial losses, however, Stevens's first thoughts were not of himself but of those who lived and worked at Caledonia. In a

July 11 letter to Simon Stevens, he wrote, "I do not know what the poor families will do. I must provide for their present relief." One historian reports that Stevens supported the victims of the Caledonia assault for nearly three years.[42] The generosity shown by Stevens at Caledonia and by Mrs. Smith after the Battle of Gettysburg—these two incidents alone—should be sufficient to give pause to anyone attempting to portray either or both of them as vindictive, vengeful people who simply hated the South.

From destruction *by* soldiers, we must turn to destruction *of* soldiers. On September 19, 1863, Captain Alanson Stevens and his battery joined in the Battle of Chickamauga in far northwestern Georgia, just across the southern Tennessee border. Military historians tell us the combatants were "hotly engaged," and on the third day, September 21, Captain Stevens was shot and killed. Major Thaddeus Stevens Jr. was dispatched immediately to retrieve the body. In a letter dated September 28, Major Stevens told his uncle that "Alanson was shot through the left brest. His body is in the hands of the enemy and I do not suppose it can be obtained."[43] Southern historian David A. Powell provides a more fine-grained explanation: "Captain Stevens was hastily buried on the field, and almost certainly was later reinterred as an unknown soldier in the National Cemetery created the following year in Chattanooga [Tennessee]."[44] Alanson's death heightened Stevens's concern for Thad Jr. on the front lines. Confident that his nephew had had enough of war, he reached out to Secretary of War Edwin Stanton. In short order, Major Thaddeus Stevens Jr. was discharged from active duty and reassigned as provost-marshal, in charge of military police, back home in Lancaster.[45]

Alanson's death brought Mary Primm, a widow at the age of eighteen, face-to-face with Thaddeus Stevens and probably Mrs. Smith as well. Mary testified later that she and Stevens exchanged letters after Alanson died, and that led her to visit Lancaster. Mary was probably greeted by Mrs. Smith when she knocked on the door of Stevens's home on South Queen Street. Mary was ushered into Stevens's presence; we don't know whether Mrs. Smith stayed for the conversation. She would certainly have known about Alanson's involvement with Mary.

"I spoke to him in regard to the note," Mary recalled later. Stevens had written a $2,400 promissory note to Alanson and a smaller one to Thad Jr., backed by money left them by their father. Mary claimed Alanson gave her his note for safekeeping, while he did his three months' service, and took it with him when he reenlisted. Mary testified that she "asked him

[Stevens] what he would do for me, and regards this note. I told him it was not for the interest of myself, but my child." As Mary told the story, Stevens did not refute her claim to be Alanson's widow. Instead, she said, he directed her to Thad Jr.: "He replied that Thaddeus Stevens, Jr. had the notes in his hands and whatever agreement he and I would come to he would be satisfied and would try to see Thaddeus."[46]

She apparently pursued the issue with Thad Jr., but without success. "Thaddeus Stevens Junior kept me under the impression that he had them, but I could never get him to show them to me," she said. Thad did have his brother's note. Years later, one of the men in Alanson's battery told the court how he got it. John Cole, who had worked with Alanson at the Caledonia Furnace, testified that he first saw Alanson's promissory note as he and Thad Jr. examined the contents of Alanson's trunk by candle-light after Thad's unsuccessful attempt to retrieve his brother's body in Georgia. Shown the note as he testified, Cole said that he opened a package "and got hold of something like this, and handed it to Jr. and said, 'What's this?' Jr. says, 'That is a note which Alanson J. Stevens held against his uncle. This we will certainly take.'" Cole said Thad put the note in his pocket book with some other papers.[47] By the time Thad returned to Lancaster, the story had changed.

Simon Stevens, called to testify in Mary Primm's claim against Stevens's estate, said he was with Stevens, along with Thad and O. J. Dickey, at Stevens's home when "Mr. Stevens turned around to Thad, whom he called Major and said,—'Major, it is strange that that note of mine never turned up,' the Major replied, 'Maybe the Rebs may present it to you.'" In his testimony, Simon said, "I first heard Mr. Stevens speak of the widow of Alanson Stevens and his child a week or ten days or two weeks after the death of Alanson, as near as I can tell. I think, in fact, I know it as Thad was present, that this conversation occurred in Lancaster." Simon said he was not aware, in 1863, that Thad Jr. had assumed responsibility for administering Alanson's estate.[48] Thaddeus Stevens died without ever learning the truth about Alanson's note. Mary Primm went away empty-handed, but she didn't give up on her fight to be recognized as Alanson's widow. She returned to Lancaster several years later, with her daughter—Alanson's daughter—Jennie in tow.

CHAPTER II

"In Health or in Sickness"

Lydia Hamilton Smith and Thaddeus Stevens soldiered through a great deal of sadness in 1863. In addition to losing Alanson, they lost their friend Ann Louisa Carpenter, the young wife of Dr. Henry Carpenter, on January 9. Ann Carpenter was the daughter of ex-mayor John Mathiot of Lancaster, but more importantly, for Mrs. Smith and Stevens, she was the mother of three daughters, Mary (fifteen), Catherine (twelve), and Sarah (ten).[1] As we've already noted, the Carpenters were part of the inner circle of Lancaster society with which Mrs. Smith and Stevens spent the most time. In her will, Mrs. Smith bequeathed small legacies to the three Carpenter daughters as a token of her fondness for them. Losing Ann Carpenter at the age of thirty-five touched Mrs. Smith deeply; her love and concern for Ann's daughters endured for many years after their mother's death.

The rebel attack on his Caledonia ironworks was another source of sadness for Stevens, but not for self-centered reasons. Stevens had long dreamed of making a grand gesture on behalf of his adopted hometown, and he feared the financial loss in Franklin County meant not only that his dream must be deferred but that it might be extinguished. We hear his thoughts from Barbara Dice Bush, daughter of Stevens's friend and neighbor Christopher Dice. After learning of the torching of Caledonia, Mrs. Bush said that Stevens rushed into her father's grocery, in tears, and exclaimed, "Christ, the Rebels have burned my furnaces and destroyed the homes of my workmen. Now I cannot carry out my plans for a school for boys, perhaps I never can, for it will require all I have left to take care of these thirty families." According to Mrs. Bush, her father, "who habitually carried all his troubles to the Lord in prayer, said, 'Let us ask the help of the Lord,' whereupon [he] offered up prayer."[2] It's not clear whether Dice's petition to the Lord assuaged Stevens's anguish, but he clung to his dream, even including a provision for a school in his will. Stevens was a lifelong advocate of public education and had long cherished the notion of endowing a school for less fortunate children. The intensity of Stevens's wish to fund a school, and his disillusionment over losing the source of that funding, might have influenced O. J. Dickey's behavior a few years later when, as one of Stevens's executors, he and Mrs. Smith clashed over an issue related to Stevens's estate. We'll examine the details later.

Lydia Hamilton Smith was fifty years old in 1863. She had been with Thaddeus Stevens in Lancaster and in Washington, DC, for nearly twenty years. She had come a long way from her childhood days in Gettysburg and had chalked up experiences few white women of her time, and fewer Black women, would ever know. Her portfolio grew steadily: she owned real estate, worked as a seamstress, and ran a livery service in Washington. As a witness in legal action Mrs. Smith initiated against Stevens's executors after his death, Simon Stevens outlined her ascendance from housekeeper to Lydia Hamilton Smith, businesswoman. Simon said that she had "limited means" when she arrived in Lancaster. But "she was [already] a keen bright business woman and Mr. Stevens encouraged and advised her to make safe investments of her little accumulation, which latter she derived from the salary he paid her during the first few years that she kept house for him and from payments made her by others for sewing, etc. These investments," Simon testified, "were made under Stevens's advice so that at the time of his death she was probably worth from $10,000 to $12,000." These investments included, according to Simon, two carriages and two pair of horses "to let" for many years in Washington "and for such uses as Mr. Stevens had for them." Simon said Mrs. Smith had free use of Thaddeus Stevens's stables, and he said Stevens told him it was cheaper for him to rent Lydia's carriages than to send for other carriages and pay each for their hire. And, Simon told the court, "she bought and let out several pieces of property in Lancaster and made some comparatively profitable speculation in real estate there."[3] All in all, a busy life, but her investments were only part of what occupied Lydia Hamilton Smith's thoughts and hours.

Those who knew her best testified (as part of her subsequent court case) to the almost incredible workload Mrs. Smith carried in Lancaster and in Washington. Jacob Keneagy, who served as an amanuensis for Stevens in his last year and also a witness in Mrs. Smith's case, said that she "seemed to have management of everything about the house, indoors and out." Hetty Franciscus, who lived with Mrs. Smith and Stevens and looked after the South Queen Street house in Lancaster when they were away, testified that she knew what Mrs. Smith had to do. "She had a great deal to do both in the house and out of it. . . . Mrs. Smith did so much that I can hardly tell you what she did, she attended to Mr. Stevens in all his sickness and to his affairs outside; she brought everything into the house; she did all that was to be done." Stevens's friend and physician, Dr. Henry Carpenter, told that same court of Mrs. Smith's success at keeping so many balls in the air. Carpenter, who knew Mrs. Smith from the time she arrived in Lancaster, said that "she accumulated considerable means during that time—she is a shrewd business woman and made money on some outside business that she had, outside of her housekeeping. I have no special knowledge, but I guess that she got all that she wanted—She managed the household and always had as much as she wanted, as far as I know." Carpenter added, "I never saw Mr. Stevens give her any money to my recollection."[4]

Mrs. Smith's industriousness and devotion to Stevens became public knowledge. By this time, she was, for better or for worse, one of the most widely known women in America. And the word had spread that to get to Thaddeus Stevens at home, you needed to go through Lydia Hamilton Smith. In a letter soliciting Stevens's assistance, one office seeker closed with, "Remember me kindly to Mrs. Smith. I desire sending her a box of Catawba wine."[5]

As overseer of Stevens's household, Mrs. Smith may have witnessed several unusual social events during the Civil War. Based largely on the testimony of Mrs. Barbara Dice Bush, W. Frank Gorrecht suggests that Thaddeus Stevens had dinner, possibly several times, with James Buchanan, US president and Lancaster's native son—and a man whose politics Stevens could not abide. Gorrecht offers no dates for the encounters, but he argues that Buchanan's wartime speeches, putting him solidly on the Union side, would have made him more acceptable to Stevens.

From that assumption, Gorrecht contends that it's not unreasonable to think the two men secretly "held a number of conferences at their respective homes . . . and only for discussion of the welfare of the Union." The linchpin of Gorrecht's argument is testimony from Mrs. Bush. According to her, Thaddeus Stevens came into her father's grocery store one afternoon and invited her mother to be a fourth guest for dinner at his house with Buchanan and his niece Harriet Lane. Mrs. Dice agreed and Stevens escorted her, still in her gingham work dress, out the door and into his home, where, presumably, Mrs. Smith had dinner waiting. Mrs. Dice reported that "all were so lively to her that in a few minutes she felt very much at home as if she were at her own table."[6] Given the enmity that had long existed between Stevens and Buchanan, it would have been significant, indeed, for the two men to lay aside their differences and think together about the welfare of the nation. Considering Mrs. Smith's status in Stevens's household by this time, it would be interesting to know how she felt about being relegated to the role of servant in a home where she was, for all practical purposes, a wife. We don't know what happened during those encounters. Nor do we know Mrs. Smith's reaction to Buchanan and his niece coming to "her" house for dinner.

Perhaps Mrs. Smith and Stevens had no choice but to play out the sessions with Buchanan the way they did. From the beginning of their time together, they had been pilloried by political enemies—the *Intelligencer* newspaper was particularly vociferous in Lancaster—for crossing the line on race relations. Had Mrs. Smith sat down at the table, Buchanan likely would have taken his niece's arm and left. He was, after all, the man who, in 1826, declared slavery "a great political and a great moral evil" but concluded that it was "one of those moral evils, from which it is impossible for us to escape." In 1836, to prevent political opponents from accusing his family of owning slaves, Buchanan bought a mother and daughter from his brother-in-law in Virginia—twenty-two-year-old Daphne Cook and her five-year-old daughter, Ann. Rather than free them, he held them as indentured servants: Daphne for seven years, Ann for twenty-three.[7] As a person of color, Lydia Hamilton Smith would not have expected to dine with that man.

Thaddeus Stevens was seventy-one years old in 1863, and his physical ailments had exacted a toll on his once-handsome face and virile physique. Carl Schurz, a German revolutionary who immigrated to the United States in the mid-nineteenth century and became deeply involved in Lincoln's Republican party,[8] got an up-close-and-personal look at Stevens when he lodged with Stevens and Mrs. Smith in Lancaster while stumping through Pennsylvania at Stevens's urging. Schurz, who would attain the rank of general fighting for the Union during the Civil War, was impressed by the intensity of Stevens's hatred of slavery and his "argumentative pith and sarcastic wit." But, Schurz wrote, "the impression his personality made upon me was not sympathetic; his face long and pallid, topped with an ample dark brown wig which was at first glance recognized as such; beetling brows overhanging keen eyes of uncertain color which sometimes seemed to scintillate with a sudden gleam, the underlip defiantly protruding; the whole expression usually stern; his figure would have looked stalwart but for a deformed foot which made him bend and limp."[9] Schurz said what Stevens "seemed to enjoy most in his talk was his sardonic humor, which he made play upon men and things like lurid freaks of lightning." But, Schurz cautioned, that wasn't the true essence of the man. "There was behind his cynicism," he wrote, "a rich fund of human kindness and sympathy," which, Schurz observed, made Stevens "eminently popular. They [Lancastrians] had no end of stories to tell about the protection he had given fugitive slaves, sometimes at much risk and sacrifice to himself, and of the many benefactions he had bestowed with a lavish hand upon widows and orphans and other persons in need; and of his generous fidelity to his friends."[10]

General Schurz made no explicit mention of Mrs. Smith in his memories of Lancaster, but he must have met her, and he may have been alluding to her when he touched on how Lancastrians felt about Stevens's personal life. "They did, indeed, not revere him as a model of virtue," he wrote, "but of the occasional lapse of his bachelor life from correct moral standards, which seemed to be well known and talked about, they spoke with affectionate lenity of judgment."[11]

Stevens, as we know, was engaged in the most important work of his life during and immediately after the Civil War. He had staked his claim to true leadership in Congress with the introduction of the Emancipation Resolution two years before Lincoln proclaimed the slaves emancipated. He championed the Draft Law and supported drafting free Black men to provide the Union Army with the manpower it needed to crush the Southern rebellion. In a speech to the Union League of Lancaster in April 1863, he became the first to advance the theory that, as parts of the South came under Union control, they should be considered conquered provinces.[12] That set the stage for Stevens's later arguments that the rebel states should be treated as conquered enemies when it came time to "reconstruct" the Union.

Stevens was among the first to realize that Lincoln's Emancipation Proclamation lacked the force of law, leaving the nation open to a resumption of slavery when the fighting was over. To prevent that, on March 28, 1864,

Stevens proposed an amendment to the Constitution that would abolish slavery forever. After nine months of debate, Congress narrowly passed the amendment on January 31, 1865. (Stevens's fight for the Thirteenth Amendment is featured in Steven Spielberg's popular 2012 film, *Lincoln*. The movie implies that Mrs. Smith's presence in Stevens's life was a major factor in his crusade for the new law. Near the end of the film, we see Stevens climb into bed and hand the official Thirteenth Amendment document to Mrs. Smith, who lies beside him, looking very pleased. Needless to say, Spielberg's treatment set off spirited debate on whether Mrs. Smith and Stevens were an "item.") The amendment outlawing slavery in the United States was ratified by the required three-fourths of the states and became the law of the land on December 6, 1865.[13]

This catalog of Stevens's contributions isn't offered as a salute to his critical efforts during and after the war, although he played a crucial role in guiding the nation through a turbulent time. The point of reviewing his record here is that he might not have been alive to accomplish any of it if Mrs. Smith had not assumed the increasing responsibility of caring for him as his health deteriorated. There is ample testimony to support that assertion.

Stevens himself reportedly credited Mrs. Smith with keeping him alive. Catharine Effinger, who ran the tavern next door to Stevens's home on South Queen Street in Lancaster and was also a witness in Mrs. Smith's later legal action, testified that he "often heard Mr. Stevens speak about Mrs. Smith, he said she was good. He said he thought if he had not had such good attendance he would not have lived as long." Stevens's physician Dr. Henry Carpenter agreed. Carpenter later said that Stevens "was almost a constant invalid the last fifteen years of his life—constantly taking medicine," and Carpenter was adamant about the impact of Mrs. Smith's nursing care: "Thaddeus Stevens' life was prolonged six or eight years by faithful nursing and close attention and the continual use of remedies calculated to sustain his dynamic powers. . . . She devoted the best period of her life to him."[14]

Caring for Stevens would absorb more and more of Mrs. Smith's time and energy. Those who watched her do it said it was exhausting and, at times, unpleasant work, but Mrs. Smith allowed no one else to do it, and Dr. Carpenter doubted whether Stevens would have allowed anyone but her to minister to him. Carpenter confirmed that she "had principal care of him during his sickness—he required a good deal of attention—sometimes he was quite ill. She was very faithful in her attention to him. . . . She attended to Mr. Stevens as faithfully as it is possible for any person to do."[15]

John Warfel, who lived in Stevens's Washington home from 1863 to 1867, testified, in Mrs. Smith's case against Stevens's executors, that "Lydia Hamilton Smith was always very kind to Thaddeus Stevens," even after Stevens grew so "feeble he had to be carried downstairs by two colored men," transferred into Mrs. Smith's carriage, "and driven in it to the House. . . . He [Stevens] always regarded her as very kind to him." Jacob Keneagy, the amanuensis we've already heard from, said Mrs. Smith "attended to him personally in every little matter; no matter what it was; she attended to all his wants; she bandaged his leg, it had to be kept bandaged all the time, she was very constant in her attention, more so than many would be." Keneagy offered that she performed some truly difficult duties. "What I meant when I said Mrs. Smith did things that I would not have done," he said, "was that she attended and cleaned him as if he were an infant, this kind of attention was during the whole period that I was in Mr. Stevens' house."[16]

In Lancaster, Catharine Effinger said that Mrs. Smith attended "him in every way he needed. There was some kind of sickness that I would not have attended him, she waited on his person day and night, the most of the time he was sick she sat up all night, she had to wash him like a child; indeed, she was faithful in her attention to him." In his testimony, Dr. Carpenter stressed that Mrs. Smith "was his only nurse during that time; she devoted herself to the services of a nurse. When it was very much needed, almost like that of a mother to a child. . . . There were times when his condition was such that she would not get into her bed or change her clothing for weeks at a time. I remember several occasions when such was the case for weeks at a time." Dr. Carpenter echoed the language of the other witnesses: "She would tend him as one would a child. He was too feeble to dress himself very often." Dr. Carpenter endorsed the value of Mrs. Smith's care. After she helped him dress, "Stevens would then be carried to a carriage and into his House seat—in a chair—he went to every session if he could hold his head up."[17]

Dr. Carpenter was asked whether Stevens would have accepted such care from another nurse. "I think there would have been no one," he replied, "to attend upon Mr. Stevens with such devotedness, patience and endurance as Mrs. Smith did, and from my knowledge of Mr. Stevens, I think he would not have tolerated any other person about in the capacity in which Mrs. Smith served. . . . Mr. Stevens was very sensitive to any intrusion upon his privacy, and he would have been uncomfortable in the hands of any other person."[18] Simon Stevens fully endorsed Dr. Carpenter's version of events: "For the last six years of Mr. Stevens' life Mrs. Smith in addition to being housekeeper had to nurse Mr. Stevens in his frequent illnesses and did so with great care, attention and self-denial and in the last two years of his life this duty devolved on her with a great deal of weight but was always met with true patience by her and appreciated by Stevens."[19]

To add to Lydia's burden, her son Isaac had not adjusted well to military life. He enlisted on July 10, 1863, in Lancaster, and by April 1864, records showed him "absent without leave." He may have been absent without leave, but it appears he was absent with a purpose. It seems likely he was in Washington, with Lydia and Stevens, trying to get out of the army. Isaac's military file contains a deposition taken in Washington, DC, on April 12, 1864, from a man named Hugh Kennedy, who testified that Isaac was "subject to paralysis." Kennedy told a DC justice of the peace that in 1860, while he was getting a shave in Isaac's barbershop in Lancaster, Isaac was "seized with a fit of palsy." Kennedy reported that "Smith was so temporarily paralyzed that he was unable to finish shaving [him]." Kennedy said he saw Isaac experience similar fits at other times, seizures so debilitating they "forced him to suspend business for a time."[20]

The deposition was presented to military officials, possibly by Lydia or Stevens, but it didn't produce immediate relief for Isaac. Records indicate that he was back with Company D in May and June and fought with them in Virginia at Baylor's Farm, St. Petersburg, and New Market Heights. Sometime that year, Isaac was reassigned from the infantry to the drum corps. He was still with Company D in August, when they reached Dutch Gap, near Jamestown, but by December, he was gone again. The record indicates Isaac left in Norfolk as the regiment began its first expedition to Fort Fisher, near Wilmington, North Carolina. The 6th US Colored Infantry mustered out of service at Wilmington in September 1865, but Isaac wasn't there. The final entry on his card listed him as a deserter.[21]

But that's not accurate. In Isaac's military file is a copy of Special Order 37, dated January 24, 1865, which states, "By direction of the President, Private Isaac Smith, Co. D, 6th US Colored Troops, having been illegally drafted will be discharged the service of The United States, on receipt of this order at the place where he may be serving. By order of the Secretary of War, E. D. Townsend, Assistant Adjutant General."[22] Did Isaac seek Thaddeus Stevens's help to make an early exit from the army? His mother was house manager and confidant for Stevens, and Stevens was the most powerful man in Congress in 1864, with direct access to President Lincoln himself. Stevens had already used his connections to get Thad Jr. out of harm's way. It seems possible he would have tapped that same influence if Lydia asked him to and if he believed Isaac had been dragooned illegally into military service.

As 1864 gave way to 1865, and the war dragged on, Stevens kept pushing for a stronger Union effort. Lincoln's bodyguard at the White House, Colonel William H. Crook, later recalled that Stevens paid a visit to the president in late March to "urge 'a more vigorous prosecution of the war,'" which, Crook wrote, "was the watchword of those men of his own party who criticized the President." Crook considered Stevens "one of the ablest, as well as one of the most radical men then in Congress." But, Crook said, Stevens "was a very impatient man." Crook said Lincoln "listened patiently to Mr. Stevens' argument, and when he had concluded he looked at his visitor a moment in silence. Then he said, looking at Mr. Stevens very shrewdly, 'Stevens, this is a pretty big hog we are trying to catch, and to hold when we do catch him. We must take care that he doesn't slip away from us.'" Crook concluded that "Mr. Stevens had to be satisfied with the answer."[23] There can be no debate about that. That encounter, in late March, was the last time Stevens saw Lincoln alive.

Less than a month later, on April 9, 1865, the Confederate Army surrendered at Appomattox Courthouse in Virginia. Six days after that, the *New York Herald* reported tragic news on the front page. The tiered headline read: "Important, Assassination of President Lincoln, The President Shot at the Theatre, Last Evening, Secretary Seward, Daggered in His Bed, But, Not Mortally Wounded."[24]

Thaddeus Stevens reportedly learned the dreadful news from his friend William Wright in Lancaster. Wright knocked on Stevens's door at 45–47 South Queen Street in the dark hours of April 14 to 15, bringing Stevens to his bedroom window on the second floor. When Stevens appeared, Wright told him the president had been assassinated. Stevens, stunned by the news, exclaimed, "Betrayed again, by __,"[25] and immediately thought of the disastrous results when past vice presidents John Tyler and Millard Fillmore ascended to the presidency. Stevens realized immediately that the man who would succeed the president, Vice President Andrew Johnson, a poorly educated Democrat from Tennessee who opposed rigid Republican rules for readmitting Southern states to the Union, would be as great a disaster in the White House as Tyler or Fillmore.

Stevens and Lincoln had never been particularly close. As historian Hans Trefousse put it, "While Stevens was direct, often harsh, and usually ahead of his constituents, Lincoln was careful, never acerbic, and always on guard not to move too far forward of public opinion." The two men were united in their opposition to slavery and support for preserving the Union, but it's fair to say they were not fond of each other.[26] On the distaff side, Mrs. Smith admired Mary Todd Lincoln enormously. We've already seen that Mrs. Smith always gave great attention to her appearance; when the Lincolns dominated the social scene in Washington, a neighbor recalled that Mrs. Smith "took great delight in having her clothes made to resemble those of Mrs. Lincoln."[27]

Mrs. Lincoln was always elegantly and fashionably attired when she presided over social occasions at the White House. On New Year's Day, 1864, she received guests wearing a dress of "purple silk trimmed with black velvet and lace," and, according to one observer, "looked exceedingly well, receiving her guests with much apparent ease and grace."[28] Mrs. Smith presented an equally fashionable image in an 1868 photograph (the only photo of her known to exist). In it, she wears what appears to be a black silk dress. Black was becoming à la mode for women in Paris at the time. Mrs. Smith's hairstyle was also popular; for fashion-conscious women of her day, "the hair was usually arranged in braids at the back and turned up and pinned close to the head, while the front hair was crimped, parted in the middle and drawn back above the ears."[29]

But Lydia Hamilton Smith and Mary Lincoln shared something more than fashion sense—something insidious. They both bore the uninvited burden of heartless, often venomous, criticism and condemnation that spilled onto them as Southerners and other defenders of slavery spewed their hatred onto Thaddeus Stevens and Abraham Lincoln. These haughty racists wrote that Mrs. Lincoln was "as short and plump as her husband was tall and gawky," and that, at forty-five, she was "middle age[d] and medium height, her face plain, her nose and mouth ordinary, her appearance 'homely.'"[30] Rose O'Neal Greenhow, a Southern spy held under house arrest in Washington during the war who was said to hate every Northerner, saw Mrs. Lincoln in person only once. In that encounter, Greenhow refused to see anything cultivated or attractive about her. "Mary Lincoln," she wrote, "is a short, broad, flat figure, with a broad flat face, with sallow, mottled complexion, light gray eyes with scant, light eyelashes, and exceedingly thin, pinched lips."[31]

By this time, Lydia Hamilton Smith was known and despised by critics across the country. In 1863, the *Idaho Semi-Weekly World* newspaper used a news brief from Lancaster to belittle her. The story, headlined "Mrs. Thad. Stevens," snidely informed readers, "The mulatto paramour of Thad Stevens generally known as 'Mrs. Thad Stevens,' was robbed in Lancaster (Pa.) lately at a railroad depot, of $100 in greenbacks, three Mexican silver dollars, one diamond breastpin, a safe key, a bunch of household keys, and *free passes* over the railroads from Lancaster to Washington." Having disposed of the objective facts of the matter, the writer went on: "This woman's former name was Smith. She was the wife of Jacob Smith, a respectable colored barber of Harrisburg, but through the influence of Thad Stevens she left her husband and became his mistress and his housekeeper, which double position she has filled for many years!"[32]

The writer used that slanderous content as a springboard to full-blown editorial condemnation of Thaddeus Stevens and the entire Republican party. "What a leader for the 'God and morality' party to bow down to and worship—a man who is a gambler and a libertine—a man who has been an open practitioner of his doctrine of miscegenation for years! Yet this is the party, recognizing and honoring such a leader, and supporting a notorious tippler for the highest office in the country, which was esteemed worthy of special commendation and indorsement [*sic*] by the political persons recently assembled in Boston."[33]

In 1866, the *Bolivar Bulletin* in Tennessee picked up a nasty editorial from the *LaCrosse Democrat* in Wisconsin, based on a report that Stevens was "growing weaker and weaker every day." The Wisconsin editors used it to denigrate him and Mrs. Smith in one breath: "A pretty picture—pallid cheeks, brilliant eyes, beetling brows, massive forehead, pathos, sorrow, tremulous triumph! Ah—good Thaddeus! Sweet paramour of the mulatto wench of Lancaster! Excellent Stevens! The best thing we have heard yet is that you are 'growing weaker and weaker every day, thank God!' The effects of your 'youthful piety,' Thaddy—Moxa Morton could give you some valuable hints on that subject—but Thaddy, old boy, go on with your weakening—it is a good symptom, and pleases us much."[34] The Tennessee editors followed those un-Christian sentiments with word that the Baptists were building a new church in Bolivar.

As we know, Thaddeus Stevens had long been the target of slanderous accusations, and Abraham Lincoln had endured rough political weather on his way to the White House, but Lydia Hamilton Smith and Mary Lincoln surely had not. It's difficult to see the world through the eyes of the individuals who inflicted such abuse on these two women. It's hard to understand what they hoped to accomplish with such hatred. The fact that the women managed to carry on in the face of such withering criticism is testimony to the strength they both brought to the roles fate asked them to play. Mary Todd Lincoln returned to Illinois after her husband's death and lived with family members until she died in 1882. Lydia Hamilton Smith was still in the crosshairs and heading into the most challenging years of her life in 1865. If she ever complained about her treatment at the hands of the American public or the responsibilities she was asked to shoulder, we have no record of it.

CHAPTER 12

THE BATTLES AFTER THE WAR

As Mrs. Smith battled to keep Thaddeus Stevens alive, he and his fellow Republicans battled to prevent the new president—Andrew Johnson, a Southern Democrat—from pardoning the rebellious states and welcoming them back into the Union if they simply swore an oath of allegiance to the nation they had fought a bloody war to bring down. We know that Stevens's constituents backed his efforts. They were waiting for him when he (with Mrs. Smith, we presume) reached the Norris Locomotive Works in Lancaster after pleading with Johnson not to pardon the insurgents. He was "welcomed by a large crowd, cannon, and a regiment escorted over part of the city by his nephew, Chief Marshal Thaddeus Stevens, Jr."[1]

Fearful that Johnson's stance made freed African Americans vulnerable to mistreatment at the hands of former slaveowners, Republicans, with Thaddeus Stevens and Senator Lyman Trumbull of Illinois in the lead, pushed through the nation's first civil rights law, defining citizenship and affirming that "*all* citizens are equally protected by law,"[2] in 1865. Johnson vetoed it. And Johnson rejected it again when Republicans brought it back in 1866, but Congress overrode the presidential pen and made it the law of the land that "all people born in the United States were United States citizens and had certain inalienable rights, including the right to make contracts, to own property, to sue in court, and to enjoy the full protection of federal law."[3]

Response to the override was immediate and joyous, as Lyman Trumbull's biographer Horace White reports: "After three days of extremely ardent debate signalized by a speech of singular cogency and power from Senator Trumbull, the father of the bill, the vote was reached about 7 o'clock on Friday evening. When the end of the roll was reached and Vice-President Foster announced the result, nearly the whole Senate and auditory were carried off their feet and joined in a tumultuous outburst of cheering such as was never heard within those walls before."[4] Republicans would spearhead passage of several other measures related to the nation's recovery from the Civil War, including creation of the Freedmen's Bureau, "which provided assistance to tens of thousands of former slaves and impoverished whites in the Southern States and the District of Columbia," and several Reconstruction Acts, establishing military rule over Southern states awaiting new governments, limiting voting rights for former Confederate officials, and granting former male slaves the right to vote and hold public office. They also led the way to passage of the Fourteenth and Fifteenth Amendments—to protect African Americans from discriminatory state laws and to guarantee freedmen the vote, respectively.[5]

These are the things Thaddeus Stevens labored to accomplish as his health declined, and these are the things he was able to attempt thanks to the vigilant care provided by Lydia Hamilton Smith. These are also measures the South reacted to with revulsion and violence, seeing people they had considered no more than property elevated to fully human status. In Tennessee, the *Memphis Argus* wrote, "Would to God they were back in Africa, or some other seaport town, anywhere but here."[6] The *Memphis Avalanche* adopted a harder tone in its May 1866 edition: "Since the radicals cannot in this part of the state assassinate, kill and murder rebels, and take possession of their property, they propose to give a greasy, filthy, stinking negro the right to crowd them from the polls, to exercise those rights of franchise which belong not to Indians or Negroes but to white men."[7]

As Southern cities chafed under the military governors imposed by Reconstruction, tension readily boiled over into violence. On April 30, on South Street in Memphis, several African Americans and four Irish cops tangled with fists and clubs. When the cops returned the next day and started arresting the rowdiest elements of a crowd of a hundred Black people, shots rang out. That night, two hundred Irish police officers showed up with white volunteers and proceeded to attack the entire African American population of the city. As they waded in, local judge John C. Creighton urged them on, intoning, "Boys, I want you to go ahead and kill the last damn one of the n[—]r race and burn up the cradle." The attacks raged on for three days, leaving forty-six Black and two white people dead, five Black women raped, and more than seventy-five people wounded. The white cops and volunteers torched ninety-one houses, four churches, and twelve schools and committed more than one hundred robberies.[8] New Orleans was ripped by anti-Reconstruction violence, too. Stevens demanded an investigation of the violence as Congress debated the Fourteenth Amendment. He had known long before the war ended that it would be necessary to pass legislation to protect newly freed slaves from retaliation by angry Southerners. The violence against African Americans in many cities and towns across the South proved he was right. The Fourteenth Amendment helped, but it didn't head off the wicked "Jim Crow" laws Southerners rammed through in decades to come, all designed to keep the Black man "in his place."

While Reconstruction played out across the South in 1866, the much smaller drama of Mary Primm, Alanson Stevens's paramour and possible widow, arose in Lancaster for the second time. She reportedly came to enroll Jennie, Alanson's daughter, in school. Alanson Stevens never knew Jennie because he was fighting a war when she was born; the child was nearly five when her mother arrived in Lancaster. Mary apparently approached the educator Dr. Thomas Burrowes, Stevens's neighbor, about enrolling Jane in a Lancaster school. When Burrowes asked Stevens about it, Stevens reportedly disavowed the young woman. But Mrs. Smith had concern for the child. She wrote an inquiring letter to Thad Jr., who was then working at the Caledonia ironworks, where Mary and her daughter were living when Alanson was killed and likely were still living in 1866.

Mrs. Smith told Thad that "Mary Primm has been applying to this district . . . to get her child in [school] representing herself as the widow of Alanson Stevens and Mr. Burrowes inquired of your uncel about it and he told them that thair was no such widow. Mr. Stevens, have you seen the child?" Thad's attitude toward Mary Primm had not changed. He offered her no assistance, and she left Lancaster empty-handed for a second time.[9] We will see Mary Primm again, but Jennie will not be with her. In her claim against Stevens's estate, Mary testified that Alanson Jane Stevens died on August 22, 1873—she was eleven years and four months old—while Mary was living at Monroe Forge in northeastern Lebanon County, Pennsylvania. Jennie was buried in Fredericksburg, about fifteen miles southeast of the forge.[10] Mary Primm wasn't the only person who hoped Mrs. Smith's place in Stevens's life would facilitate access to the congressman. Word had apparently spread far and wide that dropping Mrs. Smith's name might make things happen. On July 2, 1866, a Black soldier from New York, John H. Quarles, wrote to Stevens seeking his help in getting his back pay. Quarles began his letter with, "I was informed by my mother who is now in Washington City that having seen your good lady on my behalf you would forward my interest in a plain matter of fact manner." We can assume that Mrs. Smith did put in a good word for Quarles, but we don't know whether Stevens was able to solve his problem.[11]

Being home in Lancaster in the summer and fall of 1866 did little to mend what ailed Thaddeus Stevens. When Mrs. Smith packed their trunks for the trip to Washington, DC, in late November, he was very weak. His friend and law partner Alexander Hood wrote that he was "so feeble as to be unable to sit up in the [railroad] car, and a bed was made for him on the floor. Those who knew his condition had great fear whether he could survive the journey." But the old man surprised everyone once again. "After his arrival at Washington," Hood wrote, "he rallied and during most of the session he remained comparatively well."[12] The Stevens-Smith household received sad news from Indiana in January 1867. Lizzie Kirlin Stevens, the vivacious young wife of Stevens's nephew Dr. Thaddeus Morrill Stevens, had died in Indianapolis. Lizzie had kept up a lively correspondence with Stevens over the years, always including Mrs. Smith in her greetings. In an April 1865 letter, after visiting Stevens in Washington, Lizzie had written to him, "much love to you and Mrs. S. How is she. I'd like to hear from her—she was so kind to us and made our visit so pleasant. I always think of her with many pleasant thoughts. If any thing should happen to influence you to come out this spring tell her she has a standing invitation also."[13]

Stevens was quite fond of Lizzie, and it's not hard to see why. Her sparkling personality shines through in a letter she wrote to Stevens a year before she died. "Why are you raising such a commotion," she wrote, "you'll begin to think you are of great importance to create such sensations will you not? Oh, what a splendid thing it is to be great, as well as good—I almost wish I was a man I'd never rest until I'd accomplished something worth striving for."[14]

Lizzie's awareness of Stevens's declining health led her to offer some spiritually freighted advice. "I suppose you'll work yourself to death this winter[.] don't work so hard—you haven't but one life to live in this world, take it easy but hope you'll reap a glorious reward in the future one—where the weary are at rest, welcome sound!" Lizzie closed as she always did, "Give my love to Thaddeus and Mrs. S. Lovingly, Lizzie

Stevens."[15] The couple had visited Mrs. Smith and Stevens in Washington in early July 1866, and both of them had been ill when they left. When Lizzie wrote to say they were back in Indiana, Stevens responded, "I am glad to hear that you safely arrived at home well, and improving—but I regret that the Doctor is still feeble. . . . My health is something better—But I fear Old Age will afflict me to my death." Stevens was apparently looking forward to a visit from Lizzie in the autumn. He told her, "[Tell] the Doctor to come in with you this fall."[16] Dr. Stevens regained his health in time; Lizzie did not. Less than six months after her last visit with Stevens and Mrs. Smith, she was gone. She was just twenty-seven years old when she died.

As the intensity of the battle over Reconstruction and the fate of freed people of color rose, so did the vicious criticism Stevens's enemies hurled against him and Mrs. Smith. Early in 1867, Stevens briefly considered standing for the US Senate (senators were then chosen by state legislatures) at the urging of A. E. Roberts and others. Stevens's enemies reacted to the idea with renewed attempts to assassinate his character. As they had done for years, they homed in on his religious life and his relationship to Lydia Hamilton Smith.

The religious attacks charged him, again, with being an "infidel." He was accused of not believing in God or hell and criticizing the Bible. As these latest indictments spread, Harrisburg farmer John T. Keagy wrote to ask Stevens if the allegations were true, observing that Stevens's opponents said that he was "an infidel, that you said the Bible was the production of a barbarous age, and that you do not believe in the existence of a God nor of a hell. . . . My curiosity was excited and I write you for personal information. The committal of the matter to me shall not tarnish your fair fame."[17]

In the twenty-first century, a letter like that would seem awfully suspicious, but in 1867, after long ignoring such talk, Stevens fired off an immediate response to Keagy. "All of the statements which you said were made are false," he asserted, "as the author well knew if he had any knowledge on the subject. I have always been a firm believer in the Bible. He is a fool who disbelieves the existence of a God as you say is charged to me. I also believe in the existence of a hell for the especial benefit of this slanderer." Stevens informed Keagy that he normally didn't respond to such irresponsible accusations, but "I would not be thought to be an infidel. I was raised a Baptist and adhere to their belief."[18]

We don't know why Stevens, one of the shrewdest lawyers and politicians ever to walk under the Capitol Dome in Washington, responded to Keagy's letter. Historian William Hall introduces Keagy as "an ardent admirer of Mr. Stevens,"[19] so it may have been simply a courtesy for a friend. Whatever the reason, it marked the beginning of a different Thaddeus Stevens. After silently absorbing the slings and arrows of those who, for decades, had tried to destroy him, Stevens began to speak out about his personal life and to defend himself and Mrs. Smith against the vicious attacks they had both withstood for so long.

In May 1867, a Southerner named George Drake visited Stevens and Mrs. Smith in Lancaster. As the editor of the *Union Springs Times* in Alabama, Drake was firmly embedded in the camp that believed Thaddeus Stevens's efforts to punish the South grew directly out of his high regard for all people of color, especially Lydia Hamilton Smith. When he got home, Drake crafted a sarcastic piece incorporating what he had seen and heard in Lancaster into an article he published on June 12. His target was Stevens, but he used Mrs. Smith to do it. "Radicals [like Stevens]," he began, "have a good deal to say about the close relationship some of the former slaves bear to their masters and their masters' friends. They tell Southern people that numbers among their servile class are too yellow to be white, and too white to be black." (Drake was referring to Northern accusations of slaveowners fathering children with enslaved women.) "They must stop this. It is horribly unkind to their great leader and master." Then he got to Mrs. Smith. "In the city of Lancaster, Pa.," he told his readers, "in the godly North, nigh unto the pure city of Philadelphia, Thaddeus Stevens has for years lived in open adultery with a mulatto woman, whom he seduced from her husband, a full blooded negro." Drake cranked up the level of his insinuations and indulged his deep-seated racist views. "This mulatto," he said,

> manages his households, both in Lancaster and at Washington, receives or rejects his visitors at will, speaks of Mr. Stevens and herself as "we," and in all things comports herself as if she enjoyed the rights of a lawful wife. I have no word of unkindness or abuse for her. She is a neat, tidy housekeeper, and appears to be as polite and well-trained as negroes generally are. As to Mr. Stevens' connection with her, it is his own business, and entirely a matter of taste. I only mention the fact, that the ultra-godly, super-sanctified saints of the African ascendency

may get the beam out of their own eye before they gouge so merci-
lessly at the mote in ours.[20]

The article was reprinted by a number of other newspapers that shared
Drake's sentiments, which might explain how Stevens's friend W. B. Melius
became aware of it in Albany, New York. Melius sent it to Stevens, who,
again, overrode his tendency to ignore such things and penned a response
to Melius in September: "In the course of my life I have rec'd a very large
number of such attacks—Perhaps no man in the State has received more
slanders or been charged with more vices or more great crimes than I have.
It has been my fortune for forty years to be the bitter object of attack by
violent partisans. I have seldom noticed them . . . unless they affected my
moral character aside from politics or was required by the interests of others. You tell me that this charge may influence your next election—Hence
I notice it."[21]

Then Stevens carefully addressed Drake's slanderous remarks about
Mrs. Smith and his household. "As to the domestic history," he wrote,
"I have only to say that the whole is totally without foundation except as
follows. From the time I began business (40 odd years ago) I have kept
house through the agency of hired servants, having no female relatives.
Those servants were of various colors; some white, some black and others of all intermediate colors. My only inquiry was into their honesty and
capacity. They have resided with me for various periods from one month
to fifteen years. Generally more than one at a time."[22]

Here Stevens addressed Drake's most insidious insinuation. "I believe
I can say that no child was ever raised or, so far as I know, begotten under
my roof. Sometimes husband and wife have worked the one for me and
the other for another, generally at the same time, cohabiting on Saturday
nights. But I believe none of them became pregnant during the time." Stevens told Melius he was disclosing more of his personal life to him than
he had ever done before. He saved his condemnations for the end. "These
calumnies and worse have been perennially published against me by fellows living within sight of my door—I know of no one who has believed
one of them, or scarcely pretended to believe them. Having no ambition
for office, no aspiration for fame, I have not found it pleasant to turn aside
to encounter the offensive odor of diseased dog secretions."[23]

Some biographers suggest Stevens's declaration that "no child was
ever raised or, so far as I know, begotten under my roof" was a clever and

technically truthful way to avoid talking about Mrs. Smith. There is no evidence to suggest that she had any other children after Isaac was born, so Drake's insinuation of mixed-race children born to Stevens and Mrs. Smith doesn't hold up. And it's fairly certain that Mrs. Smith did not sleep in Stevens's house until her sons were old enough to look after themselves, which supports Stevens's assertion that no child was raised in his house. But nowhere in his letter to Melius does Stevens categorically deny a romantic relationship with Lydia Hamilton Smith. It would have made his political life a bit easier if he had, but he didn't, and that may tell us a lot about his feelings for her.

The *Lancaster Intelligencer*, a longtime nemesis of Stevens's, likely knew about Drake's malevolent editorializing but didn't need his encouragement to add its latest contribution to the chorus of Stevens's critics. On July 6, 1867, the paper told readers, "Here, where his [Stevens's] domestic arrangements are so well known, his practical recognition of his pet theory is perfectly well understood. . . . There are few men who have not given to the world such open and notorious evidence of a belief in negro equality as Thaddeus Stevens. A personage, not of his race, a female of dusky hue, daily walks the streets of Lancaster when Mr. Stevens is at home. She has presided over his house for years. Even by his own party friends, she is constantly spoken of as Mrs. Stevens, though we fancy that no rite of Mother Church ever gave her a right to it."[24]

The *Intelligencer* editor was motivated to write the piece after learning that Stevens had returned a burial plot he purchased because the cemetery refused to inter people of color. The editor—a white man—found that offensive. "If Thaddeus Stevens insists on being buried side by side with the woman he is supposed to have taken to his bosom," the editor wrote, "it is entirely a matter of taste. But why did he not purchase a lot in an African burying ground at once? There no white man's bones would have jostled his own, and she who has so long been his most intimate associate might have been gathered to his side without exciting public scandal."[25] Stevens made no reply to this attack.

By 1866, Lydia Hamilton Smith apparently had grown tired of the *Intelligencer*'s racist insinuations and decided to confront the editor. The paper, in a piece probably written by its owner, Henry G. Smith, reported on February 3 that an angry woman, "with eyes that flashed a vengeful fire" and "a torrent of accusing words [issuing] from her lips," had entered their offices and demanded to know "'Why—why did you publish me in your paper?'" Henry Smith claimed to be so stunned by the confrontation that a colleague stepped in to respond to Lydia before he could recover. Nowhere in the piece is Lydia acknowledged by her proper name; she is referred to only as "Thad. Stevens' housekeeper."

According to the article, Henry Smith's "partner" toyed with Lydia (much to the newspaper publisher's obvious delight), but he eventually permitted her to say she was there to protest the *Intelligencer*'s publication of an accusation (common among Stevens's enemies) that he so idolized his mixed-race housekeeper that she was able to control his political thoughts and actions, especially with regard to people of color. The publisher reported that his partner asked Lydia directly, "(with a leer in his eye), 'Are you his idol?'" to which she replied "excitedly, and with a convulsive gasp that threatened to choke her, 'No—no!'" Henry Smith reports that Lydia explained that she had come to complain about the paper's treatment of herself and Thaddeus Stevens at the urging of "'more than a dozen highly respectable white ladies and gentlemen, all of whom have insisted that I ought to come and demand an apology.'" Henry Smith told his readers that his colleague responded with "a towering dignity commensurate with the occasion, 'Madame, we have no apology to make.'" When he asked, "'Why didn't you send some of your white backers here? We might have known better how to deal with them,'" Lydia reportedly replied "(In a fury) 'If—if ever—If ever my name appears in your paper again—I will—*will*—*cowhide the editor*!'"[26]

It's unfortunate that none of those "white ladies and gentlemen" accompanied Mrs. Smith to the *Intelligencer* office. It might have made Henry Smith and his colleague at least think twice before treating her in such abysmal fashion. But the fact that she undertook the mission on her own underscores her courage and self-confidence, traits she'll demonstrate again when she takes on Stevens's executors after his death.

No amount of slander or criticism could deter Thaddeus Stevens from his mission to accord full human equality to the freed slaves and all African Americans. In March, he and Senator Charles Sumner of Massachusetts put legislative support behind the actions of General William T. Sherman. After the war, Sherman "ordered that a half million acres of land in South Carolina, Georgia and Florida be given to the former slaves in 40-acre lots with mules, horses and other provisions." Stevens and Sumner's bill directed that even more land—three million acres—be given to the freed slaves in forty-acre plots. Congress passed the measure, but President Andrew

Johnson vetoed it and withdrew Sherman's order. "Forty acres and a mule" was reduced to a slogan, still familiar today, for a promise never kept.[27]

Later in the year, in a letter to his friend Dr. Michael D. G. Pfeiffer, Stevens "first elaborated his opinion that suffrage was an inalienable right guaranteed to every American citizen by our National Bill of Rights, the Declaration of Independence," and he further claimed that the federal government had the right to "regulate suffrage in all national affairs."[28] Stevens's letter to the good doctor was widely read and widely celebrated at the time, but his beliefs about the right to vote have been sorely tested over many generations of Americans, all the way down to the twenty-first century.

Stevens's longtime friend Rev. Jonathan Blanchard visited him in the winter of 1867. Blanchard was the preacher who converted Stevens to the abolitionist cause in Gettysburg and became his dedicated friend and admirer. Writing about the visit later, Blanchard said he knew his old friend was "a dying man." Stevens was also a soul Blanchard had endeavored to save for many years. Blanchard knew Stevens very well. He had recruited him to the antislavery cause because he had, as he confessed to Stevens, "an almost superstitious belief in your talents."[29] He knew Stevens still embraced the essence of his mother's Baptist faith; he knew Stevens had supported several promising ministerial candidates at Gettysburg and Mercersburg Colleges. He knew Stevens had given up strong drink long ago and now consumed only milk and water. He also knew Stevens enjoyed gambling and used profanity. But what bothered Blanchard most of all was that, as he put it, Stevens "should be guilty of illicit commerce with the sex." "How, then, shall we account for his personal errors and vices, and what shall we say of these?"[30] he had asked himself. Blanchard had met Mrs. Smith and knew she was a mixed-race woman who had tended to Stevens's needs for nearly a quarter of a century "with the ability and fidelity of a wife."[31]

On that cold winter's day in 1867, Blanchard put the question to Stevens directly and Stevens gave a clear, if not exactly direct, answer. As he spoke, it seems to me, he confirmed the suspicions so many, friends and enemies alike, had held for so long. He responded by comparing himself to other notable figures of his age. Stevens first measured himself against Henry Clay; he told Blanchard he wasn't lewd like the senator from Kentucky. Clay was heralded as the Great Compromiser for shepherding through Congress two historic compromises that brought new territories and states into the Union and allowed slavery to flourish. He was, however, attacked by critics for his lewd lifestyle. Even friendly biographers admit that Clay was "a 'wretched father,' drank excessively, and was 'quite possibly' unfaithful" to his wife, Lucretia.[32]

Next, Stevens said he was not as profane as Ben Wade. Historians acknowledge that Wade had a foul mouth. When Andrew Johnson advanced to the White House, Wade, a Republican from Ohio, was elected president pro tempore of the Senate. That raised concern for some in the august body: "If Johnson were convicted [in an impeachment trial], rough-edged Ben Wade, with his impressive command of profanity, would inherit the White House. It was not his cursing that made Wade an anathema to all Democrats and many conservative Republicans; it was his lifelong fight for the rights of blacks, women, and working-class men."[33]

Stevens enjoyed playing faro, a card game, from time to time, but he told Blanchard he wasn't in the same league as General Daniel Sickles when it came to gambling. Sickles, a New Yorker who fought for the Union in the Civil War, was widely known in Stevens's day for his drinking, gambling, and womanizing. According to one historian, he "was continually embroiled in some sort of financial, legislative, sexual or homicidal crisis" from his mid-thirties until he died at the age of ninety-four. His most notorious involvement with homicide arose in Washington, when he shot and killed Philip Barton Key, brother of Francis Scott Key, after he discovered that Key and his wife were lovers. Sickles made history in that case as the first homicide defendant to be acquitted on the grounds of temporary insanity.[34]

Stevens held himself up against Lord Lyndhurst, the British lord chancellor, and said he was not as avaricious as the noted Englishman. Lord Lyndhurst, otherwise known as John Copley, was the son of the famous painter John Singleton Copley. Born in America, Copley grew up in England, where he gained quite a reputation as a lawyer and member of Parliament. But even his fawning biographers admit that he occasionally exhibited "a sinister smile of great cunning, and some malignity, which obtained for him the sobriquet of Mephistophiles," the demonic character who facilitated Dr. Faustus's deal with the devil in German folklore.[35]

After Copley came Daniel Webster. Stevens told Blanchard that his personal habits were "less vicious" than Webster's. Webster was frequently attacked by critics who accused him of abandoning the religious values of his youth once he reached the halls of power. One detractor wrote that "his veracity, his honesty, his temperance, his chastity all were submerged in his intense and overmastering worldliness before he died." Another condemned him for his public language, accusing him of "uttering in very uncharacteristic language a threat against 'you damned abolitionists.'" Yet another charged that in congressional debate, Webster had "thrown the whole weight of his influence into the scale against the slave."[36] Stevens may have had those indictments in mind when he described Webster as more vicious, but he might also have been remembering the events of 1840, when Stevens believed that President William Henry Harrison would appoint him postmaster general only to see Webster and Henry Clay steer the position to someone else. Stevens apparently never forgave Webster.

In the end, Stevens said his life might compare most favorably to former vice president Richard M. Johnson, except that Johnson owned slaves and lobbied for mail delivery on the Sabbath. It's interesting that Stevens willingly placed himself alongside Richard Johnson. He obviously had nothing but disdain for Johnson's advocacy, on behalf of mail contractors, to permit Sunday mail delivery. Stevens, the champion of the common man, believed that forcing poor working men to deliver the mail on the Sabbath robbed them of their only day of rest.

But we should note that Stevens condemned Johnson, a Kentucky congressman who became vice president under President Martin Van Buren, for *owning slaves*, not for his controversial practice of making enslaved women his mistresses. According to historian Milton Meltzer, Johnson "lived openly with his Negro housekeeper [and slave] Julia Chinn. He had acknowledged their two daughters and educated them. Later, under his guidance they married white men and inherited his estate." When Chinn died, Meltzer writes, "Johnson fell in love with another slave . . . but she escaped. He caught her and sold her into the deep south." During his 1836 campaign for vice president, Meltzer reports, "Johnson formed an open alliance with the fugitive slave's sixteen-year-old sister." The "country flared with excited talk of Johnson's actions," Meltzer says, but elected him vice president just the same.[37]

It was Johnson's "slaveholding" that appalled Stevens, not his love for a woman of color. He complained to Blanchard that Johnson's "slaveholding and disregard of the Sabbath sanctified his vices, so that a family of mulatto children did not prevent his being the idol of the negro-hating democratic party: and his 'Report' setting aside God's law of the Sabbath made him Vice-President of the United States, while [he, Stevens] with three times [Johnson's] ability and a thousand times his honesty, never held any office but that of a direct representative of the people."[38]

Stevens talked to Blanchard like a man who had harbored these resentments for a very long time. He made clear that he saw himself as the victim of an unjust society that had robbed him of political opportunity because he lived with Lydia Hamilton Smith. Without saying it in so many words, Stevens implied that his relationship with a free woman of color meant that "he could not be a United States Senator ever and though he *made* presidents he could not be a member of their cabinets! 'I have lived my life through as you see me here,'" he told his friend. "I have tried to deal justly with my fellow-man. . . . I have tried to be charitable."[39] Blanchard wrote that he "was deeply moved, and interrupted him with this direct question: 'Mr. Stevens, do you know anything about Christ? Do you love him?'" To which Stevens replied, "'When one looks at him—his truthfulness: for he *was* truth—*not* to love him would be to be a wretch! But'" (at this point, Stevens's "voice died away into the tones of one who was musing") "—for my own case, I must make that a matter of trust."[40] Blanchard had his answer and, I would submit, so do those of us who wonder about the true nature of the relationship between Lydia Hamilton Smith and Thaddeus Stevens. Blanchard returned to this topic after Stevens's death, and we'll hear more testimony, but Stevens's own testimony in the presence of his abolitionist friend is enough. Stevens *owns* his relationship to Mrs. Smith in this conversation. In Blanchard's terms, we could say he *confessed* to it. And he did so without apology.

If Stevens wanted to deny it, why would he have chosen Richard M. Johnson as the political figure most like himself on the question of a sexual relationship? Johnson loved Black women he *owned*; Thaddeus Stevens loved a free Black woman who chose him as her companion. If there is any condemnation due here, it is of a society that elevated to high places a man who owned human beings and denigrated a man (and woman) who, in terms of racial awareness, were simply many years ahead of their time.

With Mrs. Smith constantly at Stevens's side, the pair maintained a fairly demanding schedule throughout 1867. In Washington, as President Johnson worked to thwart Republican-led Reconstruction efforts, Stevens and Senator John Sherman, an Ohio Republican and brother of well-known Union general William T. Sherman, wrote measures related to Johnson's impending impeachment. Those bills were passed into law on March 2, March 23, and July 19. Southern historians chronicling this work later couldn't resist taking a shot at Stevens and Mrs. Smith in passing: "Chief among his [Sherman's] assistants in this work was wig-wearing, club-footed old 'Thad Stevens,' frank and bold, with his grimly sharpened hatchet-face, soured on all the world except his Negro housekeeper, believed to be his concubine, and her race."[41]

On July 22, the couple's friend Dr. Henry Carpenter married Laura W. Miller of Oil City, Pennsylvania. It was Carpenter's second marriage; his first wife, Ann, had died four years earlier, leaving the doctor with three daughters of whom Mrs. Smith was especially fond. Mrs. Smith and Stevens were on hand for the festivities, as was former president (and Stevens's enemy) James Buchanan. That reportedly inspired some of their mutual acquaintances to attempt a reconciliation at the wedding reception.

According to newspaper editor W. Frank Gorrecht, Fulton Bank president John C. Carter's father claimed he was one of several men who tried to arrange a friendly meeting between Stevens and Buchanan in a nonpartisan setting. Before telling the rest of the story, Gorrecht impresses upon the reader that "no one, unless they lived through that period, can have the least conception of the intense hostility that existed between the respective adherents of Stevens and Buchanan in Lancaster." With that in mind, we can picture these well-intentioned individuals guiding Buchanan through the crowd and up to Stevens, where, at someone's urging, he reached out a friendly hand. The plan failed because, Gorrecht tells us, "Thaddeus Stevens simply did not see Buchanan extend his hand." The two men parted; their differences were never reconciled.[42]

There is, however, another version of this story, one offered by Stevens's former law student and partner Alexander Hood. Hood reminds his readers that the trouble between Stevens and Buchanan had started forty years before Dr. Carpenter's 1867 wedding, when Stevens rejected Buchanan's invitation to employ his considerable rhetorical and political talents on behalf of the Democratic Party. The way Stevens said "no" may have contributed to the hostility generated between the two men, if he brushed off the Lancastrian's overture in the same curt manner with which he dismissed many of his political opponents. Hood's account of the Stevens-Buchanan encounter in 1867 begins in similar fashion to Gorrecht's, but when the two men found themselves face-to-face, Hood says, it was Stevens who offered to greet Buchanan, perhaps extending a hand of friendship, only to be snubbed by the former president.[43]

Stevens and Mrs. Smith spent five days at the Bedford Springs Resort in Pennsylvania during the summer of 1867. The resort at Bedford Springs, about 150 miles due west of Lancaster, was founded in 1796 by Nicholas Shauffler after he discovered "high mineral content in the natural fresh-water springs." Shauffler wasn't actually the first person to stumble across the springs; Native Americans had been drinking and bathing in what they considered healing waters for centuries before white men happened along. By the mid-nineteenth century, the resort at Bedford Springs had become a place to see and be seen for the rich and famous from Philadelphia, New York City, and Washington, DC. President James Buchanan had spent considerable time there from 1857 to 1861—he referred to it as the "Summer White House."[44] Stevens wasn't interested in politicking during his stay at the resort that summer. He was seeking the restorative powers of the mineral springs. And he took Dr. Henry Carpenter, as well as Mrs. Smith, along to help him find them.[45] The mineral waters may have helped. Alexander Hood thought Stevens "seemed better" when he returned to Washington in November. That train trip would prove to be Stevens's last to DC.

In August 1867, while Stevens, in weakened condition, was at work in the first session of the 40th Congress, Lydia traveled back to Lancaster to deal with a very different problem. Her son Isaac, now thirty, was losing his battle with the bottle. We don't know exactly when Lydia arrived in Lancaster or what Isaac was doing when she got there, but his behavior was serious enough that Lydia swore out a warrant to have her son arrested and charged with "drunken and disorderly conduct." On August 28, Isaac was convicted and sentenced to thirty days' hard labor in the county jail.[46]

It's not clear whether Lydia's "tough love" got Isaac back on the right path. Other than her charge against him, we don't know very much about what was happening in his life in the summer of 1867. But at some point he must have moved, invited or uninvited, into Stevens's house at 45–47 South Queen Street. Hetty Franciscus, the woman who looked after the house while Stevens and Lydia were away, might have reported that to Lydia. She might also have informed Lydia and Stevens that Isaac returned there when he was released from the county jail. We know he was there afterward, because Stevens wrote to him at that address on November 9.

Lydia likely told Stevens what she found when she got to Lancaster in August, and Franciscus surely kept them apprised of Isaac's behavior after he was released from prison. By November 9, Stevens had had enough.

He wrote an angry letter to Isaac: "Sir, take notice that before Tuesday night next you have all your things away from my house and that you do not yourself enter my house during my absence to sleep or for any other purpose, under penalty of being considered a Housebreaker."[47] It appears Isaac did as he was told. When the census takers canvased Lancaster three years later, Isaac was living elsewhere.

Some biographers have interpreted Isaac's expulsion as evidence that Stevens's affection for Mrs. Smith did not, as Richard Current puts it, extend to "all members of her race or even of her family."[48] I think we err if we try to understand this story in racial terms. It seems to me that what we're dealing with here is a parental problem—admittedly with an "older" child, but a child, nonetheless. If we accept that Lydia served as a surrogate mother for Stevens's nephews (and in 1873 she was still playing that role for Thad Jr.), then why shouldn't we see Stevens's reaction to Isaac's behavior as that of a frustrated surrogate father? Considering that Lydia made a special trip to Lancaster to initiate charges against her own son, it's easy to imagine her venting some serious frustration in conversation with Stevens when she returned to Washington. It seems probable that she and Stevens were in accord as he booted Isaac from his house.

Surely, Mrs. Smith must have sometimes felt overwhelmed by the responsibilities she was asked to bear. But we have no evidence suggesting that she ever shirked any of them. If anything, she seems to have thrown herself into the fray with even more determination. We can illustrate that with a brief incident from the fall of 1867. According to one account, a Philadelphia minister Stevens had heard preach years before in Harrisburg came to call "on the invalid . . . [and] desired to kneel by his bedside and pray for his soul. But Old Thad was sleeping, and Lydia Smith would not let the visitor go upstairs."[49] Vigilance was not just another word to Lydia Hamilton Smith. In early November, Dr. Thaddeus Morrill Stevens wrote his uncle from his home in Indianapolis to say that he'd seen "by way of the papers that you are enjoying very good health. I am glad of it, don't [work?] too hard you can't stand it." It had been nearly eleven months since Dr. Stevens's wife Lizzie had died. The doctor told Stevens his political views were attracting a lot of attention in Indiana. He endorsed Stevens's call for universal suffrage as an excellent campaign issue going into the 1868 elections. He closed by telling his uncle, "I think I shall come to Washington soon, tell Mrs. Smith that I shall bore her awhile."[50] That would have been welcome news to Stevens and Mrs. Smith as they grappled with the dual challenges of his health and the mounting case against President Andrew Johnson.

The news from Lancaster in December 1867 would have been far less welcome. On Sunday, December 22, Isaac Smith was arrested again. District Attorney William Atlee charged that "Isaac Smith . . . with force and arms, willfully, and unlawfully did disturb and interrupt a meeting, society and congregation, the said meeting, society and congregation then and there being convened for the purpose of religious worship."[51] The service Isaac disrupted was at Bethel African Methodist Episcopal Church on Strawberry Street, the same church whose members had worked so faithfully, along with Stevens and Mrs. Smith, to guide fugitive slaves to safety on the Underground Railroad. We don't know why Isaac broke up the service at Bethel A.M.E.; given his record to this point, it's a safe bet alcohol was involved. He pleaded guilty to the charge and was sentenced to "six weeks separate and solitary confinement at labor, fined $1.00, and ordered to pay court costs of $22.32.[52] If Lydia came to Isaac's rescue on this occasion, we have no record of it.

We should note here that Thaddeus Stevens wrote and signed his last will and testament in the summer of 1867. In it, we find further evidence of his profound attachment to Lydia Hamilton Smith. In section 2, he wrote, "I give to Mrs. Lydia Smith, my housekeeper, five hundred dollars a year during her natural life, to be paid semi-annually, or at her option, she may receive five thousand dollars." Stevens then put what might seem like a reasonable condition on her legacy. "She may make her selection," he wrote, "and then release all further claim on my estate." That innocuous-sounding provision would cause no end of headaches for Mrs. Smith after Stevens died. In the twenty-first century, Stevens's gift to her would be worth nearly $90,000. The large legacy adds more evidence to the argument that Stevens had much more than a normal regard for his loving housekeeper.[53]

The next paragraph of Stevens's will paints a very clear picture of how intermingled their lives had become since she came to live with him in 1844. "Mrs. Smith," Stevens wrote, "has some furniture of her own, used in common with mine, some bought with her own money, as well as others, which would be difficult to distinguish; now she must be trustee on honor to take such as she claims without further proof." If she began working and sleeping in Stevens's house in 1856, as the record seems to indicate, that means she'd been mixing his furniture with hers for a decade, providing a comfortable living space, as any good "wife" would do. When Stevens pointed out that she had purchased some of the furnishings in the house on South Queen Street, he was admitting that they had shared a life together for a long time. Most ordinary hired housekeepers of the day would not have been willing to spend their hard-earned money buying furniture for the householder for whom they worked.[54]

Two paragraphs later, Stevens made provision for Mrs. Smith and his nephew Major Thaddeus Stevens Jr. to live in his house for three years after his death. Then, if Thad chooses to live elsewhere, the trustees are to dispose of the property. Two paragraphs after that, Stevens is still talking about Thad Jr. but the subject addressed will eventually involve Mrs. Smith. Acknowledging that his nephew still has a drinking problem, Stevens lays out an abstinence plan that would eventually make Thad the heir to his entire estate after outstanding debts and legacies had been paid. As we'll see, Thad was unable to meet the challenge, and it would fall to Mrs. Smith to tend to him as he destroyed himself with drink.[55]

Stevens also instructed his executors to use the remainder of his estate, if large enough, to endow a school for poor and orphan children in Lancaster. As we know, he had intended to finance his bequest through the sale of his Franklin County ironworks. Apparently, in the summer of 1867, he hoped his estate, when liquidated, would still yield enough to start the school. That provision would also complicate Mrs. Smith's life in days to come.[56]

All in all, the year 1867 was an arduous and mostly disappointing one for Lydia Hamilton Smith. Its final days ticked away with her younger son imprisoned in solitary confinement, her companion's health—his very existence—dependent on her round-the-clock nursing care, and many in the nation waiting for Stevens to lead the charge against President Johnson and his persistent efforts to undo Reconstruction programs designed to guarantee the equality of people of color. And as Stevens and Mrs. Smith grappled with the uncertainties of their life together, their enemies continued to taunt them.

A vicious and threatening letter arrived in late December. It was apparently written on Christmas Day in Washington by a racist too cowardly to sign his (or her) name. The writer told Stevens, "It seems that even in this festive time, when most human hearts soften, yours is without one emotion of pity for the cruelty, injustice and oppression which you have inflicted on a suffering and outraged people. May God forgive you for these great crimes, and make you realize their enormity."[57] What had Stevens done to trigger such a venomous holiday-season condemnation? The writer appears to be inverting Stevens's message to the House as he introduced a house bill in March 1867: "Relative to Damages to Loyal Men and for Other Purposes" (H.R. 20). In his speech, Stevens portrayed the Confederacy as the villains. The letter writer attempts to turn that argument on its head and make the rebels the victims of the Union's (that is, Stevens's) vindictiveness. Stevens's bill, like Confiscation Acts passed during the Civil War, called for punishment of Confederate "traitors" by confiscation of their land. That land would then be redistributed, in allotments of forty acres, to "liberated slaves." (Such a plan had been instituted by General Sherman under Secretary of War Stanton during and immediately after the war, only to be upended by President Johnson. Those actions became a central part of Republican calls for Johnson's impeachment.) In his speech, Stevens asked whether the American people were satisfied to see the president allow "a murderous belligerent"—the Confederacy—to escape accountability for its actions with "impunity." And he repeated his belief that the nation owed a massive debt to those enslaved for so long: "It [H.R. 20] is important to four millions of injured, oppressed, and helpless men, whose ancestors for two centuries have been held in bondage and compelled to earn the very property, a small portion of which we propose to restore to them, and who are now destitute, helpless, and exposed to want and starvation, under the deliberate cruelty of their former masters."[58] To the contrary, the indignant letter writer would have us believe it was the white slavemasters of the South who were the aggrieved party here, not those who had felt the overseers' whips for hundreds of years.

Early in his speech, Stevens informed the House, "To this issue I desire to devote the small remnant of my life." As one of the most powerful members of Congress, Stevens's failing health had long since become news, and the letter writer homed in on it as his (or her) rant continued: "You are at the gate of the tomb, looking into the grave, and yet you dare to defy the Almighty with profane utterances, and vindictive vengeance. And all for what? To elevate your black bastards in the Social Scale . . . and to inflict punishment for the destruction of your ironworks." (We noted earlier that Stevens's ironworks was specifically targeted when Confederate troops made their way into Pennsylvania.) The correspondent, writing with the white heat of self-righteous hate, conjured up the accusations of "corruption, vice, and contempt of religion" with which Stevens's critics had long assailed him, warning the congressman that he would pay for his sins. "There is a day of retribution for us all, which you cannot escape. There are those here in Washington, who know the motives and influencers that control your actions, and the price paid for certain legislation. Those facts must come out. Still we pray for your repentance."[59] If the anonymous writer intended to expose Thaddeus Stevens, there wasn't much time left to do it. In the end, would such a letter have clouded the holidays for Lydia Hamilton Smith and Thaddeus Stevens after all of the abusive rhetoric they had already absorbed? I doubt it.

CHAPTER 13

A COMPANION LOST

Mrs. Smith was in Lancaster in the fall of 1867. Perhaps she had delayed her return to Washington while Isaac served thirty days of hard labor in the county jail on the drunk and disorderly conduct charge she had sworn against him in late August. But she didn't stay in Lancaster much longer—Thaddeus Stevens needed her at his rented house on South B Street. She told a reporter, later, that Stevens "requested me to come to Washington and get his house ready and keep it up in the event of his death until the lease expired in March, 1869, and said that whoever came in his place might, if they desired, occupy his late residence."[1]

Stevens needed Mrs. Smith in Washington for more than housekeeping; he needed her so that he could keep going. The drumbeat to impeachment was growing louder and louder as Stevens was growing weaker and weaker. His amanuensis in Washington, Jacob Keneagy, testifying on Lydia's behalf when she took Stevens's executors to court, described Stevens's condition in late 1867. He said Stevens needed to be "carried up and down stairs and from his house to his carriage and from his carriage to the House by the managers and back again." John Warfel, who knew Mrs. Smith and Stevens in Lancaster and Washington and was another witness in her case, said that Stevens's health was "frequently very poor." He said Stevens was "frequently so feeble he had to be carried downstairs by two colored men— and carried to the carriage and driven in it to the House." Stevens's body man (personal assistant), Lewis West, testified that Stevens grew so weak that Mrs. Smith had to dress him before he was carried downstairs to one of the carriages she maintained in Washington and taken to the Capitol.[2] She personally delivered his lunch to the House later in the day. When

Stevens reached Capitol Hill, two young Black men would hoist him onto their shoulders and carry him to his desk. But as his body faded, his wit remained sharp. Many historians have shared his quip to the young men, apparently overheard by a good many at the Capitol, as he rode to his seat: "What will I do for someone to carry me," he deadpanned, "when you boys are dead and gone?"[3]

Stevens sorely needed that clarity of mind, but he was losing the battle to preserve his body. In late January or early February, he reportedly suffered a heart attack. According to biographer Richard Nelson Current, it wasn't his first. That occasioned a telegram to Dr. Carpenter in Lancaster (probably sent by Mrs. Smith) urgently requesting more of the "powders" that had exerted "good effect" in the past.[4] The powders may not have been very efficacious this time. It was a very weak Thaddeus Stevens who was carried to his seat on February 24, 1868, when the House of Representatives voted, for the first time in American history, to impeach the president of the United States. The vote was 126 to 47. The following day, February 25, Stevens and Congressman John A. Bingham, Republican of Ohio, presented the articles of impeachment to the Senate.

The articles focused on what Radical Republicans considered Andrew Johnson's illegal firing of Secretary of War Edwin M. Stanton as part of his campaign to derail the Reconstruction programs already implemented by Congress. Johnson hoped to replace Stanton with someone more amenable to the lenient Reconstruction policy he enacted for bringing the South back into the Union after he succeeded the slain President Lincoln in April 1865. Vehemently opposed by Thaddeus Stevens and other Radical Republicans, that policy provided almost total amnesty for ex-Confederates, set up a program that allowed Confederate states to rapidly regain their status as part of the United States, and approved new, local Southern governments. Those governments proceeded to enact "Black codes" that "preserved the system of slavery in all but its name."[5]

Stevens had recovered little of his strength when the impeachment trial began in the Senate chamber. One Southern historian writes that "the old man was sustained only by the intensity of his hate. His eye was bright, but his face bore the crooked autograph of pain." Stevens stood to deliver his opening speech, the historian says, but "after he talked a few moments, he sank into his chair," and Massachusetts congressman Benjamin Butler read the rest of Stevens's prepared remarks.[6] The trial lasted several weeks; in the end, when several Republicans defected from their party's cause, Johnson was acquitted by one vote. The Senate adjourned as a court of impeachment on May 26.

By the time the trial ended, Stevens was physically exhausted, but the fire of his Radical Republicanism was still red-hot. In comments preserved in the *Congressional Globe* (third session of the 40th Congress, 1868), he predicted that never again would a president be "removed by peaceful means. If he retains the money and patronage of the government, it will be found, as has been found, stronger than the law, and impenetrable to the spear of justice." "If tyranny becomes intolerable," Stevens told his colleagues, "the only resource will be found in the dagger of Brutus."[7]

At no point in these months did Stevens ever use his illness as an excuse to shirk his duties in the House. Alexander Hood, Stevens's former law student and partner, attested later to Stevens's faithful attendance on Capitol Hill. Hood wrote that Stevens "was always present attending to his duty," despite being so feeble he needed to be carried into the building. "Nor, when the impeachment trial was over, did he fail to attend, but continued to appear almost daily to the end of the session, which closed on the 17th of July. Mr. Stevens was at this time too weak to attempt the journey to Lancaster."[8] Unable to travel home, Stevens delivered on his promise of new articles of impeachment, but they did not garner much support; Andrew Johnson served out his term without facing another trial.

Lydia did return to Lancaster that spring, but it's not clear whether she was there for business or pleasure. On April 7, Isaac was in trouble again. District Attorney William Atlee charged him with stealing from Jacob Effinger, who was then tenant and proprietor of Kleiss's Tavern (which Stevens owned), next door to Stevens's and Lydia's house at the corner of South Queen and Vine Streets. Court documents show that Isaac was accused of stealing two shirt studs (each valued at one dollar) and a breastpin (also valued at one dollar), and the district attorney offered the court six witnesses, including Effinger, willing to testify.[9] Isaac was found guilty, but it's not clear what punishment he received.

Is it possible that Lydia made a special trip to Lancaster to support her son in his latest difficulty? We don't know. We do know that she was in Lancaster on April 30, when Catherine "Kate" Mathiot, sister of Dr. Henry Carpenter's first wife, Ann Louisa, and daughter of late Lancaster mayor John Mathiot, married Dr. Isaac McKinney. Catherine was in her forties in 1868, as was Dr. McKinney. The couple wed at Dr. Carpenter's home on a Thursday morning.[10] It was Dr. McKinney's second marriage. His first wife, Susan, died sometime after 1860, leaving three children, who were ten, eleven, and thirteen when their father married Catherine Mathiot.[11] At the age of forty-two, the mayor's daughter had inherited an instant family.

In a letter from Washington dated May 3, Mrs. Smith told the bride, who appears to have been a good friend, that she had just arrived home safely "after having a delightful tim[e]" at the festivities after the wedding. Among the partiers were many of Mrs. Smith's and Stevens's friends and neighbors, and the celebration appears to have extended into the next day, Friday.[12]

In her letter, Mrs. Smith reports that Dr. Carpenter's daughter Catherine spent a good part of Friday evening in tears. Catherine— Mrs. Smith calls her Katy—and her sisters, Mary and Sarah, lost their mother, Catherine Mathiot's sister, Ann Louise, in 1863. Their father had married his second wife, Laura, in 1867, with Mrs. Smith and Stevens in attendance. Mrs. Smith reports to the new bride that her nieces, whom Kate likely knew quite well, were all still grieving the loss of their mother. "They kept up the fun until Friday night," she wrote. "They all try to hide thair greaf and do it prety well but Poor little Katy." (Catherine was sixteen in 1868.) Lydia watched Catherine closely that night, and she told Kate that she "notizt hir leav the Room and Run to the part of the yard and thair Remain until she coud [?] dry up hir Pretty brown eyes and she would Return and try to be merry with the Rest. They all try thair best but in spight of all thair strong nervs it will show."

Mrs. Smith was deeply moved by Catherine's suffering. She told Kate that her departure (perhaps for a wedding trip or simply to return to Jersey Shore, more than a hundred miles north of Lancaster) had made young Katy even sadder. "About 700 oclock," Lydia wrote, "she began to realize that that you had gon and she made A vizit over the temporary bridg to yates cunningham['s] Garden to that Conty spot to have A quiet cry by hirself." Yeates Cunningham lived next to the Carpenters in 1868. He was apparently well to do; in 1870, the census taker put him down for $20,000 in real estate and a personal estate worth $1,000. How he made that money, we don't know. When asked his occupation that year, he responded, "Never had occupation."[13]

Mrs. Smith couldn't bear to watch Katy Carpenter sobbing alone in Cunningham's garden. She told her friend, "I went out and brought hir up and Mrs Kerfoot and Mrs Eshbough Mrs. [Brinton] and Kitty kept it up till after 10 oclock."[14] Kate Mathiot McKinney and Mrs. Smith must

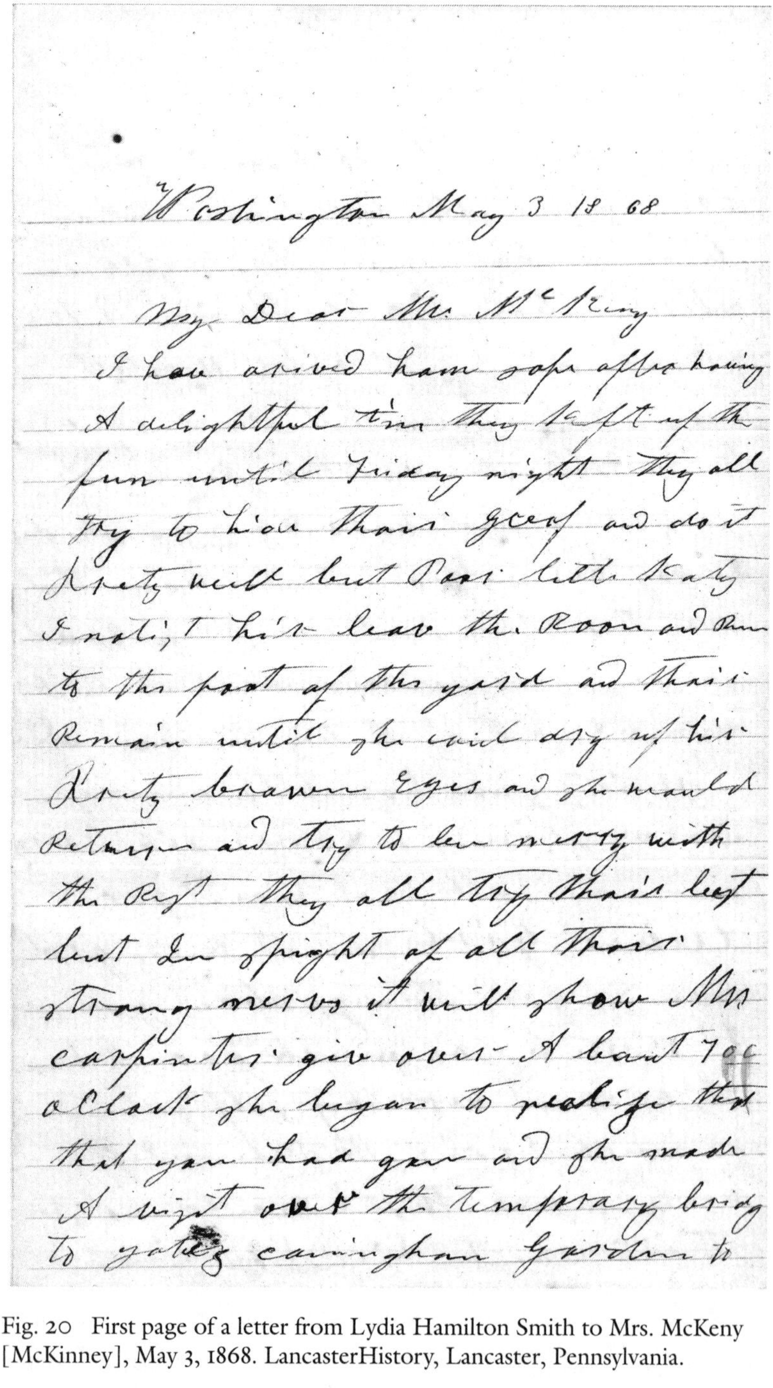

Fig. 20 First page of a letter from Lydia Hamilton Smith to Mrs. McKeny [McKinney], May 3, 1868. LancasterHistory, Lancaster, Pennsylvania.

have been very close. In her letter, Mrs. Smith moves on from the Carpenter girls' sadness to share with Kate how highly regarded she was in Lancaster. "Dear Mrs Mc You hav left menny warm friends in ower city Evry one says well Kate was A good Clever Girl and a verry grate menny good things about you and It done me as much good to hear It as if it was my self getting so much prais."[15]

Mrs. Smith obviously shared her experience with Stevens as soon as she arrived home, because she adds his opinion to the letter. "Mr Stevens regret verry much that he could not be thair when he hird how much fun they had," she told Kate, "and hop that you and the Dr Mc may live long and happy life. he says if ever he did wish A good girl happiness It is Kate—see how Much the old gentelman thinks of you[?]" Kate likely knew virtually everyone in Mrs. Smith's and Stevens's social circle. Mrs. Smith begins her closing with, "harriet and lewis wishes to be Remembered to you and wishes you good luck lewis says."[16] (Lewis West was Stevens's body man; his wife, Harriet, worked for Mrs. Smith.) And then she wrote, "I almost forgot to say that Dr Stevens [Dr. Thaddeus Morrill Stevens, Stevens's nephew] was hear when I got home and he says that he is In love with A widow and is sorry he did not get the Invitation in time to go to your wedding. he was in harrisburg at the time and new nothing of it." Finally, Mrs. Smith tells her friend, "Pleas write to me and tell me how you got up hom I left[?] anxious about you as you was not well. may god bless you. good night. L Smith."[17]

In addition to giving us a sense of Mrs. Smith's travels in this crucial period of her life, this letter gives us a deeper appreciation for how affectionate and sensitive Lydia Hamilton Smith was with those who were within her circle of acquaintance. She was already fifty-five when she wrote this letter, yet her buoyant spirit and sparkling personality still shine through. It seems safe to observe that many people experiencing the challenges she confronted in this period might struggle to present such a positive face to the world.

Stevens, too, put on the best face he could as he was carried to and from the Senate during Andrew Johnson's impeachment proceedings. There were moments when the possibility of recovery flickered ever so briefly, but those closest to him, beginning with Mrs. Smith, knew that was increasingly unlikely. Long accustomed to hiding the whole truth of their relationship, Stevens and Mrs. Smith kept the full truth of his illness between them. Fawn Brodie reports, "Few of his visitors knew that there was torment in his prolonged dying. Only Lydia Smith, who massaged his swollen feet and saw to it that he followed the orders of his Lancaster physician [Dr. Carpenter]—iron tonic, blue pills, nourishing food, with as much punch, wine, brandy, or beer, as may be necessary and agreeable."[18]

The Reverend Jonathan Blanchard, Stevens's old abolitionist friend, apparently understood Stevens's increasingly dire situation better than most. On February 15, as Stevens was about to grit his way through the impeachment trial, Blanchard, who harbored a sincere love and appreciation for Stevens, wrote him an urgent letter. In the strongest terms yet, he begged the ailing statesman to repent. "You are five years beyond the allotted time of man," he told Stevens.[19] "At present, in every part of the United States, people believe that your personal life has been *one prolonged sin*; that your lips are defiled with blasphemy! Your hands with gambling!! And your body with women!!!"[20] Blanchard told his old friend, "The good you have done the country (and none have done more, if so much) is no offset for vices such as I have named above. . . . What makes bad government is bad and sinful men."[21] In the spring, Blanchard traveled to Washington to see Stevens. What he learned made the burden on his heart even greater. "Toward the close of his life," Blanchard later wrote, "when he saw that he must soon go, his cries by night upon his bed almost resembled howlings, and when one ran to him asking him if he was in agony, or what was the matter, he would answer 'nothing in particular,' or 'nothing in this world,' but when my informant listened silent outside the door, his agony of mind was heard venting itself in 'strong crying and tears,'—crying for God, if there were one, to come to his relief."[22] Who could have known these things but Mrs. Smith?

Although he doesn't give us an exact date, it was probably during this visit that Blanchard learned of Stevens's deep desire to spend eternity with Mrs. Smith by his side. "I saw him cry," he wrote, "till the big tears ran heavily down his sunken cheeks while relating his efforts to get his bones into a spot where a devilish spirit of caste and proscription could not cast out as a dead brute the corpse of the woman who had taken care of him for more than twenty-five years with the ability and fidelity of a wife, though not permitted by a law mightier far than the statute, to become his wife."[23]

Stevens's relationship with Mrs. Smith put Blanchard in a difficult position. He went on at some length, trying to reconcile his tremendous regard for Thaddeus Stevens as a crusader for freedom and justice with what Blanchard could only think of as a life of sin. "I shall not cater to a prurient curiosity," he wrote,

> by describing the person of the woman, who was in complexion a dark brunette; nor seek to throw a soft light on the shame and sin of fornication by contrasting with this case that of Abraham, who cast off his swarthy concubine, while Stevens stuck to the last gasp by his. It is ours to learn the lesson which this case of crime against Christ's laws of purity teaches us; to see a great and mighty and fearless spirit cowering, and covering his domestic life with life-long secrecy; to writings of a great soul under perpetual conviction of sin; to see him send the purest and most pious young men he could find to college and into the ministry, in hope to atone for his polluting example by giving a gospel to the world which condemned him![24]

We know that by 1868, many Americans, especially Southerners and Southern sympathizers, regarded Stevens as a godless wretch worthy of nothing but hatred and disdain. But millions of people considered him a hero of the Republic. On August 3, one of those people, a particularly wealthy one, demonstrated his respect. Mrs. Smith told the story to a *New York Times* reporter. "On Monday, the 3d inst.," the *Times* reporter recorded her as saying,

> when Mr. Stevens received a letter from Mr. Garrett, President of the Baltimore and Ohio Railroad, offering him the use of a special car to convey him home, he appeared more gratified than I had ever before seen him. He said he knew he was not able to go home in the regular passenger car, and as the offer presented an opportunity for going home without being crowded, he seemed very much cheered. Upon Thursday, the 6th inst., when Dr. Carpenter went in to bid him goodbye, he said he was so much better that if the Doctor would stay another day he believed he should be able to go home with him.[25]

Dr. Carpenter, who had come to Washington specifically to check on his patient, nixed the plan. Mrs. Smith said, "Dr. Carpenter told him that it would not be safe for him to go then, but that he might go in a few days." As we listen to her account, we can sense the closeness that had grown up between Mrs. Smith and Stevens. "The next day [Friday]," she continued,

> he said we should have to defer going home for the present, as he was growing weaker, and that it did not make any difference now whether we went home or not; we might just as well stay here. He said, "This is as good a place as any." He continued: "I have pretty nearly wound up my business here; I have my affairs nearly settled at the furnace and my preparations are about all made." He intimated his readiness to die, but added: "I see some bright prospects in the future that could almost tempt me to desire to live a little longer, but no matter."[26]

Mrs. Smith apparently shared Dr. Carpenter's assessment, on August 6, that Stevens wasn't fit to travel home to Lancaster. In fact, she was so concerned about Stevens's condition that she wrote a note to Thad Jr. the next day, August 7, apprising him of the situation. Thad was in Franklin County, at the ironworks. "Dear Thad," she wrote, "Your uncel has bin quite low I had almost given up but he is better he had diarhear which would sit hard on him he was so weak. I will write to you every day and let you know how he is. Yours, Lydia."[27] Thad was soon on his way to Washington.

Mrs. Smith remained by Stevens's bedside throughout the weekend, administering medications around the clock, doing everything she could to ease his physical suffering, and, no doubt, praying for his health and his soul. She was assisted in both tasks by Sister Loretta O'Riley and Sister Genevieve Ewers, "colored sisters of charity of the Providence Hospital who had been visiting him daily in his illness and whose benevolent and charitable work had been so heartily supported by Stevens in personal and legislative efforts." Specifically, Stevens "had secured a special Congressional appropriation of thirty thousand dollars for this institution in spite of great opposition. It was a Washington charity for negroes."[28] Stevens was quite fond of the Black nurses. Mrs. Smith told the *New York Times*, "Last year when he was sick he said he would sooner send one hundred miles for Sister Loretta to be with him in his last hours, than to have many preachers he knew of." The sisters were obviously a comfortable choice for Mrs. Smith. As a devout Catholic, she would have been heartened to have nurses from a Catholic medical order present. As it turned out, the sisters contributed far more than nursing services in Stevens's final hours.[29]

According to Mrs. Smith, "On Tuesday morning [August 11th] he [Stevens] thought he was better, and I thought so too, though we could not get him to take much nourishment. He lay quietly, at times asleep apparently, but really in deep meditation. Mr. Stevens thought more of the future than was generally supposed. He was always a man of a few words on that subject."[30] But Stevens was fairly talkative that day. Mrs. Smith said that Thad Jr. came into his uncle's room around two o'clock in the afternoon, having just arrived from the furnace. Stevens brought up the work at Caledonia; during the war, Confederate soldiers had burned off thousands of acres of timberland around the forge. Mrs. Smith said he "talked to him [Thad] about his clearing off land there and the affairs of the furnace as clearly as he ever did, and also conversed with him about deposition taken and the points of law in a certain suit, telling him what was necessary to be done and what was not, just as loudly as he would have done at any other time, though he lay with his eyes shut all the while." Earlier in the day, Stevens talked with the Reverend Dr. Ewing and J. Scott Patterson of the Interior Department.[31]

A rumor flashed around the city on that hot August afternoon. Stevens was "better," someone had said, but, of course, that was not the case.[32] He was lying on his bed at 279 South B Street, surrounded by those who loved him most, waiting to die. Thad Jr.'s arrival brought the number of friends in the room to at least six—Mrs. Smith, Simon Stevens, Sisters Loretta and Genevieve, Thad Jr., and Lewis West, who had carried Stevens to and from this second-floor bedroom for months. Historian Frank Gorrecht suggests that grocer Christopher Dice, Stevens's neighbor in Lancaster (and his most intimate and confidential friend, in Gorrecht's estimation), had been summoned to Stevens's deathbed to employ his considerable powers of prayer, but no other accounts of these hours mention him.[33]

The details of these final hours vary a bit, but all sources agree that someone, either Thad Jr. or Mrs. Smith and the nurses from Providence Hospital, took turns fanning Stevens and feeding him pieces of ice. He dozed, off and on, through the afternoon but remained surprisingly lucid when he woke. He talked public affairs with Simon, telling him that Seward's purchase of Alaska was the biggest thing in his career. When he fell silent for a moment, Simon mentioned that he'd seen General Rosecrans and that the general had spoken highly of Alanson's military service. Stevens observed, "He was a brave boy." He dozed again, awoke, and told Simon he believed that Grant would be elected president and the Reconstruction laws he and the Radical Republicans had worked so hard to pass would, finally, be carried out. Stevens reportedly spoke to everyone in the room, in turn, and finally told Thad, "We'll have a nice trip home; I'll visit the foundry with you, perhaps." At that point, Stevens's Washington physician, Dr. Noble Young, came into the room and cautioned those present not to disturb Stevens or let him fatigue himself with talking.[34]

The room was mostly silent until early evening, when two African Methodist Episcopal ministers arrived. According to Mrs. Smith, the Reverend Mr. Hall and the Reverend Mr. Reed had visited Stevens on New Year's Day. She told the *Times* that "when asked whether he would have persons pray with him he [Stevens] said he would." She said, "The clergymen . . . were sent for and sang and prayed with him." Her next comment was especially poignant. She said, "While they were praying he responded to them twice, but I could not understand what he said." When they finished praying and singing, the clergymen told Stevens, "You have the prayers of all the colored people in the country." Stevens "nodded his assent." The nursing sisters prayed with Stevens, as well. Mrs. Smith said, "When Sister Loretta O'Riley and Sister Genevieve . . . knelt by his bedside and prayed, Sister Loretta took him by the hand. His breast heaved with emotion though he did not speak. The last that I recollect of his saying, was when we wanted to move him to another bed, when he said, 'Don't move me,' and motioned for ice." In telling her story, Mrs. Smith revealed aspects of her life with Stevens that very few would have known. "For the last two years," she told the reporter, "he requested to be talked to about death freely, saying that he had not that horror of it which he once had."[35] Surely, she was one of the people Stevens had talked to "about death," and his openness to Jonathan Blanchard's repeated entreaties to get right with God might reflect the change in attitude she talked about.

At ten minutes to midnight, Mrs. Smith told the *Times* reporter, when Stevens "was asked if he would allow Sister Loretta to baptize him he consented. This was a very short time before he died." Perhaps to deflect later suggestions that Stevens didn't know what was happening, she added, "He was conscious to the last."[36] She would later confess to orchestrating Stevens's baptism and to being relieved that it happened. "I believe," she told a reporter for the *Philadelphia Times*, "that he is safe in heaven today."[37]

Biographer James Woodburn gives a particularly sensitive description of the baptism and the moments that followed. "No objection [to the baptism] being offered," he writes, the impressive ceremony was performed amid reverential silence. Mrs. Smith the colored housekeeper knelt at the foot of the bed, while the sisters, also kneeling, continued to read the prayers for the departing soul. The plaintive tones of the holy sisters, the repressed and troubled breathing of the dying man mingled with the sobs of his nephew and of his faithful friend and housekeeper, Mrs. Smith, were indications of coming death. The annalist relates that the clock struck twelve and in three minutes, he was dead . . . when death came he passed calmly and peacefully away as though falling into a sweet slumber.

Mrs. Smith and Thad, overcome by emotion, had to be escorted from the room.[38]

Word of Stevens's death spread quickly around Washington and, by telegraph, to the nation. Thomas Frederick Woodley reports that Andrew Johnson, still recovering after surviving impeachment, "sighed in relief" at Stevens's death and "showed no magnanimity by the silence that he invoked. . . . He issued no word of notice of the passing nor did he proclaim any sign of national mourning."[39] Lydia Hamilton Smith's battle to preserve Thaddeus Stevens's life was over. But new battles, engendered by his death, were just beginning. Those battles, largely financial in nature, would pit her against the three trusted friends Stevens appointed to carry out his last wishes.

CHAPTER 14

"It Was Mr. Dickey"

President Johnson may have chosen to ignore Stevens's passing, but Congress, the city of Washington, and the Northern half of the nation rose to honor a great American. Stevens was embalmed under the direction of the surgeon general and laid out in his South B Street home, but, according to Thomas Frederick Woodley, the officers of the Butler Zouaves, a Black military unit from Washington charged with guarding the coffin, "had difficulty in handling the crowds that flocked to view the body. Next day, the body was moved to the Capitol, where it lay in state in the rotunda, on the same catafalque that had supported the casket of the martyred Lincoln." *Harper's Weekly* reported that "the coffin was borne to the Capitol by five colored and three white pall-bearers." The *Times* identified them as "Messrs. Chauncy, Reese and several other employees of the House of Representatives, aided by Lewis West, Mr. Stevens' old body servant." Stevens's family—Mrs. Smith, Thad Jr., and Simon Stevens—arranged for the Butler Zouaves to stand honor guard. Photographs from those days show the Zouaves standing guard as some six thousand people paid their respects to the great civil rights warrior. The Zouaves' somber bearing added to the significance and solemnity of the proceedings in Washington; in Lancaster, unfortunately, it would be another matter.[1]

In the Rotunda, the coffin was positioned in front of a statue of the late martyred president, and flowers piled up around it, many "placed there by black hands." Stevens's body was enshrouded in a black suit with a scarf around his neck. The *New York Times* reporter observed that Stevens's features had "changed but very little, and he looks quite natural, though

Fig. 21 Thaddeus Stevens's body lying in state in the Rotunda of the Capitol, Washington, DC, August 14, 1868. Photo: Wikimedia Commons (Alexander Gardner).

emaciated by his long illness. The mouth and eyes are closed, but the eyes are somewhat sunken, and the right temple is a little dark."[2]

The *Times* described Stevens's coffin as "rosewood, covered with fine black cloth, and lined with white satin. Upon the lid is a large silver plate bearing the following inscription: 'THADDEUS STEVENS: born April 4, 1792; and died Aug. 11, 1868 at midnight.' The plate is in the form of a shield, handsomely chased, and around it a row of silver tacks. Upon each side are three very heavy silver handles, the hinge portion being the national coat of arms, and an eagle emblazoned on the handle. The coffin is heavily trimmed with silver, and upon the lid rests a beautiful chain of white ribbon."[3] The family had moved quickly and made a number of important decisions by the time Stevens's coffin reached the Rotunda. The elegance of the coffin and its ornamentation suggest that Mrs. Smith played a large and likely determinant role in those decisions.

A funeral service was held in the Rotunda on Friday morning, August 14, after which the Zouaves, "preceded by a colored brass-band from the neighboring city of Georgetown," escorted Stevens's body to the depot, where it was placed on a special train for the trip to Lancaster.[4] As the train

Fig. 22   Oliver Jesse Dickey.
LancasterHistory,
Lancaster, Pennsylvania.

wound its way northward it stopped at Harrisburg and York, where "minute guns were fired."⁵ When the train pulled into Lancaster Friday night, many Lancastrians were waiting to greet it. The family's plans for honoring Stevens had been carried out with dignity and respect in the nation's capital, but in Lancaster they encountered resistance in the person of O. J. Dickey, Stevens's former student and law partner. Dickey chaired the Committee of Arrangements for Stevens's funeral in Lancaster. Trouble was already brewing before Lydia, Thad Jr., and Simon Stevens left Washington. A reporter for the *Philadelphia Inquirer* who tracked down details of what happened prefaced his account with the observation that Stevens's family had not totally approved of O. J. Dickey and the Committee of Arrangements. The reporter explained that the family, assuming Stevens would want some of "that race whose freedom and enfranchisement he had been instrumental" to take part in his funeral, "had arranged the Butler Zouaves, colored independent militia organization of D.C. to accompany his remains to Lancaster and stay through the funeral." The family's wishes had apparently been communicated to Dickey and the committee while Mrs. Smith, Thad, and Simon Stevens were still in Washington, because they triggered a telegram from Dickey telling them that "arrangements there [in Lancaster] would admit of no military display of colored men at the funeral. To this Mr. Simon Stevens replied that the arrangements had already been completed, and it was too late to alter the programme. The colored body guard of honor, he said, would go to Lancaster with the body, and after that the committee of Lancaster could do as they deemed."[6]

Mrs. Smith, Thad, and Simon may have stepped off the train in Lancaster hoping for the best, but they were met with the worst. The *Inquirer* journalist reported that "the committee used the discretion thus given them, by sending the colored men home the next morning after their arrival." The reporter apparently spoke with the honor guard members before they left the city. He wrote, "It is needless to say that the colored men were at once mortified and chagrined. They had contemplated remaining to attend the funeral of the man whom their race almost worshiped while he lived."[7]

Why would Dickey do such a thing? He had known Stevens a long time by 1868 and knew as well as anyone how much he was loved and respected by people of color. The *Inquirer* reporter grappled with this question, too, and, after talking to people in Lancaster, offered up this explanation. "This action is accounted for," he wrote, "on the ground that Mr. Dickey, who is anxious to take Mr. Stevens' place in Congress, wants to conciliate all branches of the Republican party in order to get the nomination." The *Inquirer*'s correspondent didn't think much of that. Thaddeus Stevens's funeral is one of the biggest in US history, he said: "The city of Lancaster presented a slight that will long be remembered by its denizens; and one of the most striking occurrences that will retain a place on the minds of the rising generation of Lancaster will be the remembrance of Thaddeus Stevens' funeral."[8] This account helps us understand why Stevens's family had not "totally approved" of Dickey and his committee. If he chose to insult the Butler Zouaves and thwart the family's wishes for Stevens's funeral to advance his political fortunes, it worked. Local Republicans nominated Thaddeus Stevens for Congress in 1870, as tribute to the "champion of freedom and justice." The Democratic *Lancaster Intelligencer* "mocked the idea of voting for a 'corpse for Congress.'"[9] In the end, Dickey won the nomination and the election. He served two terms as congressman from Thaddeus Stevens's district.

When the train reached Lancaster, Stevens's body was taken to the home on South Queen Street where he and Mrs. Smith had lived for nearly a decade. He lay in state there, in the front parlor, for two days. The family hadn't planned to hold a viewing, but, the *New York Times* reported, when hundreds of mourners showed up outside the door, their eagerness to pay respects to Stevens "caused the relatives [Mrs. Smith, most likely] to admit many to see the remains." The *Times* said the large crowd outside filled the streets, "the scene exceeding anything witnessed here for years."[10] Many of those outside were people of color who had, as Woodley puts it, "already realized how largely responsible the Old Commoner had been for bringing the country to act on their behalf." Woodley writes that many Black people endured the hardship of long travel to mourn the loss of Stevens. He estimates that at least half of those attending Stevens's funeral ceremonies in Lancaster were Black.[11]

Those invited inside Stevens's house witnessed Mrs. Smith's talents as a housekeeper. The *Inquirer* reporter told Philadelphia readers that "a few portraits of his relatives and friends hung around the parlor . . . a bright Brussels carpet upon the floor gave it a real homelike, cheerful look." (Was Mrs. Smith's portrait among the others?) Mrs. Smith had arranged some of Stevens's papers on the coffee table. One document, from his agent, referred to a case involving the ironworks; two of the papers were from poor people seeking Stevens's assistance in cases from Washington. Of those inside and outside of the house, the *Inquirer* reporter said they were the "bone and sinew of old Lancaster." Not rabble, the reporter wrote. They were "men whose hands were hard, but whose hearts have beaten only for suffering humanity for a quarter of a century; men whose faces bore the imprint of freemen, who knew their rights, their liberties, and how to guard them."[12]

Preparations for Thaddeus Stevens's funeral in Lancaster began at five in the morning on August 17. The streets of the city began filling up, as the first of an estimated twenty thousand mourners poured in. The *Inquirer* reporter said the streets were impassable all day. Woodley writes, "In the sultry quiet of that August day, a deep gloom hung impressively over the city."[13] After a small service at Stevens's home, the hearse and ten carriages lined up on South Queen Street for the procession to Shreiner's Cemetery (now Shreiner-Concord Cemetery). Stevens chose Shreiner's for his final resting place because it did not exclude people of color.

Sixteen pallbearers carried Stevens's coffin to the hearse, which was a plain black vehicle drawn by two black horses. Stevens's nephews Thaddeus Stevens Jr. and Dr. Thaddeus Morrill Stevens (from Indianapolis) and Stevens's close friend and confidant Simon Stevens rode in the first carriage behind the hearse. Lydia Hamilton Smith rode in the second with Mr. Patterson, Mrs. Retrauff, and John Sweeney, manager of Stevens's ironworks in Franklin County. The household staff Mrs. Smith managed (the newspaper referred to them as servants and did not name them) occupied the third carriage. In the fourth carriage were Mr. and Mrs. Faroff and their daughters. The *Inquirer* reporter did not record the occupants of carriages five through eight but mentioned that the funeral procession included several Black dignitaries from Philadelphia. They were not identified by name. Perhaps those dignitaries were riding in one of the four middle carriages. In carriage nine, we find the Honorable Simon Cameron, secretary of war under Lincoln at the start of the Civil War. In the last carriage, we find Thomas H. Burrowes, Stevens's good friend and neighbor and an acclaimed educator, and Dr. Henry Carpenter, Stevens's friend and physician, who traveled many miles and spent many long hours, with Mrs. Smith's assistance, trying to keep Congressman Thaddeus Stevens alive.[14]

With church bells tolling across the city, the procession rolled slowly up South Queen Street to Centre Square and turned east on King Street, taking a circuitous route away from its destination on the west side of the city, likely to allow more citizens to salute the fallen statesman. The procession proceeded up King Street to Lime and turned north toward Chestnut Street. At Chestnut, the hearse turned back west, slowly processing past houses draped in mourning to the cemetery at Mulberry Street.[15] By the time the procession reached Shreiner's Cemetery, a relatively small burial ground, mourners of "all ages, sexes, and color" had crowded inside its "rude and dilapidated wooden fence," according to the *Inquirer*. The *Times* estimated no more than a tenth of the thousands gathered could fit inside the enclosure.[16]

The graveside service was conducted by several clerics, one each from the Moravian, Presbyterian, Lutheran, and Episcopal churches. Rev. Jacob Mombert, of Lancaster's St. James Episcopal Church, delivered an address on Stevens's life and service to the nation.[17] The epitaph Stevens wrote for his tomb was meant to remind anyone who saw it of the driving force behind his lifetime of work. It reads:

I repose in this quiet and secluded spot,
Not from any natural preference for solitude,
But finding other cemeteries limited as to race by charter rules,
I have chosen this that I might illustrate in my death
The principles which I advocated
Through a long life:
EQUALITY OF MAN BEFORE HIS CREATOR.

Newspapers and magazines across the country took note of Stevens's passing. Many saluted him as a crusader for equality and justice. *Harper's Weekly* called him "one of the most positive characters this country has had in politics for many years, and the widespread influence which he wielded was due to that particularity of character."[18] Even some Southern newspapers, in reporting his death, called him the "best of the radicals." But some, like the *New Orleans Bee*, couldn't resist referring to him, even in death, as "this malignant old man."[19] But the lowest shot of all may have been fired by the newspaper right up the street from his home. The *Philadelphia Inquirer* noted that the evening Democratic paper in Lancaster went to press, on the day Stevens was buried, "without a word or line of notice of the tributes being laid at the grave of Lancaster's most noted citizen. This was a striking contrast to the respect lately shown at the funeral of ex-President Buchanan by the Republican papers of the city. Can meanness go further!"[20]

Lydia Hamilton Smith returned home from the cemetery on August 17 without the man who had walked beside her for nearly a quarter of a century. We have no written evidence of what she was thinking and feeling that night. As Thaddeus Stevens's companion, she had been part of the great dramas played out in the United States during the nineteenth century. She had taken great risks, working with Stevens and other courageous people who ran the Underground Railroad in Lancaster County and across much of southern Pennsylvania. With Stevens's advice and assistance, she had established herself as a successful businesswoman. Much of the last five or six years she had dedicated to caring for Stevens, as his declining health threatened to derail the important work he was doing in Washington. Was she anxious about facing what she knew could be a cruel and vicious world without her partner? Any ordinary person would have been. But, as we know by now, Mrs. Smith was no ordinary person. She was smart, shrewd, determined, and deeply religious. Perhaps she was counting on those things, and her many friends, to move on without Thaddeus Stevens. She couldn't know, in that grief-stricken moment, that she would need all of them to meet a challenge that lay just ahead. At the center of that challenge stood the man who had denied her wish, and Thad Jr.'s and Simon Stevens's wish as well, to have the Black Butler Zouaves escort Stevens through the streets of Lancaster to his grave—O. J. Dickey.

Dickey was one of three men, all friends and colleagues, whom Stevens asked to serve as executors of his will. Stevens was intimately acquainted with all of them. Dickey worked in Stevens's Lancaster office from 1846 until 1857. He was elected Lancaster County district attorney in 1856 and moved to larger quarters the following year. A. E. Roberts moved to Lancaster from New Holland, Pennsylvania, after he was elected sheriff of Lancaster County. He was appointed US marshal for the Eastern District of Pennsylvania in 1850 and led the platoon of police officers who arrested the defendants in the Christiana Resistance in 1851. Earlier we noted that prosecutors accused him of sympathizing with the prisoners. In 1854, Stevens championed Roberts's successful bid for the congressional seat he himself had lost in 1852. Edward McPherson became an admirer of Stevens and his political views after he moved from Gettysburg to Lancaster to join Stevens's practice. He took his new convictions with him when he moved back to Gettysburg; he was elected to Congress from that district. Stevens had him appointed clerk of the House of Representatives in 1863.[21]

Mrs. Smith's trouble with Thaddeus Stevens's executors began on Wednesday morning, October 28, when she sent Lewis West to fetch executor A. E. Roberts. West, Stevens's former body man in Washington, and his wife, Harriet, now worked for Mrs. Smith. Mrs. Smith still had business in Washington—the lease on Stevens's South B Street house ran through March 1869, and she still owned the horses and carriages that had carried Stevens to and from the House. Shortly after Stevens died, Mrs. Smith had given the executors an itemized bill for funeral expenses, totaling $586.01, that she'd covered with her own money. She summoned Roberts to her home that October morning, hoping he would reimburse her for those expenses before she left for Washington.

Lewis West returned that morning and told Mrs. Smith that Roberts had said he would come "right away." But time passed and Roberts didn't come, so Mrs. Smith sent West back to Roberts. West came back a second time with the report that Roberts had said he would come "after breakfast." More time passed before Roberts finally showed up. West, in Mrs. Smith's later court case, said that when Roberts came in, Mrs. Smith asked him, "Why didn't you come before?" Roberts did not answer her; instead, he turned to West and told him to get grocer Christopher Dice from his store next door. Dice was summoned, along with Jacob Effinger, proprietor of Kleiss's Tavern, on the south side of Stevens's home.[22] West said Roberts handed Mrs. Smith a receipt that she signed before accompanying Roberts to the bank.

Jacob Effinger, another witness in Mrs. Smith's case, told the court that Roberts had asked him to come over to Stevens's house that day (October 28) to witness the payment of money to Mrs. Smith. He said he saw Mrs. Smith sign the paper but didn't know how much money she received or what it was for. Dice testified that he asked what the money was for, and Roberts said "it was for part payment of Mrs. Smith's wages." Note that the bill Mrs. Smith submitted was for funeral expenses, not wages. After she signed, both Dice and Effinger added their signatures to the document.

Mrs. Smith told her own story after Lewis West testified. She was immediately asked by her attorney if she'd read the receipt Roberts brought to her. She admitted she had not, and added, by way of explanation, "I am not a very good hand at reading." If she had taken the time to read the paper Roberts put in front of her, she would have spared herself a great deal of mental and legal anguish, and she would not have signed it. As it was, she told the court "A. E. Roberts did not read the letter marked 'A' J. H. B. [the receipt's court exhibit designation] to me before I signed it." Her next comments reflect the larger claim that took her to court against Thaddeus Stevens's estate. In addition to the itemized funeral expenses, she intended to file a claim for back wages that Stevens had promised her, in front of several witnesses, before he died. We've already heard those people testify about her almost superhuman exertions nursing Stevens in his last six years. We'll hear more from them shortly, but, at this juncture, it is important to know that before October 28th, the executors had somehow learned of Mrs. Smith's intentions. They may have heard it from Mrs. Smith herself, or Simon Stevens, or perhaps someone else who'd been in that second-floor bedroom in Washington and had informed the executors of Stevens's very generous pledge to her. However they became aware, the executors, and apparently O. J. Dickey in particular, were not happy about it. Stevens had already bequeathed Mrs. Smith $5,000 in his will, and they feared she would be asking for thousands more in an upcoming claim. On top of that, there was that provision—Stevens's dream provision—of using $50,000 to endow a practical school for orphans and poor children in Lancaster. Bear all of these things in mind as we listen to the rest of Mrs. Smith's testimony.

After admitting she hadn't read the receipt A. E. Roberts brought to her, nor had it been read to her, Mrs. Smith said, "He did not tell me that it was a release of all demands against the estate except about what was willed to me [the $5,000 legacy]. I did not read it myself. I did not tell him that this receipt was for all demands against the estate except what was willed to me." But, as we already know, Mrs. Smith did sign the document. Then, on the way to the bank, where she expected to receive $586.01 to cover Thaddeus Stevens's funeral expenses, she asked Roberts, "Mr. Roberts when will you pay me my wages?" That sounds as if Mrs. Smith had already asked for the wages Stevens pledged to pay her. We have no exact date for when she submitted a formal request for the money, but when she did, she itemized it. A copy of her "bill," updated to 1875 to reflect nonpayment of the wages for more than seven years after Stevens died, is in Stevens's estate files at the Lancaster County Archives. It reads:

> Estate of Hon. Thad. Stevens dec'd to Lydia
> Smith D[ue]
> To five years services as housekeeper etc of deceased
> extending to a period one year previous to his death
> at 50 dollars per month— $3000.00
> To one year's service as housekeeper of dec'd during
> the last year of his life at 200 dollars per month   2400.00
>   5400.00
> Interest from Aug. 11, 1868 to Nov. 11, 1875
> 7yrs 3 mo.   2349.00
> $7749.00

Mrs. Smith's original request, in 1868, was apparently for $5,400. As she and Roberts walked to the bank on October 28, after she asked about the back wages, she testified that he "said that paper that was signed was that you would not ask for wages." Realizing that something was very wrong, she asked A. E. Roberts, "Why do you treat me this way?" and he replied, "Don't blame me it was Mr. Dickey." When she and Roberts reached the bank, Roberts wrote out a check that read:

> Lancaster, Pa. Oct. 28, 1868
> First National Bank of Lancaster
> Pay to Lydia Smith—on order
> Five hundred and eight six 01/100 dollars

The check did not indicate what the payment was for. With the cash in her pocket, Mrs. Smith left Roberts, but she didn't go straight home. She testified that "on my way back from the bank I ran over to Mr. Dickey's office and said to Mr. Dickey, 'Why do you treat me so?' When he said, 'Do you want to be paid for nursing the old man when he has left you five thousand dollars?'" Mrs. Smith said she responded, "I said I wanted all that was due me and he allowed that I should be paid." According to her, "there was nothing said about the receipt in Mr. Dickey's office." At that point, Lydia testified, the omnibus—a horse-drawn forerunner of the trolley—"was waiting for me to go to Washington and I was obliged to leave."

O. J. Dickey's testimony in the case helps us understand what A. E. Roberts and Dickey were up to that morning. On the stand, he was shown a receipt, dated October 28, 1868, marked "A" J. H. B. (The transcript is a bit difficult to read at this point, but Dickey seems to say Roberts brought a receipt or voucher—marked exhibit "B" J. H. B. in court—to him the morning of the 28th, asking if it would be satisfactory for paying Mrs. Smith's bill.) He testified that the receipt was in his own handwriting and went on to explain how it came to be. "Mr. Roberts came to my office at the time that the will is dated and I said it was a good voucher for the payment of money, but that as Mrs. Smith made a claim for wages we had better settle it all at once." At this point in the record, someone inserted: "Mr. Roberts asked me to draw up a 'marker' that would [word illegible]. It is right to say that Mrs. Smith after Mr. Stevens death claimed that her legacy was independent of her wages and I told her [based] on my conversations of this she could not get both. She always claimed it was on account of her claim for wages that I drew up this receipt in that way."

"I never had any information from Mrs. Smith to draw up the transfer nor on that subject," Dickey said. "She never came to me." The next several words in the transcript are indecipherable. But Dickey's next statement suggests he had assumed the role of chief executor of Thaddeus Stevens's estate. "I told Mr. Roberts not to pay her," he said, "unless she signed the voucher that I drew up."

Two versions of the "receipt" Lydia signed appear in the court record. They testify to Dickey's intention to prevent Lydia from pursuing the back wages Stevens had promised her. One of them, likely the one A. E. Roberts wrote and showed to O. J. Dickey, reads:

Received Lancaster Oct. 28, 1868
from A. E. Roberts + O. J. Dickey—

Executors of the will of Hon. T. Stevens
deceased Five Hundred and eighty six
dollars and one cent **in full of the amount
of the above bill**
Witness M. C. Daicz [Dice] Lydia Smith [emphases mine]

The second version, written by O. J. Dickey, reads:

Lancaster, Oct. 28th 1868
Received of A. E. Roberts & O. J. Dickey, Executors of
Hon. T. Stevens five hundred and eight-six
dollars **in full of all demands on account of
everything except what is willed to her.**
Witness Jacob Effinger [signed] Lydia Smith
W. C. Daicz [Dice]

When Roberts took the stand, he confirmed that it was Dickey's version of the receipt he had pressured Mrs. Smith to sign. He was asked why she made out the bill. He told the court that she demanded to be paid for her claims against the estate, and he had asked her for her terms. She had handed him a memorandum, an itemized bill, he said, with items from which her bill on account was drawn up. He said he had told her he would talk to Dickey. He may have had that conversation with Dickey the morning of October 28; it would explain why he was so long getting to Mrs. Smith's house.

Roberts confirmed that as Dickey wrote out the receipt, he said that if she signed, then she would get no more money. Roberts claimed he told Mrs. Smith that if she signed the receipt she would have no trouble with other claims. He said he told her, "I did not think there would be any trouble for her to obtain payment" for claims not covered by the $586. (That's certainly not what Dickey had just told him.) Roberts said, "I told her the executors were quite willing to pay her every claim that the law allowed her or would allow."

In cross-examining Roberts as he testified, Mrs. Smith's attorney asked him who reviewed exceptions (petitions for actions or payments not explicitly spelled out in a will) to Stevens's will. The executors apparently considered Lydia's request an exception. Roberts didn't answer directly. He said he didn't think Mrs. Smith had presented him with a claim for wages and services. "She made the claim to O. J. Dickey," Roberts said. He then explained that the executors had divided the labor in executing Stevens's will. He said any claims involving money went first to Dickey, who sent the claimants to Roberts if they needed to be paid.

Roberts then shed more light on how the executors, especially Dickey, viewed Mrs. Smith's claims. He said Dickey told him he saw that Mrs. Smith was talking about other claims, and he wanted this one signed by her agreeing to release all other claims beyond her legacy in the will. Apparently, no one had shared that information with her as she innocently sought reimbursement for her expenses. Roberts said he didn't think he told Mrs. Smith about Dickey's condition before she signed the paper. "I don't think I told her before she signed the receipt," he said, "that the effect of the receipt would be to preclude her from [future] collection of her claims for wages or any other claims."

Roberts went on to admit they'd kept Lydia in the dark about all of this. "Mrs. Smith was not present at the conversation between Mr. Dickey and myself," he said, and he repeated his admission that he had not told her the effect that signing the receipt would have on her claims on Stevens's estate. Roberts gave his testimony on August 16, 1875, seven years after Mrs. Smith had first filed her claim with the executors. He had apparently maintained communication with her during that time. He told the court that he had spoken with "Mrs. Smith last night [August 15] on this subject. I told her last night that if she had any claims against his estate not covered by this receipt the executors were willing, anxious and bound to pay it if the law allowed it."

Mrs. Smith's attorney asked Roberts if the previous night's conversation had included telling her that the executors had, so far, paid her nothing for the wages she sought, and that if she had a claim against the estate for wages that it was not covered by the receipt. Roberts replied, "I said to her that as an individual I could see no good reason why she should not be paid for wages if the law could allow it under his will and the receipt she had given." Roberts's next statement may have been an attempt to put some distance between himself and O. J. Dickey. He said, "I think I went a little further and said that *I was quite as willing to pay her all she was entitled to for wages as to create a big fund for building the asylum*" (my emphasis). Roberts's mention of "building the asylum" was, of course, a reference to Stevens's dream of endowing, through his estate, a "refuge for the relief of homeless indigent orphans."[23]

Was Roberts telling us as much about O. J. Dickey as he was about himself with this comment? It would help us understand why Dickey was so adamantly opposed to Mrs. Smith asking for anything from the estate beyond her $5,000 legacy. If Dickey was rejecting claims on Stevens's estate so there would be enough money left for Stevens's dream school, we have to ask why. Did he see some political benefit in it? Announcing such an important project for the community would likely reflect well on the individual making the announcement. Or had Stevens spoken so often and so fondly of the "asylum" in Dickey's presence that he, too, had become dedicated to making it happen? We don't know. But if Dickey saw himself simply as Stevens's executor, doing what Stevens wanted done, then he was either tragically unaware of or willfully in disregard of what Stevens wanted for Lydia Hamilton Smith. Simon Stevens knew, but we don't know whether he shared that information with the executors before October 28, 1868.

Simon Stevens was living in New York City when he was deposed in 1873, but his story took the court back to Washington in 1868, to the second-floor bedroom at 279 South B Street, where he had kept his deathly ill friend Thaddeus Stevens company and assisted him with legal work. We've already heard Simon describe Mrs. Smith's ceaseless labors as Stevens's illnesses took their toll. Since Mrs. Smith was pursuing a claim for back wages against Stevens's estate, Simon was asked to estimate what her care was worth in dollars and cents. "In my judgment," he said, "her services as housekeeper and nurse for the six years previous to Mr. Stevens' death were well worth eight hundred and fifty dollars a year."[24]

Simon was asked if he ever heard Stevens put a value on Mrs. Smith's service. He responded, "On several occasions during the last year of his life, he stated to me in Washington City that Mrs. Smith ought to receive out of his estate at his death five thousand dollars more than he had provided for her in his will." Simon said he heard Stevens tell Mrs. Smith how much he valued her. "In the last few months of Mr. Stevens' life at Washington I heard him speak to Mrs. Smith on several occasions of the value of her services to him particularly when she was washing and dressing him."

Simon said he heard Stevens promise to do right by Mrs. Smith many times. He testified that Stevens "said repeatedly that he would make provision in a new will for paying her five thousand dollars extra to the amount already provided for her in his will and told her that in the event of his not making another will she could receive from his estate six years' services at $50 a month." Stevens turned that promise into an order for Simon to carry out. "He stated to me," Simon said, "that he wished me to draw a new will for him to sign and dictated instructions. Among these instructions was one to prepare an item giving to Mrs. Smith for her service and as a gratuity ten thousand dollars instead of five thousand dollars as named in his former will."

And, according to Simon, Stevens took into account the possibilities that lay ahead. Simon told the court, "On the Saturday previous to his death which occurred the following Tuesday, he told me that in the event of his dying before executing another will, I should see that Mrs. Smith got at least fifty dollars a month for six years previous to his death in addition to the bequest of five thousand dollars given by his will and stated that he was particularly desirous that this should be done for the reason that he had paid her no salary for more than that number of years." Simon testified that Mrs. Smith's well-being was one of the last matters Stevens thought about. "On the next day, Sunday," he said, "Mr. Stevens slept nearly all day and was too weak in the evening to converse about it but said, 'We will attend to that document early Monday morning.' On Monday he was [illegible] and continued sinking, until he died at 12 o'clock Tuesday night." Simon Stevens's testimony extended over two sessions, and in the second session he repeated his understanding of Thaddeus Stevens's wishes with regard to Lydia Hamilton Smith. He said Stevens told him, sometimes with Mrs. Smith present, that "Mrs. Smith's extra care entitled her to five thousand dollars more than he had provided for in his will and that she should have it as a mark of his appreciation of and gratitude for her services to him and his nephew, Thaddeus Stevens, Jr. To carry out that intention," Simon told the court, "Mr. Stevens directed me to prepare a new will as I have already stated." Virtually everyone who had been part of Stevens's household before he died testified (on Mrs. Smith's behalf) that they, too, had heard Stevens assure her that she would be well compensated for her service. And by October 1868, someone, perhaps Mrs. Smith, had told the executors what Stevens wanted to do for her. O. J. Dickey was obviously not prepared, in 1868, to grant Stevens's wish, no matter who testified to the truth of it. Mrs. Smith was not one to accept such rejection meekly. She took action in court to win her wages, and neither race nor gender appears to have held her back. It would be a long and frustrating journey. We'll track the progress of her case in the months (and years) ahead.

On November 17, 1868, the Reverend Jonathan Blanchard was still struggling to reconcile Thaddeus Stevens's involvement with Lydia Hamilton Smith with Stevens's accomplishments as a crusader for equality. It seems likely that Blanchard would have read of Stevens's deathbed baptism by Sister Loretta O'Riley from Providence Hospital, but he took no notice of it in the November 17 issue of his newspaper, the *Christian Cynosure*. Blanchard told his readers he had just returned from a church conference in Marietta, Ohio, where the conversation had apparently touched on Thaddeus Stevens. In that discussion, Blanchard wrote, the noted African Methodist Episcopal (A.M.E.) minister Bishop Daniel Payne had declared, "Mr. Stevens lived with a colored woman as his wife without marrying her."[25] Payne had first met Stevens as a twenty-five-year-old seminary student in Gettysburg in 1837. That was the year Stevens helped Blanchard set up debates in Gettysburg; the topic was slavery. Blanchard, of course, argued against it, and Payne, who would become the first Black Lutheran minister when his seminary studies were completed, also spoke out on the antislavery side. Payne moved to the A.M.E. church in 1841 and led the Philadelphia Vigilance Committee from 1842 to 1843. The Vigilance Committee "provided enslaved black women and men food, clothing, and temporary shelter, and also assisted them in escaping to Canada." Philadelphia's proximity to Lancaster and the Stevens household, as deeply involved in Underground Railroad activity as Payne was, may explain the certainty with which he announced Mrs. Smith's and Stevens's sin. Payne became the first Black American to lead a college when he assumed the presidency of Wilberforce University in Xenia, Ohio, in 1856.[26] He was still there in 1868.

After sharing Bishop Payne's pronouncement with his readers, Blanchard assured them he was only using the word of this "clear-minded, capable man" to confirm his earlier contention that "Mr. Stevens' sin was that of Richard M. Johnson, that is, engaging in sexual relations with a woman to whom he was not married, not that of a Webster, or even of Henry Clay." But, Blanchard insisted, Stevens differed from Johnson, who "[enslaved] the race of his own offspring," while Stevens returned a graveyard plot because the cemetery refused people of color, and after having made the mistake once in his early career as an attorney, never again allowed a fugitive slave to be taken back to slavery.[27]

Blanchard praised Stevens for doing "more to tone up Congress to treat the rebellion as a rebellion than any and all other members of Congress put together," but he couldn't overlook Stevens's "fornication," his intimate relationship with a woman to whom he was not married.[28] Did the fact that Mrs. Smith was a person of color factor into Blanchard's thinking? If she and Stevens had wed, could Blanchard, a lifelong fighter for racial equality, have accepted their interracial marriage? The answer is not clear from his writing in 1868, but it was in 1884, when he wrote about Frederick Douglass's second marriage—to a white woman.

Several years after his first wife had died, Douglass married Helen Pitts, the daughter of a New York abolitionist. In the February 7 issue of the *Christian Cynosure*, Blanchard quoted the Apostle Paul and alluded to Shakespeare as he blessed their union: "This marriage of Douglass is asserting in practice that 'God has made of one blood all nations of men' [Acts 17:26]. This wedding was the funeral of caste; and though people will still ordinarily prefer companions of their own color, no tempest will arise if Desdemona shall love Othello." Blanchard left no room for doubt about what he meant. "This marriage is America's protest and proclamation," he wrote, "against the harems and seraglios of the lethargic caste-ridden nations that Christ's law of marriage (whose complexion was about an average of them all) must wipe out all lines drawn by fingers of caste, that affection is to be left free under law."[29]

In the end, Blanchard chose to relegate sexual matters to the background as he declared Thaddeus Stevens "the most wonderful man of his age. . . . He has not left his peer in his fidelity to human rights combined with ability to defend them." In benediction, Blanchard intoned, "Blessed be he that considereth the poor; the Lord will deliver him in times of trouble, and such, to a sinner, is the time of his death."[30]

CHAPTER 15

MRS. SMITH GOES TO WASHINGTON

Thaddeus Stevens may have dreamed of endowing a "house of refuge" (a school) for "homeless indigent orphans" of all "races and colors," but it was the people and places dearest to his heart that he thought of most as he wrote and signed his will in November 1867. He used $1,000 to create an annual source of income for the Juvenile Library Association in Peacham, Vermont, where he grew up. He gave $500 to the Peacham town cemetery, where his beloved mother, Sarah, and brother Alanson were buried. The money was to be invested and the interest used to keep "the graves in good order and plant roses and other cheerful flowers at each of the four corners of said graves every spring."[1]

To Lydia, Stevens granted an annuity of $500 a year for the rest of her life, with the option, as we've already noted, to take a one-time payment of $5,000 and "release all further claim on my estate." (These are the words on which O. J. Dickey based his rejection of Lydia's claim for wages.) Stevens granted Thad Jr. an annuity of $800 a year, with the added provision that "if by reason of sickness he may need more, he is to have it at the discretion of the trustees." Stevens bequeathed one-time legacies to a number of people, but he instructed his executors that "none of the legacies except the annuities will be paid for three years, during which time the house I now live in [45–47 South Queen Street] and furniture and books will remain as they are."[2]

Stevens was clearly concerned about how Lydia and Thad Jr. would get on after he died. He told the executors, "Mrs. Smith may occupy the house the first year, and if Thaddeus Stevens, (son of Morrill), prefers to keep house to boarding, he may keep house there with her or with any one else during the three years or any part thereof. If at the end of three years Thaddeus Stevens prefers some other mode of living, then the trustees shall dispose of said property as they deem best."[3]

We've already seen Lydia at the house on South Queen Street in the months after Stevens's death, but it's not clear that Thad Jr. was living there. He was helping manage operations at the Caledonia Furnace in Franklin County, but the duration of his work there was uncertain. Stevens had stipulated in his will that "the furnace and all other real estate may be rented or sold. The furnace must not be worked longer than to consume the stock on hand."[4] Before and after the Civil War, when he looked after his uncle's law practice in Lancaster, Thad lived at Shenk's Hotel in the first block of West King Street. He did show up at 45–47 South Queen occasionally, especially as he failed to meet the provision in Stevens's will promising him the entire estate if he gave up drinking. Stevens's provision for endowing "a house of refuge for the relief of homeless indigent orphans" was predicated on Thad Jr.'s failure to stay sober. But the fact that he put Thad first in line to inherit his estate, ahead of his lifelong dream of creating a school where no needy student—"neither poor Germans, Irish or Mohammedans, nor any others on account of race, or color"—would be turned away, suggests that he cared very deeply for his nephew.[5] Of course, Stevens was a practical man who did not entertain delusions. Having watched Thad battle his demon since his academy days, he may have expected him to fail, but in his will, he gave him a chance, nonetheless.

Depending how long Mrs. Smith remained in Washington, in late 1868, she might have been present for the dedication of a new school built by people of color and dedicated in honor of Thaddeus Stevens. Thaddeus Stevens School, still operating today at 1050 Twenty-First Street, NW, was the first public school building in the District of Columbia with "facilities for African Americans considered comparable to those provided for white students." The city's public schools were still segregated at the time.[6] *The Elevator*—a Black-owned San Francisco newspaper—wrote that "no tribute could have been more appropriate nor more grateful to the venerable statesman, who always deemed his labors in behalf of the common school system of Pennsylvania to be the crown of his life."[7]

Late in 1868, O. J. Dickey had begun paying Stevens's creditors. Many of the names are familiar. In October, Dr. Henry Carpenter received $50. Hetty and Jacob Franciscus—part of the household staff Mrs. Smith supervised—drew what may have been their wages. Dickey paid Jacob $8.75 and

Fig. 23 Newspaper Row in Washington, DC, 1873–74. Mrs. Smith's boardinghouse is the four-story, six-bay building just left of the trees in this rendering, occupied at that time by the *New York Tribune* and *New York World*. From *Harper's New Monthly Magazine*, January 1874. National Archives, Washington, DC.

Hetty $10. On September 3, Lydia received $33 in payment for "railroad coupons" (the railroad might have been one of the investments Stevens guided her in making). A year later, on December 15, 1869, Dickey paid Lydia $400 "legacy interest" on her $5,000 legacy from Stevens. Apparently, the legacy had not yet been given to her. Dickey's records show that she also received $100 interest on a "note" Stevens held for her.[8]

Sometime between Stevens's death and the first half of 1870, Lydia Hamilton Smith made a very big decision. Exactly when she made it, we don't know, but when census takers knocked on the door of a boardinghouse at 515 Fourteenth Street in Washington, DC's Fifth Ward on June 24, 1870, the head of the household was Lydia Smith. The census taker put her down as fifty years old; she was actually fifty-seven. She was also listed as "white." The census record gives us some idea of how Lydia was surviving financially. She reported owning $9,000 worth of real estate, which would have included the boardinghouse in DC, property in Lancaster, and possibly the livery service she ran out of Stevens's rented stable on B Street.[9]

Mrs. Smith's boardinghouse was just two blocks from the White House on a street known as Newspaper Row, so called because big city newspapers had their offices there. She was across the street from the famous Willard Hotel, where Ulysses S. Grant coined the term "lobbyist" for the stream of self-promoters who constantly bothered him as he sat in the lobby and enjoyed his cigar and brandy. A Lancaster newspaper article later described Mrs. Smith's house as "genteel lodgings for gentlemen." She reportedly boarded many dignitaries during her boardinghouse years in Washington.[10]

In buying the house on Fourteenth Street, Mrs. Smith graduated from the three-story brick rental property she had built on East Vine Street in Lancaster to a four-story, six-bay structure in Washington. And she had quite a household to look after, right from the start. Counting Mrs. Smith, the census taker tallied ten people living in her new abode, and some of their names are familiar. Lewis West, Stevens's body man, was there, working as a house waiter; his wife, Harriet, was listed as a house servant. Two other women, Theresa Davis and Caroline Johnson, were identified as house servants. And there were several boarders: a young Pennsylvania woman named Annie Davis, who worked in a confectionery (candy store); James Patterson, another Pennsylvanian, who worked as a clerk for the Department of the Interior; and Lot and Leonora Bayless. Lot was recorded as a "PGH Rep," while Leonora was "at home."[11] There was one other Pennsylvanian in the house: Mrs. Smith's son Isaac was there. The census taker put him down as a barber and as white.[12]

Isaac was thirty-three in 1870. He had been making his way in Lancaster as a barber and band leader for some time, with, as we know, a couple of alcohol-fueled wrong turns. We can only wonder whose idea it was for him to accompany his mother to Washington. And that wonder increases when we examine 1870 census records for Lancaster. There we find thirty-three-year-old Isaac Smith, a Black barber, with a yearly income of $150, living at 327 North Street,[13] and he wasn't living alone. According to the record, Isaac had two companions: thirty-year-old Sarah Fillkill, a young Black woman who is listed as "Housekeeper" (the record indicates she was illiterate), and ten-month-old Clara Smith, a Black infant whose relation to Isaac and Sarah is not noted in the record.[14]

Sarah Fillkill's presence in Isaac's home raises several questions. What was her relationship to Isaac? And, if they were "keeping house" together, was baby Clara Smith their child? We don't have ready answers to those questions, but census records tell us something about Sarah. In 1860, twenty-year-old Sarah Fillkill was living with her husband, a free twenty-two-year-old Black man named David Fillkill, in Mercersburg, Franklin

County, Pennsylvania. David owned no property but reported a personal estate of $15.[15]

On May 30, 1864, David, then twenty-seven, was drafted into the Union Army. He was given the rank of private and assigned to Company C of the 45th US Colored Infantry. David didn't serve long. Military records indicate that he "died Aug. 24, 1864 of dysentery, in the Hospital at Camp Casey, Va."[16] Camp Casey was established in Arlington, Virginia, as "an active training ground for hundreds of former slaves willing to take up arms against 'the historic crime of black enslavement.'" But the camp vanished shortly after the war. As recently as 2015, historians were still trying to find it. One historian suggests that Camp Casey might have been located "where the south parking lot of the Pentagon is today."[17] Sarah Fillkill applied for a widow's pension on April 10, 1866. Her husband's regular pay, for his brief time in uniform, amounted to $12.46.[18] We don't know what brought Sarah Fillkill to Isaac Smith's home. And we know little to nothing of little Clara Smith's fate. She does not appear in Isaac's household in the 1880 census record.

In February 1870, the nation officially ratified the Fifteenth Amendment to the US Constitution. It was the third of three Reconstruction Amendments Thaddeus Stevens helped draft; he did not live long enough to shepherd the Fifteenth into law. The Fifteenth Amendment granted all American males, regardless of race, color, or condition of servitude, the right to vote. (It would be another fifty years before women were granted the franchise.) Stevens and other Radical Republicans believed the right to vote was critical if African Americans were to successfully fight off white Southerners' efforts to take away the rights and freedoms they'd only recently won in the Thirteenth and Fourteenth Amendments.[19]

Ratification of the Fifteenth Amendment was cause for celebration in Lancaster. The congregants at Bethel A.M.E. Church organized a day of festivities in April: "Local dignitaries and residents gathered at the church for a service officiated by Reverend [Robert] Boston and featuring James P. Wickersham, principal of the State Normal School at Millersville [Pennsylvania]. A large parade, rejoicing in the African right to vote, was led by delegations from Lancaster City, several nearby townships, and the Stevens Drum Corps."[20] Similar celebrations took place across the nation, including an especially elaborate one in Baltimore. We don't know Mrs. Smith's reaction to all of this. But, if Steven Spielberg's movie *Lincoln* is accurate in showing her celebrating the passage of the

Thirteenth Amendment with Stevens, then ratification of the Fifteenth would have pleased her as well.

In his will, Thaddeus Stevens had directed his executors that "none of the legacies except the annuities will be paid for three years." Lydia made her choice—$5,000 all at once rather than $500 a year—clear to the executors early on. That put her in the legacy rather than annuity category. In observance of Stevens's three-year rule for legacies, O. J. Dickey held off on paying Mrs. Smith until 1871. That year, on behalf of Thaddeus Stevens and his estate, Dickey handed her the sizable sum of $5,000. Estate records indicate the money was "paid by assignment of $5,000 of a mortgage of Jeremiah McElligott to O. J. Dickey." In turn, Dickey passed the cash to Mrs. Smith. Accountants reviewing the transaction later wrote, "Assignment of the same interest of $5,000 to Lydia Smith was made May 5, 1871."[21] Despite spending the majority of her time in Washington, Mrs. Smith was still pressing for her back wages in Lancaster. Dickey remained adamantly opposed to paying them.

Mrs. Smith continued investing in real estate in 1871. On July 8, she bought a house from Henry Lossner on North Street in Lancaster, the street where Isaac was living in 1870. We know the deed number of her new house—C-10-274—but not the address.[22] It might have been 327 North Street, the house Isaac was renting the year before. As it turned out, Isaac didn't stay on North Street. The 1871 edition of the Lancaster city directory shows him living at 227 Middle Street.[23]

A number of real estate transactions took place on Lot 134 (the property Stevens purchased at sheriff's sale in 1843), at the northeast corner of South Queen and East Vine Streets, in November 1871. On November 8, as Stevens's executors began selling some of his properties, Jacob Effinger bought "the two-story brick dwelling house and grounds at South Queen and Vine Streets"—the former Kleiss Brewery—for $5,000. That same day, Mrs. Smith (identified in the record as being from Washington, DC) sold Effinger a small strip of land behind the tavern, extending to Queen Street, for $1.00. In turn, Effinger deeded to Mrs. Smith a small strip of land between the tavern and Lydia's rental property on East Vine Street.[24]

Despite the responsibilities of running a boardinghouse in DC (and whatever other business interests she may have had) and managing her properties in Lancaster, Mrs. Smith kept up the friendships she had forged during her years with Thaddeus Stevens. We have a window into those relationships through a letter she wrote to a friend; it may have been Kate

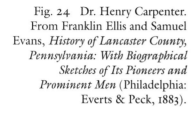
Fig. 24 Dr. Henry Carpenter.
From Franklin Ellis and Samuel
Evans, *History of Lancaster County,
Pennsylvania: With Biographical
Sketches of Its Pioneers and
Prominent Men* (Philadelphia:
Everts & Peck, 1883).

Mathiot McKinney, to whom she had written after attending her wedding at Dr. Henry Carpenter's home in 1868. The letter is undated, but its contents strongly suggest that Mrs. Smith wrote it sometime in 1871 or 1872. The letter appears to reference the death of Dr. Carpenter's second wife, Laura Miller Carpenter, who died in 1871 at the age of thirty-five, leaving Carpenter's three daughters motherless again.

Mrs. Smith began the letter inquiring about her friend's journey home, perhaps after a visit in Washington. After her marriage, Kate moved to her husband's home in Jersey Shore, a small town in north-central Pennsylvania, west of Williamsport. Wherever her friend lived, getting there was apparently a bit difficult. Mrs. Smith wrote, "I have bin verry anxious to know how you got home and how you are now. I have felt your pains quite keen, when I think of you having to ride over that ruff road." She added that she had "a lady and gentleman boarding with me that know the Dr. McKinney. She is from hagerstown, a very fine family. His [illegible] man—G Baker and hers is a cousin to Elliot down in Lancaster, the old Batch."[25]

Then Lydia Hamilton Smith, the human dynamo, confessed to her friend that time was taking its toll on her. (She was then fifty-eight years old.) "I am suffering with the heat it is very hot hear today," she wrote, "and I am so tierd of boarding hous keeping when ever this hot weather gets here I am not as strong as I wanst was and am less abel to work and I feal it Evry day and see the folly of working so hard but it seams that I cannot get Red of it."[26] Her thoughts subsequently turned to the loss in

Lancaster. "I think of our Dear friend Mrs. Carpenter [handwriting unclear, possibly "Cospint"] almost Evry day sins hir death," she told Kate. "I cannot Realize hir death. It seems to me that she must come back. It will seam verry strang to me to go thair and not see you nor hir thair with the children. It looks lonely [lovly?] when we think of it I hop the young ladies will keep good health and be A comfort to thair father."[27]

As she closed, Mrs. Smith talked a little business with her friend. She wrote, "I see Mrs. Whitehall boards quite near to me and was talking of coming to board The lady she boards with told me but she got some one to com in and keep hir borders to gether while she went north during the sumer and I am trying to do the same—pleas write me soon and lett me know how you are. Your friend Lydia Smith." There would be no reprieve from "boarding house keeping."[28] Mrs. Smith operated the boardinghouse on Fourteenth Street for the rest of her life.

Sometime during these years (we don't know exactly when), she added three or four houses on South Water Street in Lancaster to her portfolio. And on April 8, 1873, she added one more house, the one she shared with Thaddeus Stevens for a decade: 45–47 South Queen Street.[29] Accounts filed by Stevens's executors in proceedings related to her claim for wages indicate "Amount received fr. Mrs. Smith for the house and lot on South Queen Street—$7,320.00." The next line in the account reads: "Account interest fr. Mrs. Smith $549.00."[30] Mrs. Smith now owned the house where she had made a home for Stevens and cared for him in his illness. Not to read too much into it, but we should note that when she rented out her new property on South Queen Street, she reserved two rooms for her own use when she came to town—Thaddeus Stevens's bedroom and the adjoining library.[31] In the spirit of Steven Spielberg's portrayal of Stevens and Mrs. Smith in their Washington home, I am inclined to believe that she chose those rooms in Lancaster for quite personal reasons.

CHAPTER 16

MRS. SMITH VERSUS THE EXECUTORS

It's safe to assume that in her dealings with Stevens's executors—receiving the $5,000 legacy Stevens bequeathed to her and purchasing his house on South Queen Street—Mrs. Smith kept repeating her demand for the back wages Stevens promised her shortly before he died. If O. J. Dickey thought his deceitful trick with the receipt for payment of Stevens's funeral expenses had slammed the door on her claim, he didn't know Lydia Hamilton Smith.

As she pursued her claim, the executors continued to ask the same question Dickey had hurled at her in his office on October 28, 1868: Thaddeus Stevens left you $5,000, so are you "due anymore?" Mrs. Smith always insisted that her claim for wages was a separate matter from the legacy Stevens had left her. The executors, claiming her request had been "very carefully considered," used Stevens's own words, from his will, to deny that. Stevens "declares his intention in the clause bequeathing the legacy," they argued, especially the portion stipulating that, after choosing which way she wanted to receive her legacy, Mrs. Smith would "then release all further claims on my estate." The executors cited other cases to buttress their argument, and always concluded, "She herself has made her choice, and having made it is estopped from making more [money]. The claim is," they said, "therefore disallowed."[1]

On May 20, 1873, five years after Stevens's death, Mrs. Smith asked the court to order Stevens's executors—A. E. Roberts, O. J. Dickey, and Edward McPherson—to "file an account" of the financial status of Stevens's estate. In the petition, Mrs. Smith's lawyers pointed out that in January 1871, the executors had reported that Stevens's personal estate (cash in hand) amounted to a whopping $48,616.25. Yet in May 1872, as Mrs. Smith pursued her wages, McPherson reported that Stevens's estate was down to just $1,486.32 in cash, and they'd not yet paid out any legacies. Dickey and Roberts pointed to McPherson's tally and said "her [Mrs. Smith's] claim against the estate greatly exceeds the balance of the account filed by Mr. McPherson." (Lydia's initial claim, you may recall, was for $5,400 in back wages. It eventually reached $7,749, as she added interest for years of nonpayment.)

Roberts and Dickey stood firm. They responded to Mrs. Smith's petition with four points:

> 1st That the petitioner is not a creditor of the estate. 2. That all her claims or demands against the estate have been paid. 3. Stating the bequest to her under the will, of an annuity of $500 per annum, for life, or a gross sum of $5,000; her election to take the $5,000, and its payment. And 4th. Stating her rights under the will to take furniture and its delivery to her.[2]

Dickey showed no sign of budging from his earlier position.

After hearing testimony from witnesses Mrs. Smith called, including Simon Stevens (the executors called no witnesses), Judge John B. Livingston ruled in her favor, but he qualified his opinion. Livingston acknowledged that "a considerable amount of testimony has been taken on behalf of the claimant by which she attempts to show that she has a claim against the Estate for Services rendered, above, beyond, and exclusive of the legacy given her by the will." Livingston acknowledged that Mrs. Smith claimed "the testator [Thaddeus Stevens] recognized this claim, and stated that she was entitled to it, in addition to what was given her by him, in and by the will." Livingston noted that the executors had not called a single witness to refute any of the testimony Mrs. Smith had produced.[3]

Then the judge expressed some doubt about the approach Mrs. Smith and her attorneys had taken in pursuing her claim.

> Without at this time expressing any opinion as to the validity of her claim or whether she will ultimately be entitled to recover the same or any portion thereof (*which would be a very unusual thing upon a citation to executors to file an account*) we are of opinion that the petitioner has produced testimony sufficient at least to require us to call upon

the executors to file an account, and if it shall appear that they have a balance in hand in favoring the estate, she will have the privilege of presenting her claim to a board of auditors to be examined and passed upon, after a full hearing in the usual manner; & she may bring an action against the executors, and have her claim submitted to a jury.[4]

The judge seemed to suggest, without taking sides, that Mrs. Stevens wasn't punching hard enough and should have sued Stevens's estate from the start. But he granted her request, ordering Dickey and Roberts to "prepare and exhibit their account or accounts on the estate of said decedent so far as the same has come to their hands and been settled and disposed of by them" by November 10, 1874.[5]

The witnesses Judge Livingston heard from are already familiar to us. They were all part of Stevens's and Mrs. Smith's households in Lancaster and Washington or were present there on a regular basis: John B. Warfel, Jacob Keneagy, Hetty Franciscus, Catharine Effinger, Dr. Henry Carpenter, Jacob Effinger, William Dice, Lewis West, Simon Stevens, and Dr. Noble Young. We've already heard them describe Mrs. Smith's arduous task of caring for Thaddeus Stevens as his health declined. On the stand, Lewis West testified, "I heard Mr. Stevens tell Mrs. Smith frequently to make out her bill; that she would be paid for all her services. I heard him say so, during Mr. Stevens' last illness, when she was dressing him in the morning. It was at his house on Capitol Hill and also at Lancaster." Stevens's "last illness" came *after* he wrote and signed his will in 1867. West's testimony appeared to throw Dickey's argument—that the will was Stevens's last word on the subject—in doubt.[6]

When asked what compensation they thought Mrs. Smith deserved for her service, the witnesses all said she deserved to be well paid for her dedicated labor. They swore she deserved anywhere from $50 to $200 a month from Stevens's estate for the last six years of his life. Mrs. Smith was seeking wages only for the last years of Stevens's life, even though we've already heard him admit that he neglected to pay her after their first few years together. The irrefutable fact is that Thaddeus Stevens, himself, had set the terms of her claim. Six years was the period of time he dictated to Simon Stevens, in his final hours, as he fretted about Mrs. Smith being properly thanked and compensated. And Simon, no doubt, communicated that to Mrs. Smith, or Stevens might have told her himself.[7] Those wages, or a doubling of her legacy, were as much a part of

Thaddeus Stevens's final wishes as any other provision in his will. And they were sworn to by his close friend and fellow attorney Simon Stevens. Nonetheless, the executors persisted in their efforts to prevent Mrs. Smith from claiming them.

She had more than her claim for wages to keep her busy when she returned to Lancaster. She had decided to rent out the house on South Queen Street as soon as she purchased it. By 1878, she was renting to a man named George Heiss. Judge Landis, in his defense of Mrs. Smith and Stevens, noted that Heiss had rented the "old Stevens mansion." Landis said "Mr. Heiss was, in his day, a prominent tobacco dealer, and, for several years, 3rd Ward Council member." Heiss would be the last tenant at 45–47 South Queen Street with whom Mrs. Smith dealt.[8]

There was sad news for the extended Stevens-Smith family in 1873, but there's no evidence that Mrs. Smith was made aware of it. Alanson Stevens's second child by Mary Primm, Jennie, died. Mary Primm had moved on from Caledonia Forge by then. She was twenty-eight years old and living with a new husband, a man named Kauffman, at Monroe Forge in Lebanon County, Pennsylvania, three counties east of the Caledonia Furnace, where she had met Alanson. An old friend of Mary's, Elizabeth Alwine, later said that Jennie died on August 21 or 22. Testifying in 1892, Alwine said, "I remember the day Jennie took sick just as well now as the day it happened." Alwine said that Jennie was definitely not Mr. Kauffman's daughter; she "went by Jennie Stevens" and was identified as Jennie Stevens at her funeral. Mrs. Smith had tried to assist Mary Primm in getting Jennie into a school in Lancaster in 1866.[9]

Alwine said that Jennie went quickly: "In the morning, Jennie went along with me to see my folks, and in the afternoon of the same day she took sick and died of that sickness." Jennie was buried in Fredericksburg, Lebanon County. She was eleven years and four months old.[10] There's no evidence that Thad Jr., who had become executor of his brother's estate, was informed that Alanson's child had died. Mrs. Smith had contacted Thad about Jennie when Mary Primm brought her to Lancaster, but he had not replied.

In another sad note in 1873, Lydia's son Isaac appeared in criminal court records again. A Lancaster County grand jury indicted him for larceny. According to court documents, Isaac Smith—alias Thomas Deitz—and three other men stole "a lot of pears of the value of five dollars" from Jacob Eshelman on August 17th. Eshelman produced four witnesses, two of them apparently relatives, to back up his claim. For some reason, the district attorney dropped the charge.[11] The most intriguing aspect of this episode is that Isaac was now using an alias—Thomas Dietz. Deitz, also spelled Dice, was the last name of Mrs. Smith's and Stevens's neighbor, the grocer Christopher Dice. Dice witnessed the bogus receipt O. J. Dickey and A. E. Roberts forced Mrs. Smith to sign in 1868. That might explain where Isaac got the name, but why would he choose to use an alias at all?

Lydia's other "son," Thaddeus Stevens Jr., was in real trouble by 1873. His uncle had made ample provision for him in his will. In addition to the enticement of inheriting the whole Stevens estate if he stopped drinking, Stevens gave "Capt. Thaddeus Stevens, now at Caledonia, my gold watch; I give to my nephew, Capt. Thaddeus Stevens, eight hundred dollars a year, to be paid half yearly." Thad must have been exhibiting signs of ill health when Stevens wrote his will in 1867. After spelling out Thad's annuity, he added, "If by reason of sickness he may need more, he is to have it at the discretion of the trustees."[12]

Thad drew regularly and heavily on his $800 annuity, and O. J. Dickey wrote him checks without hesitation. In 1869, Thad drew $1,260 from Stevens's estate, and then smaller annual amounts in 1870, '71, '72, and '73. R. W. Shenk, the executor of Thad Jr.'s estate, reported later that Dickey "had paid Thaddeus Stevens, Jr., nearly all, if not all, of the annuities coming to him under the will of his uncle."[13] The accounts Shenk compiled from Dickey's records suggest that Thad's finances had, in fact, gone into the red. The last entry in Shenk's ledger was for a loan of $25 in late 1873 or early 1874.

We know Thad spent most of his time in these years in Franklin County, looking after his uncle's ironworks. But he was drinking heavily and began showing up in Lancaster in distressing condition. When that happened, the call went out for Mrs. Smith. And, despite her many responsibilities in Washington, she came. According to those who were there, she cared for Thad as faithfully as she had his uncle, just a few short years before, in the house she had shared with Thaddeus Stevens and purchased in 1873.

Jacob Effinger, proprietor of the tavern next door, testified in Mrs. Smith's legal efforts to recover from Stevens's executors her expenses in caring for Thad Jr., saying that Mrs. Smith took care of Thad "when he was sick . . . off and on for several years. She took him over to her own house. He was so sick he could not help himself." Effinger expressed his personal distaste for Lydia's task. "It was a disagreeable job," he said.

"Persons would not come to my house [the tavern] when he was there. Some customers left he was so dirty." Effinger's account was quite explicit: "He had human filth on him." And he commended Mrs. Smith's dedication to this young man she had treated like a son. "She was sent for when we could do nothing for him. She had more control over him than anybody else. She was in Washington, D.C. sometimes when we sent for her; she always came when we sent for her. She came from Washington at least a half a dozen times." Effinger said Mrs. Smith's care of Thad was comprehensive. "When he was at her place she nursed him, boarded him and he slept there. She would get a doctor for him. I don't believe there were many persons who could attend to him."[14]

John P. Schaum, another witness in Mrs. Smith's case over Thad Jr., confirmed Effinger's account and added, "I saw T. Stevens Jr. brought into Dr. King's office, which was in Mrs. Smith's house; he was sick and completely exhausted from dissipation, he was undressed there, he was very dirty and filthy, it was too dirty a job for me and I left the room." He, too, thought Mrs. Smith was an extraordinary person. "Some people," he said, "would not have attended to him under any circumstances." Hetty Franciscus was living in Stevens's house in 1869. She remembered Thad showing up in rough shape. Franciscus said that Mrs. Smith was summoned from Washington several times in that year alone. She said Thad "was there sick a half a dozen times during the year I was there. He was there sick two and three weeks at a time, she would nurse him, provide for him and would have to wash him like a child." Franciscus said Lydia met all of Thad's needs. "She furnished bed, bedclothes, fire and everything for him. When he was sick he was helpless. When he was able to get out again she would take him along with her often take him to the depot buy his ticket and start him off to his place of business at the Caledonia Furnace." Hetty said she never saw Thad give Mrs. Smith any money for her care. "I don't suppose he had any when he came," she said. "I suppose Mrs. Smith had to furnish him money. I don't believe there are many persons who would attend to him."[15]

Railroad ticket agent W. F. Hambright testified to Mrs. Smith's generosity toward Thad. "I recollect of selling at different times tickets to Harrisburg, Chambersburg, Baltimore and Washington, D.C. to Mrs. Smith. She usually purchased two, one to either Harrisburg or Chambersburg and one to either Baltimore or Washington." Hambright had kept an informal tally of her visits to the depot with Thad in tow. "Mrs. Smith may have purchased tickets according to recollection a dozen times more or less." Hambright said that was just the number of tickets he sold Mrs. Smith. He thought his father, also an agent, had likely sold tickets to her and Thad during his shift. Hambright said each ticket to Harrisburg cost $1.10; at that time, a ride to Chambersburg was $2.50.[16]

Last to testify in the Thad Jr. proceedings was Dr. George A. King, who rented the space at 45–47 South Queen, where Thaddeus Stevens had his law office. Dr. King testified that Mrs. Smith reserved two rooms in what was then her house for Thad. "He would come home drunk and completely debauched," Dr. King said. "Would often be in a very filthy condition. When in this way he would have to have sanitary care as well as professional attention." Thad was still in his thirties at the time, but King said his drinking was exacting a heavy toll. "When brought home in this condition," he said, "he would have to remain there from three days to a week on the average." And, as she had done with his uncle, Mrs. Smith sat by Thad's bedside. "Mrs. Smith always cared for him. Sometimes she would have to have assistance. He would have to be washed and completely cleaned. He came there in a filthy condition and always went away very clean and neat to the best of my knowledge." Even the good doctor admitted being a bit repulsed by the state Thad was in when he arrived at Mrs. Smith's door: "You could hardly get any person to take care of him, because he was in such a filthy condition. This happened about half a dozen times a year."[17]

Dr. King then offered details the other witnesses had not mentioned. "On one occasion," King said, "Mr. Dickey, one of the Ex'ors [executors] of Hon. T. Stevens, sent for me and told me not to pay any rent to Thaddeus back to him as Thaddeus was in no condition to receive rent when he came there [between 1869 and 1873], and also that Smith should fix him up and send him off that night, meaning near Gettysburg. Mrs. Smith would have to provide for him and give him her personal care and attention while he was here." O. J. Dickey may not have intended any disrespect toward Mrs. Smith in his conversation with Dr. King, but referring to a sixty-year-old widow only by her last name seems a bit rude when measured by the social standards of his time. It seems unlikely that Thaddeus Stevens, with his insistence that Mrs. Smith be addressed respectfully, would have approved of Dickey's language.[18]

Dr. King and the others were called to testify about the value of Mrs. Smith's care for Thad Jr., and King spoke directly to the point. He said,

"I would not have cared for him as she did for $100 a week. She came from Washington, D.C. on several occasions to my own personal knowledge to take charge of T. Stevens, Jr. and when he was ready to go, she would leave town with him, except for one or two occasions. He was always broke when he came to Mrs. Smith's. It seemed from conversation I had with Mr. Dickey, that it was understood that Mrs. Smith was to take care of Thaddeus. He had no one else to take [care] of him, nor he did not want any one else to take care of him, he would always say wait till Smith comes."[19]

Five years beyond the death of his uncle was all Thad got. Unable to shed his addiction to alcohol, and ravaged by its effects, Thaddeus Stevens Jr. died on April 1, 1874. The demon he'd been fighting since prep school had won. Court records show he "died insolvent," and in fact, his executor had to petition his uncle's estate for $1,013.85 to pay his debts. The executor said that all of the debts "were due to illness." One of them was the bill from Mrs. Smith, who asked for $350 to cover her expenses in caring for Thad in his final years.[20] Captain Thaddeus Stevens was buried beside his uncle's tomb in Shreiner's Cemetery in Lancaster. He was thirty-nine years old.

Mrs. Smith returned to Washington after Thad's funeral, while her claim for back wages inched forward in court. By 1875, O. J. Dickey and A. E. Roberts had presented their accounts of Stevens's estate. Lydia's claim had not excited much press attention until then, but when the court appointed three auditors to review the executors' work, the *Gettysburg Times* took notice. In its June 17, 1875, edition, the paper reported: "An account filed at Lancaster by the Executors of Hon. Thaddeus Stevens is now in the hands of the auditors. Lydia Smith, his housekeeper, received $5,000 by Mr. Stevens' will, but she now puts in a claim as wages for services rendered him during the last six years of his life, at the rate of $200 per month, or $14,400 in the aggregate."[21]

The paper had the numbers wrong. As we've already seen, Mrs. Smith's claim, with interest, totaled $7,749. The paper slanted its coverage of her action, pointing out the amount of her legacy and following that with "but she now puts in a claim as wages for services rendered." The paper made sure to point out "the claim will be contested. The amount in the executor's hands is $16,339.36, with the Caledonia property unsold." The paper's readers likely would have known that Stevens owned thousands of acres in Franklin County. If the paper was suggesting that Lydia was "robbing the bank," it was a weak argument. When all of Stevens's properties had been disposed of, the executors reported the "total realized from the corpus of the estate [was] $116,663.63."[22] Many years would pass before anyone else mentioned Mrs. Smith's case publicly, and then it was just a passing reference. In talking about a portrait of Lydia, historian W. U. Hensel touched on her relationship to Stevens. He noted that when Stevens died, "she was not without the vigor to prosecute a claim against his estate."[23]

The auditors completed their review of the executors' work and submitted it to the court for review. But O. J. Dickey wasn't around to hear the verdict. He died on April 21, 1876, of typhoid pneumonia in Lancaster. The obituary in the *Lebanon Daily News* was brief but highly complimentary. It mentioned Dickey's time as Thaddeus Stevens's law partner and a two-term congressman and reported that "as a good, sound and trusted legal adviser his reputation was great." "He appeared before our courts [in Lebanon] on several occasions," the paper noted, "and made a favorable impression in this community. There are other men whose death at this time could be better spared."[24] O. J. Dickey was fifty-three when he died. His passing left A. E. Roberts and Edward McPherson to await the outcome of Mrs. Smith's case, without the man who was, from the beginning, the driving force behind their efforts to deny her claim.

In the middle of January 1876, Mrs. Smith sold a piece of property. Deed indexes don't describe the property, but the buyer was the Quarryville Branch of the Lancaster and Reading Narrow Gauge Rail Road Company. That transaction took place on January 14. In May, on the eve of the International Exhibition of Arts, Manufacturers and Products of the Soil and Mine—more commonly known as the nation's Centennial celebration—Mrs. Smith opened a boardinghouse in Philadelphia and offered lodging to visitors who attended the six-month-long event. Her friend and physician Dr. Henry Carpenter noted in his records that he loaned her $25 on May 5, as she was starting her boardinghouse in Philadelphia. Carpenter's memorandum indicated he helped oversee her business interests in Lancaster (mostly paying taxes and house maintenance expenses) from at least 1875 to 1881.[25]

The Centennial opened on May 10. Like most of Mrs. Smith's business ventures, her new boardinghouse did well. The *Lancaster Intelligencer* wrote later that "she conducted a large boarding house in Philadelphia [in 1876], where she was also very successful."[26]

The final ruling in Mrs. Smith's claim for back wages arrived just before Christmas. Because O. J. Dickey had determined that Mrs. Smith was "not a creditor of the estate," her bill for back wages now fell into the category of an "exception," that is, a request that the executors suspend the rules with regard to Stevens's will. She was asking for special consideration, arguing that the usual rules for executing a will didn't apply in her case. All of her efforts, in and out of court, were an attempt to demonstrate to O. J. Dickey, A. E. Roberts, and Edward McPherson that the language in Stevens's will about her legacy was not the last expression of his intentions toward her.

She knew what Stevens had promised her, and so did many other members of their household. And she knew that Stevens had tried, too late as it turned out, to rewrite his will to express his immense gratitude for her caring presence in his life, and barring that, to be sure she was, at least, well compensated for her many labors. She was, in a sense, simply repeating the question she had asked A. E. Roberts on the street, and O. J. Dickey in his office, on October 28, 1868: "Why do you treat me this way?"

Her pleas—and all the testimony she presented to support them— were in vain. On December 21, 1876, Judge D. W. Patterson ruled that he found "no apparent clear mistakes in the auditor's findings, and the "exceptions [were] overruled and [the] report of [the] auditors confirmed."[27] It comes as no surprise that Lydia Hamilton Smith did not accept what she must have seen as an unfair and unjust decision. On January 22, 1877, Lydia appealed the ruling to the Pennsylvania Supreme Court. Her filing reads: "Lydia Smith, being aggrieved by the definitive decree of said court [Orphans Court of Lancaster County] in the above case, appeals from the same to the Supreme Court." By May, the court had made its decision.[28]

Responding to the Orphans Court of Lancaster County, where Mrs. Smith filed her appeal, the justices wrote, "A record was brought into [the Supreme Court] upon appeal by Lydia Smith from your decree made in the matter of the distribution of the balance in the hands of Oliver J. Dickey Edward McPherson & Anthony E. Roberts, Exec. [executors] of Hon. Thaddeus Stevens rejecting the claim of Lydia Smith a creditor of the said deceased overruling her exception to the auditor's report—And it was so proceeded in our Supreme Court, that the following decree was made, to wit: May 21, 1877: Decree affirmed with costs and appeal dismissed. Witness: The Hon. Daniel Agnew LLD Chief Justice of our Supreme Court at Harrisburg, the 24th day of May in the year of our Lord, one thousand eight hundred and seventy-seven."[29] O. J. Dickey had won, and one of Thaddeus Stevens's dreams—his deathbed wish to show, through a legacy, how grateful he was to Mrs. Smith for all of her love and care—was denied by the trusted colleagues he appointed to carry out his last wishes.

CHAPTER 17

An Elderly Businesswoman

In 1877, Dr. Henry Carpenter married for the third time. We have no written record of it, but Lydia Hamilton Smith was almost certainly there on May 8 when Dr. Carpenter married Sarah A. Billings Boardman. Carpenter was then fifty-seven; Sarah was thirty-five and a widow with three sons, fifteen-year-old Walter, eleven-year-old Arthur, and nine-year-old Harry. Carpenter's daughters, Mary, Kate, and Sarah, the young ladies Mrs. Smith was so fond of, had come of age by 1877. Mary was twenty-eight, Kate was twenty-six, and Sarah was twenty-two.[1]

On February 14, 1878, Mrs. Smith observed her sixty-fifth birthday. She had come a long, long way from her humble beginnings at Russell Tavern. Through a combination of intelligence, business savvy, boundless energy, and advice from her companion and confidant, Thaddeus Stevens, she had built up a considerable estate. At the same time, she had made herself available to Stevens as well as her sons, William and Isaac; Stevens's nephews Alanson and Thad Jr.; wounded survivors of the Battle of Gettysburg; and even the "widow" Mary Primm and her daughter Alanson Jane, as well as many friends and acquaintances. In the face of myriad obstacles and the condemnations of a racist and sexist society, she had shown herself to be a tower of strength and determination. But time was taking its toll. We've heard her confess to her friend Kate, in the early 1870s, that sometimes it all seemed like too much. The fact was that her health had changed direction. By the late 1870s, Lydia Hamilton Smith was forced to slow down.

Mrs. Smith's tenant on South Queen Street, George Heiss, witnessed it. He testified later that Mrs. Smith "came to Lancaster about once every three months and stopped from three days to a week each time—boarding with me." (Heiss billed her estate $50 for her use of Thaddeus Stevens's former bedroom and library.) "She said I should be paid for it," Heiss said. "This was for six years previous to her death. . . . Many times she was sick there that my daughters took her meals up to her room." Mrs. Smith had also asked Heiss to look out for her son Isaac. Heiss talked about the arrangement: "The money I loaned to Isaac and the provisions I furnished to Isaac and his family she promised to pay for. The order was given to me and they were taken off when I settled with her for the rent." Heiss apparently did some maintenance work on Mrs. Smith's houses, too. "I do not have the bill for repairing the porch," he testified. "I have no written order in which she said I should let Isaac have the money. She had always paid me for these items." Mrs. Smith's arrangement with Heiss extended to the end of her life. "The charge of $5.00 for moving Isaac," he told the auditors, "is for moving Isaac's furniture after the death of Mrs. Smith and before the death of Isaac."[2]

While every penny counted in Mrs. Smith's day (every bit as much as, if not more so, than today), it's striking to note how the people in her world related to each other in terms of finances. George Heiss testified to the fact that he stepped in to look after Lydia's struggling son on the strength of her assurance that he would be reimbursed for it—and he would be called on to do even more for Mrs. Smith in the future. We've already seen that Dr. Carpenter did the same thing after Stevens's death. American society may have been stretched to the breaking point by slavery and residual racism, but among friends, and even among more casual acquaintances, there was a sense of trust and respect that doesn't always shine through financial dealings, even family ones, in the twenty-first century.

In 1879, friendship might have played a role in Lydia's decision to sell a house she owned to Lewis (and Harriet) West. It was at 414 South Water Street, one of several she owned there.[3] The Wests had been part of the Stevens-Smith entourage for more than a decade by then. When Lewis West was no longer needed as Thaddeus Stevens's body man, the couple stayed on with Mrs. Smith, working for her in Washington and Lancaster. They were both about forty years old in 1879.

Lancaster's Bethel A.M.E. Church, where a drunken Isaac Smith disrupted a service in 1867, was hit by arsonists in April 1879. The Shiffler Fire Company, the hose company Isaac and his brother, William, helped found, responded quickly and the structure was saved. Bethel historians, writing later, describe the attack as "an unwelcome reminder of the price of freedom for Lancaster's African community."[4]

By 1879, Isaac was back on North Street in Lancaster and heading for more trouble. The Lancaster city directory for that year shows him living at 327 North Street (possibly the house Lydia bought in 1871) and operating a "shaving saloon" at 47 South Queen Street (the side of the house that had formerly served as Thaddeus Stevens's law office).[5] One block over from North Street was Middle Street, later renamed Howard Avenue. Lydia's cousin Anna Sulkey Martin, the young woman credited with recommending Lydia to Thaddeus Stevens, lived at 323 Middle Street with her husband, Dennis (also a barber); a son, Theodore, a thirty-year-old widower; and Theodore's two daughters, eight-year-old Serena and five-year-old Margaret.

Next door to the Martins, at 325 Middle Street, lived Polly Williams, an eighty-six-year-old widow working as a "washer woman." Thirty-year-old Horace Reynolds, a hod carrier, and his twenty-four-year-old wife, Emma, a housekeeper, were living with Mrs. Williams, as was her great-granddaughter, eight-year-old Kate Archie, and her eighteen-year-old granddaughter, Mary Taylor, who was "at home."[6] Isaac likely knew most, if not all, of these people. His "trouble" would involve one of them—Mary Taylor.

Isaac was forty-two years old in 1879 and married to Sarah Fillkill, who was now forty-one. When census takers canvased the neighborhood the following year, they recorded the presence of the couple's five-year-old son, David. There was no mention of Clara Smith, the ten-month-old infant noted as part of Isaac and Sarah's household in 1870. A seventy-one-year-old widow named Susan Ashton, identified as Sarah's mother, was also living at 327 North Street in 1879, as were thirty-two-year-old Jennie Walker and twenty-five-year-old Alice Williams, both listed as "washer women."[7]

Isaac seemed to have himself and his life under control by then, which makes what happened on Sunday, December 7, that much more difficult to understand. On December 8, before Alderman H. R. McConomy, eighteen-year-old Mary Taylor charged Isaac Smith with assault and battery, the most serious charge he had faced in his frequently troubled life. The indictment handed down by the grand jury in January said Isaac "did beat, wound and ill-treat, and other wrongs to her . . . and there did, to the great damage of her the said Mary Taylor." The grand jury heard from six witnesses: Mary Taylor, Brink Carter, John Hood, Nathaniel Drapper, Emma Archey, and Lydia Pinkerton. Isaac was free on $200 bail when the grand jury voted to try him on the assault and battery charge. On January

23, 1880, before the trial started, Isaac pleaded guilty. Court records do not indicate what punishment he received.[8]

Why Isaac Smith would beat an eighteen-year-old girl is hard to imagine. Given his past offenses, it's easy to think alcohol was a factor, but we really don't know. His ability to post $200 bail suggests that Lydia was in Lancaster when the assault took place or sent word for someone to get her son out of the county jail. Either way, she would have known about it. It must have added to the heartache she'd felt for her younger son for more than twenty years. And this time it wasn't just a problem for Lydia. Isaac had a wife and son. If he served time in jail for his latest offense, who would look after them while he was locked up? Isaac's horizons, long since clouded by his destructive addiction to alcohol, seemed to be growing darker.

But difficult as things seemed to be, Lydia and Isaac kept going. For her, that meant attending to both business and pleasure. New Year's Day in 1880 must not have been the holiday it is today, or else Lydia Hamilton Smith refused to give herself a day off. On January 1, 1880, she sold another of her houses on Water Street in Lancaster, this time to a man named James Prangley.[9] On February 16, she petitioned a Lancaster County court to order an account of Thad Jr.'s estate, as she sought reimbursement for the expenses she incurred in caring for him in his dying days. For care that extended over several years, she asked for $350. It would appear that once again, the executors resisted paying her bill.

Mrs. Smith's activity on February 21 tells us three things: she still enjoyed social events; when she socialized in Washington, she did it in the finest society; and she remained well known twelve years after Thaddeus Stevens's death. The *Weekly Louisianian*, a Black-owned newspaper reporting far from Washington, provided the details of Lydia's whereabouts that day. The headline read: "Society at the National Capital. Colored Teachers, Dinners, Parties, and Weddings." Beneath the headline, the paper published a letter from a correspondent in DC.

"One of the handsomest wedding parties I have ever seen," the writer begins, "assembled in the 15th Street Presbyterian Church, on the evening of the 11th, to witness the marriage of Miss Anastasia Brooks one of Washington's fair daughters by adoption to Walter S. Thomas, Esq. [from Ohio]. . . . The bride's dress was made by Mrs. Keckley of National reputation . . . the supper was furnished by 'Thomas' of Washington." Elizabeth Keckley, a former slave who bought freedom for her son and herself in St. Louis, was Mary Todd Lincoln's dressmaker and confidante. The writer then recognizes the more important guests. "A few of those present," she writes: "Georgiana Erb, of Mass., Mrs. Jennie Jakes, Baltimore, Mrs. Lydia Smith."[10] It's interesting to note that Mrs. Smith was apparently so well known that the reporter felt no need to tell readers where she lived. Given her impeccable taste in fashion, Mrs. Smith was no doubt one of the best-dressed women in attendance.

She obviously attended to her wardrobe in Lancaster as well as Washington. From 1879 to 1882, she had a running account with Abraham Hirsch, whose establishment was located at 6 and 8 North Queen Street. Hirsh was a "Dealer in Millinery, Jewelry, Fancy Goods, [&] Notions." On one visit, in 1881, Mrs. Smith purchased a shawl, a silk umbrella, a corset, a bonnet, cutlery (table, teaspoons, knives, forks), hose, twenty yards of black silk, and a black bonnet. The bill totaled $365.[11]

Hirsch's account books showed that Isaac still depended on his mother for support, even though he was working as a barber and musician. On September 27, 1880, Isaac charged "1 set of Banjo Strings," at 50 cents, to Lydia's account. In 1881, he purchased a violin ($13.50), one set of strings (50 cents), a half dozen razors ($6.00), and a suit ($17.25).[12]

Mrs. Smith also had an account with Harry Young & Sons, who had a store at 50 South Queen Street and a shop at 43 Mifflin Street. The Youngs, according to their bill, were a "Manufacturer of Spout Irons and General Jobbing, Repairing Safes a Specialty." Between August 1880 and January 1883, the Youngs made, repaired, and installed a number of locks and hinges on Mrs. Smith's houses. On January 26, 1883, they fixed the lock on Isaac's shaving saloon at 47 South Queen Street.[13]

But by 1881, Mrs. Smith's ability to keep up with things may have been declining. A Philadelphia journalist who had dined at 45 South Queen in 1860 (no doubt the meal was overseen by Lydia Hamilton Smith) returned in 1881 and 1883 and found that "the appearance of both house and housekeeper evince the flight of time . . . advancing age has wrinkled the face and whitened the hair of the once handsome and yet prepossessing quadroon woman who for twenty-four years managed the domestic affairs of Thaddeus Stevens." The reporter observed that "the exterior [of the house] looks as if the painters' brush has not touched it for many a year, at least since Mr. Stevens left it." Invited inside, the writer found himself "in what was once the plainly furnished but hospitable parlor, now used as a tobacco shop. At the end of the hall, which runs through the main building, is the dining room, which is still used for this purpose." The reporter toured the other half of the house and informed readers that "in what was once Mr. Stevens' office and law library is the usual array of dingy chairs, towels mugs and brushes seen in a third-class barber shop." The journalist noted that Stevens's old bedroom upstairs was now being used as a "sleeping apartment" by Mrs. Smith's tenants. In all, the reporter seemed discouraged by what he saw. "Today," he wrote, "it is hard to realize that this house was ever the abode of genius and fame. Ichabod! Where is the glory? Over everything hangs an air of uncleanness and decay."[14] It's interesting to note that the *Reading (PA) Daily Times and Dispatch* had a very different take on Lydia's well-being on October 20, 1883. In its "Chat By The Way" section, a collection of news tidbits, the paper reported: "Mrs. Lydia Smith, who for twenty years was housekeeper to Thaddeus Stevens, is still hale and hearty and lives near the old house in Lancaster." Reading is about thirty-five miles northeast of Lancaster. The paper did not explain why it decided to update readers on the state of Mrs. Smith's health on that particular day.[15]

Mrs. Smith's life in Lancaster had assumed a familiar rhythm in these years, but 1880 brought news of a change at her Washington boardinghouse. When census enumerator Edward F. Taylor arrived on Newspaper Row on June 14, 1880, he listed Mrs. Smith as fifty-five years old (she was sixty-seven), mulatto, and the operator of a boardinghouse. That information basically matched the entry for her in 1870. But what came next did not. Below Mrs. Smith's name, Taylor recorded the presence of forty-seven-year-old Susan Spaids, a married white woman from Ohio, and, according to the census form, Mrs. Spaids was also the operator of the boardinghouse. In the column on the form used to record the resident's relationship to the head of the household, Edward Taylor wrote "partner." The word is faint; it may have been written in pencil. Perhaps Mrs. Smith had followed through on the idea she mentioned in her letter to her friend Kate several years before, bringing in a "partner" to look after the house when she traveled north to Lancaster in the summer.[16]

Next on the 1880 record for Lydia's boardinghouse was thirty-three-year-old Lona Fitzgerald, a widow from Ohio, listed as Susan Spaids's sister and as a boarder. Other boarders included Edmund and Flora Arnold. Edward was a messenger in the US Treasury Department, and Flora was "at home." Next we find Lucille Harris, a twenty-nine-year-old widow who was "at home." Then forty-five-year-old Alfred Jackson, a widower and

"Attorney at Law," followed by James Newsom, who was thirty years old, single, and worked as a clerk for the National Board of Health.[17]

After Newsom, we see a familiar name: Harriet West. According to the census, Harriet was forty-five years old in 1880, married, and still employed as a servant in Mrs. Smith's boardinghouse. Harriet and her husband, Lewis, had hired on with Mrs. Smith after Thaddeus Stevens died, but in 1880, Lewis wasn't there. Other census records show him as a "single" man, living in a boardinghouse on C Street in Washington, working as a "servant." That house was run by Nancy W. Bushong, a sixty-four-year-old white woman from Ohio.[18] It appears that Lewis and Harriet had separated (though she still claimed to be married). Mrs. Bushong employed several female servants from Virginia in 1880; Lewis was a Virginia native. Perhaps someone in Mrs. Bushong's house had coaxed him over to C Street. The census record indicates that Lewis was "unemployed" at some point during 1880. Maybe Mrs. Smith had fired him—or perhaps he quit. We don't know, but he doesn't appear to have returned to Harriet. Six years later, after Mrs. Smith died, Harriet was living at 414 South Water Street in Lancaster, the house Mrs. Smith had sold Lewis in 1879.[19] Lewis wasn't there.

The last resident listed at the boardinghouse in 1880 was twenty-nine-year-old John Smith, a single man, employed as a servant. The record doesn't indicate how long Susan Spaids and her sister remained at 515 Fourteenth Street. They were still in Washington in 1900, living together on C Street, but the census taker did not record their occupations.[20]

The illness Mrs. Smith's Lancaster tenant George Heiss mentioned earlier continued to stalk her in the early 1880s. She sought treatment in Lancaster from her friend Dr. Henry Carpenter and from a younger physician, thirty-three-year-old Dr. Robert M. Bolenius. Dr. Bolenius seems to have provided the majority of her care, and by the latter part of 1883, she was seeing him with increasing frequency.

The doctor's record of Mrs. Smith's visits gives us a glimpse of how sick she was. She saw Bolenius once in August and in September, and then made twelve visits from October 7 to October 31. She was there six times in November. On December 31, Dr. Bolenius gave her four doses of a medication he abbreviated in his records as "sol Hyd Chenal." That portion of his bill also included a puzzling notation—"Drunken debauch."[21] Perhaps Isaac's worsening alcoholism accounted for some of the visits charged to Lydia's account. The answer remains elusive. All we know, for certain, is that Lydia Hamilton Smith was not well.

Yet she carried on. In late September 1883, Lydia traveled to Lancaster to celebrate the marriage of Dr. Carpenter's daughter Mary to Dr. Bolenius. In early October, she granted an interview to a reporter from the *Lancaster Inquirer*, who used the memories she shared to remind readers of her success in business and to recount, in her words, the sad story, from so many years earlier, of Keziah Wolrich, her errant husband, Ephraim, and their ill-fated son, Bill. While she was in town, she also took care of some business—she ordered a winter supply of pea coal for her rental properties from Russel & Shulmyer, "Dealers in Coal," in Lancaster. Sometime after December 31, she returned to Washington.[22] As she boarded the train for Washington, she did not know that she was completing the last trip she would make to Lancaster in her lifetime.

On Friday morning, February 8, 1884, Lydia Hamilton Smith got dressed and headed to an appointment. She was in Justice Walter's office near the courthouse, according to the *Washington Star*, "attending to some legal business [when she was] stricken with paralysis, and was removed to her home." The *Star* reported that Mrs. Smith "never afterwards recovered her speech."[23] Several newspapers, including the *Lancaster Intelligencer*, reported that she suffered "a stroke of apoplexy."[24] Mrs. Smith lay silent and still in her room at 515 Fourteenth Street for six days. On February 14, she died. Her death certificate listed the primary cause of death as "calcification of Cerebral Arteries" and the immediate cause of death as a "cerebral Hemorrhage."[25] Lydia died on the same day of the year on which she was born—Valentine's Day. She was exactly seventy-one-years old.

CHAPTER 18

"A Noted Woman Gone"

We don't have an hour-by-hour account of Lydia Hamilton Smith's death, as we do for her partner, Thaddeus Stevens. The *Lancaster Weekly Examiner and Express* reported that "only one son, Isaac, survives her. He was with her when she died." Surely, Harriet West, Mrs. Smith's longtime friend and household worker, was there. Given his long service in the Stevens-Smith households, Lewis West might have been summoned to the bedside as well.[1]

The *Weekly Examiner* reported that Mrs. Smith was "a remarkably intelligent woman of generous disposition and was well and favorably known." The paper informed readers that she was highly respected in Washington among both "white and colored" residents, "a fact," the paper wrote, "which was attested by a large number who attended the funeral services at St. Augustine's Catholic Church." Reverend Father Walsh, from St. Augustine's, conducted the services on February 15. Afterward, "the remains were taken by Mr. Burgdorf, the undertaker to the Baltimore and Potomac Depot and placed on the 9:30 o'clock train for Lancaster, Pa. where interment will take place."[2]

Preparations for receiving Mrs. Smith's body were already underway in Lancaster. According to George Heiss, her tenant at 45 South Queen Street, "Dr. Bolenius came and asked me if they could hold the funeral at my house." Heiss said Dr. Bolenius "had been telegraphed to make arrangements for the funeral."[3] We don't know who sent that telegram, but Isaac's presence in Washington when Lydia died suggests he might have done it. The *Lancaster New Era* reported that Isaac accompanied his mother's remains to Lancaster.[4] Heiss said, "They then brought the remains there and the funeral services were held at my house." Heiss had put black crepe on the front door. The *Lancaster New Era* reported, a few days later, that "some sacrilegious thief stole from the Stevens homestead, South Queen Street, the crape that had been hung there for the late Mrs. Lydia Smith. The larceny was perpetrated sometime during Saturday night."[5]

Out-of-town friends traveled to Lancaster to pay their respects to Mrs. Smith, and Heiss was asked to accommodate them. "Dr. Bolenius said I should board the friends," he said, "that I might as well do it as anyone else, that I would get paid for it, so I boarded them. . . . I boarded five colored people two days and a night. They had good appetites. They slept there." Heiss may have boarded Mrs. Smith's friends, but he wasn't particularly enthused about doing it. "There were five friends there altogether," he reported, "they boarded and lodged there. They came there on an evening in time for supper, bringing the corpse with them. They stayed there until the third day in the evening after the funeral. My store was in the house and I had it closed all this time . . . the remains were in the parlor in my house." Thaddeus Stevens had been laid out in that same room sixteen years earlier.[6]

Heiss charged Lydia Smith's estate $100 for "funeral services" related to her death, which included the cost of room and board for her friends. "I think the charge is a fair one," he testified in support of his claim. "I would not board them again for the same price, considering the kind of people they were, they were colored people."[7]

Mrs. Smith's body lay in the parlor of her house until two o'clock Monday afternoon, February 18. By that time, hundreds of mourners had viewed her remains, and many of them stayed in town for her funeral; the *Weekly Express* reported "the funeral was a large one."[8] The *Lancaster Intelligencer* reported on February 15 that Mrs. Smith's "remains will be brought to Lancaster for interment in the Stevens lot in Shreiner's cemetery." After a lifetime of antagonizing Thaddeus Stevens and Lydia Hamilton Smith, the paper might have made a better effort to be accurate in reporting their deaths, but that was not the case. The *Intelligencer* published not a word about Stevens's funeral in 1868, and they erred in identifying Lydia's final resting place. She had long since made a commitment to St. Mary's Cemetery. Her son William was already there.[9]

The Lancaster *New Era* reported that Mrs. Smith's funeral included "many touching tributes from those who had learned to admire the deceased for her generous nature, and among those who paid the last mournful tribute to the deceased were numbered some of our best people." The *New Era* listed the pallbearers as Joseph Lebar, James Fels, Abram Maxwell, and Edward Mellen [Millen] and reported that Dr. McCullagh officiated at the cemetery. The *New Era* reported that a funeral mass was not conducted for Mrs. Smith in Lancaster because it had already "been said" in Washington.[10]

In her will, Mrs. Smith directed her executors to "erect a plain marble monument" by her grave. They purchased a headstone for $100 and inscribed it: "Lydia Hamilton, Relict [widow] of Jacob Smith, For many years the trusted housekeeper of Hon. Thaddeus Stevens, Born at Gettysburg, Penna. on St. Valentine's Day, 1813, Died at Washington, D.C. on St. Valentine's Day, 1884."[11] We don't know who chose the epitaph on her monument; we know that Thaddeus Stevens wrote his own, and perhaps she did, too.

The length of the obituaries published in Lancaster newspapers for Lydia Hamilton Smith testifies to her stature in the community. We've seen parts of them already, but they bear repeating here. The *Weekly Examiner* pointed out that she had a "national reputation owing to her long and faithful service as housekeeper for" Thaddeus Stevens. The paper noted that she married young to a "full-blooded negro who turned out to be a worthless fellow and who ill-treated her." That mistreatment, the paper said, occasioned her acceptance of a job in Lancaster, where her employer, Thaddeus Stevens, "found that he had discovered a treasure." The *Examiner* described Mrs. Smith as "a beautiful quadroon" who "received no education, but by her unaided efforts had picked up a good fund of information." The paper said she was "generous to a fault."[12]

The *Lancaster Intelligencer*, the paper that was so critical of Stevens, was less effusive than the *Examiner* in its recognition of Mrs. Smith. She was "regarded as a 'colored' woman," the paper wrote, "but had very little negro blood in her veins, and could have anywhere passed as a Spaniard or Cuban . . . her features being finely cut, her lips thin, her hair long and wavy and her eyes black and piercing. In her younger days she was considered quite handsome, and even in her later years she retained many traces of her former beauty." The paper mentioned that she had married "a negro named Jacob Smith, of Harrisburg," and had two sons with him, but of Jacob himself, the *Intelligencer* pointed out only that he was "a musician of some note." There was no mention of his treatment of his wife. The writer did report that Mrs. Smith "died possessed of very considerable property, including Stevens' homestead and several other homes in this city."[13]

In its obituary, the *Lancaster New Era* spent considerable time on the fact that Mrs. Smith had left her husband. The paper observed that Jacob was "quite proficient as a musician" and had performed "quite successfully at the Mechanics Institute," but, like the *Intelligencer*, the *New Era* made no mention of his behavior. Instead, the *New Era* writer said he "came [to Lancaster] seeking reconciliation" with his wife, which, the paper noted, "never happened." The paper acknowledged Mrs. Smith's "magnificent" skills as a caterer and housekeeper and informed readers that, as the head of Stevens's household, she "came in contact with many of the great men of this country of whom she conversed intelligently and most entertainingly." The writer also mentioned Lydia's success in business and reputation for kindness. "Possessed of considerable means," the paper said, "she gave with [generous] hand to the deserving poor, and no one who was worthy ever appealed to her in vain."[14]

At least two other local newspapers reported on Lydia's death. On February 16, the *Christiana Ledger* in Christiana, Pennsylvania, informed readers that "Lydia Smith, formerly of Gettysburg and Lancaster, Pa., the quadroon housekeeper of Thaddeus Stevens died [in] Washington on Thursday evening." The paper didn't mention that Lydia had lived in the capital for sixteen years. The February 19 edition of the *Gettysburg Star and Sentinel*, the paper Thaddeus Stevens once owned part of, noted under "Deaths": "Smith—February 14, in Washington city, of apoplexy, Mrs. Lydia Smith, (colored), formerly of Gettysburg."[15]

Some Southern newspaper editors, still nursing animosity toward Stevens, could not resist the chance to take another shot at him through Mrs. Smith. The Raleigh, North Carolina *Farmer & Mechanic* noted her passing and referred to her as "the mulatto 'wife' of Thad Stevens, the virulent South-hater who forced the Reconstruction villainy upon our people." Other newspapers were kinder. The February 22 edition of the Pembina, North Dakota *Pioneer Express* informed its readers that "there died at Washington, on the 14th, a colored woman which had obtained a national reputation owing to her connection as housekeeper with the late Thaddeus Stevens of Pennsylvania. Lydia Smith was the name of the woman. . . . Mrs. Smith directed the affairs of his establishment and ministered to his wants. She was remembered in his will with a bequest of $5,000 in cash, certain property at Lancaster and several houses here."[16] The *Pioneer Express* was clearly engaging in the age-old practice of reprinting another newspaper's copy, but the fact that editors working so far from Lancaster and Washington picked up the story is testimony to the celebrity Lydia Hamilton Smith achieved, for better or worse, in her lifetime.

Mrs. Smith's death left her son Isaac, now forty-seven years old, as the sole survivor of her nuclear family. During her lifetime, she had witnessed his talent (as a musician) and his troubles (as an alcoholic) as he made his way in Lancaster. She knew her son, like Thaddeus Stevens's nephew Thad Jr., was losing his battle with the bottle. Over the years, she took numerous steps to help him keep his head above water: she filed charges against John Jones for getting her teenaged son drunk, she tried the "tough love" approach by charging him with drunken and disorderly conduct that earned him a month of hard labor, and she most likely supplied the $200 bail money to free him to await trial for attacking Mary Taylor.

She gave Isaac space at 47 South Queen Street for his "shaving saloon," most likely bought the house at 327 North Street so that he could live in it, and, even though he was earning money as a barber and a musician, arranged with her tenant George Heiss to provide both cash and provisions if Isaac and his family needed them. According to Heiss, Isaac and his wife took advantage of the arrangement. After Mrs. Smith died, Heiss filed a claim against her estate for $110. Included in that, he said, was money he gave Isaac to "enable him to visit his mother in Washington," money he gave Isaac's wife for "goods and provisions," the cost of repairing the porch where Isaac was living, and $5 for "moving Isaac and his family,"[17] probably to the house Mrs. Smith left him on East Vine Street. And her generosity to Isaac went even further. Her will charged her executors and their heirs with overseeing her three-story house on East Vine Street so Isaac could

> occupy the house on said lot and to reside there as long as he may desire to do so or to receive the rents and profits of said house and lot during the term of his natural life at his option and if my said son Isaac Smith shall die after the arrival of his son Isaac Alonzo Smith at majority the said Isaac Alonzo Smith is to have the said lot on East Vine Street with the appurtenances in fee simple and if the said Isaac Smith shall die before the arrival of the said Isaac Alonzo Smith at majority my executors their heirs and assigns are to hold the said property in trust for the said Isaac Alonzo Smith until his coming of age when he

is to have the fee simple aforesaid and my Executors their heirs and assigns are hereby directed and ordered and authorized to make as my executors, all proper and necessary arrangements for bringing this trust into effect.[18]

Lydia's will is the only official document in which we find Isaac Alonzo Smith's name. He's not in the census record for Isaac's household in 1870 or 1880. There was, as we've already seen, a child in Isaac's home in 1870—ten-month-old Clara Smith—but she's not there in 1880, by which time Isaac and Sarah appear as a married couple. A different child was living with Isaac and Sarah in 1880—five-year-old David Smith. Isaac Alonzo must have been born sometime between 1870 and 1877, when Lydia wrote her will; we don't know exactly when.[19]

The next provision in Lydia's will also reflects her attempt to make Isaac's life as secure as possible. "I direct my executors," she wrote,

to sell my lot of ground on South Queen Street Lancaster, Pennsylvania to the best advantage and to invest the proceeds of said sale securely at an interest not less than six percent per annum and said interest to be applied to the payment of the taxes and manage affairs of the property in East Vine Street Lancaster, Pennsylvania, herein before conveyed in trust for my son Isaac Smith and the residue of said interest if any to be paid to my said son for his support in such ways and in such amounts as may seem advisable to my said executors.[20]

Mrs. Smith also left Isaac and his son Isaac Alonzo her piano and as much of her furniture as would comfortably fit in the East Vine Street house.

In all, Lydia left Isaac a considerable estate. When the auditors calculated the value of her assets in 1886, they totaled $11,373.80, the equivalent of more than $300,000 in twenty-first-century money. Sadly, Isaac had little time to enjoy his inheritance. Less than two months after he buried his mother, Isaac joined her in death. On April 7, 1884, the *Lancaster Daily Intelligencer* ran a death notice that read: "Smith—April 7, 1884, in this city, Isaac Smith, in the 48th year of his age."[21]

The following day, under a headline that read, "Death of Little Ike Smith," the *Daily Intelligencer* informed readers, "Isaac Smith, colored, the well known barber, died last evening, at his home, on North Street of gastritis, after an illness of about two weeks." The paper reported that the "deceased was 48 years old, and the only son of the late Lydia Smith, who died but a short time ago." The paper wrote approvingly of Isaac's presence in the community: "He was known by almost every one as 'Little Ike.' Besides being a good barber, he was an excellent banjo player and whistler. For a number of years past he had a barber shop on South Queen Street near Vine." With its death notice on April 7th, the paper provided funeral information: "The relatives and friends of the family are respectfully invited to attend the funeral from his late residence, No. 327 North Street, on Wednesday morning at 1 ½ o'clock. Interment at St. Mary's cemetery."[22]

The *Lancaster New Era* more precisely told readers Isaac was "the only surviving son—indeed, the only surviving child—of the late Mrs. Lydia Smith, who became famous as the colored housekeeper of Thaddeus Stevens, when the latter entertained the most distinguished men of the land." The paper reported that "Ike . . . made his home for years in the house of Mr. Stevens" and that he "knew many of the distinguished visitors, helped to wait on them and loved to talk about them." The *New Era* staff knew Ike as a barber and musician, informing readers that he "was quite a good performer on the banjo. Indeed Ike and his banjo were almost inseparable."[23] The *Harrisburg State Journal*, an African American–owned newspaper, published a less complimentary obituary for Isaac. The headline read, "Death of a Well-Known Character," and the article informed readers that "Isaac Smith, who died Monday in Lancaster, was the son of Lydia Smith, who left $500 by her will to keep the grave of her old employer, Thaddeus Stevens, green. She also left her son a snug fortune of $25,000. Ike, as he was familiarly known, roamed about the country and was a noted banjoist. He was dissipated in his habits, and only enjoyed for a few weeks the fortune which his mother left him." The last line of the *State Journal's* article did not bode well for Isaac's wife, Sarah, and his son, David. The paper reported that Isaac "died without a will."[24]

Mrs. Smith made provision for Isaac's son Isaac Alonzo in her will, but, as we've already seen, did not mention Sarah or David. In the end, Isaac Alonzo had no chance to enjoy his grandmother's largesse, either. In the auditor's report on Mrs. Smith's estate, we learn that "Alonzo died before his father, before he turned twenty-one, and before Lydia Hamilton Smith died." Mrs. Smith apparently had made no revisions to her will after Alonzo's death. That left the executors without a legal heir to her estate. The auditors noted that Isaac was survived by his wife, Sarah Smith, who "had one child living when Lydia died: David Smith," but Lydia's failure to recognize them in her will meant that the executors did not consider them legal heirs. Isaac could have provided for them, perhaps, if he had written a will. But he didn't write one, and that left Sarah and David without a home or means of support. The executors put the money that would have gone to Isaac and Alonzo in the "general fund," to use in paying other obligations spelled out in Mrs. Smith's will.[25]

The two men Mrs. Smith appointed as her executors—Walter M. Franklin, in Lancaster, and Sidney A. Fitch, in Washington—began liquidating her extensive estate shortly after she died. In Washington, they held an estate sale in which "the portrait of Thaddeus Stevens, which had been so long in her possession, was bid off by Mr. George T. Cline of Frederick [Maryland], for the mere sum of $12." A Washington correspondent of the *Lancaster Intelligencer* observed, "I should think some historical society of Pennsylvania would have sent a representative to contest that bid." Lydia's effects in Washington also included "a gold snuff-box presented to Mr. Stevens, if I remember rightly, by citizens of Colorado, and a watch that was owned by his father." The watch was probably the same one Stevens left to Thad Jr. in his will. On March 29, 1884, completing a transaction Mrs. Smith had actually initiated while she was alive, the executors transferred the deed for the house she shared with Thaddeus Stevens, 45–47 South Queen Street, to E. O. Henry, who sold "Reapers, Mowers, French Burr Chopping Mills" there in 1884.[26] By the end of 1886, the executors had sold Lydia's three remaining two-story houses on the west side of South Water Street (Nos. 416, 418, and 420) and her three-story, semi-detached house at 21 and 23 East Vine Street, on the corner of East Vine and South Christian Streets.[27]

The executors used the money from the real estate sales to pay outstanding claims against Mrs. Smith's estate and to pay the bequests and legacies she spelled out in her will. She instructed her executors to invest $500 and use the interest to care for "sodding, preservation, and repair" of her cemetery lot in St. Mary's Cemetery. That provision attracted little attention from those curious about her will. But a similar provision, ordering the executors to invest $500 at not less than 6 percent and use the interest "to keeping the grave of the late Thaddeus Stevens at Lanc. Pa. properly sodded and repaired and for the preservation and renewal of the flowers planted on said grave,"[28] was noted in many obituaries. The fact that she left careful instructions for the care of Thaddeus Stevens's grave site suggests that she may have been tending his grave herself in the years after he died. Given the closeness of the relationship between them, it's easy to picture her visiting his tomb as she faced a sometimes harsh world without him.

Charles Smith, the young man from New York who claimed to be Lydia Hamilton Smith's grandson—born to Lydia's son William and Charlotte Foster in Lancaster—entered his claim to part of Mrs. Smith's estate shortly after she died. After hearing testimony from Charles, his second cousin Drucilla Waters, and Lydia's cousin Anna Sulkey Martin, the auditors rejected his claim, saying in their report, "Charles was the illegitimate son of William Smith, [his] mother: Charlotte Foster never married William."[29] Therefore, he was not entitled to any part of Lydia's estate.

We have seen, by this point, how very generous Lydia Hamilton Smith was in her lifetime. Through her will, she was still giving to others long after the hourglass of her life had run out. The largest of her legacies went to her half sister, Jane Cooper, who (according to Lydia's will) was born in Gettysburg but was raised by the very wealthy Alexander Reiman family in Baltimore. Jane was still living in Baltimore when Lydia composed her will in 1877. Lydia left Jane $500, a gift that would be worth more than $12,000 today. Census records show Jane Cooper, a widow in her fifties, Black, living at 115 Jasper Street in Baltimore in 1880. According to the record, Mrs. Cooper had three children, Hannah (twenty), David (eighteen), and Mary Ann (sixteen).[30] Lydia directed her executors to invest the $910 dollars from the sale of her three houses on South Water Street and give the interest to Jane "for the education of her children." If the children all died before Jane, Lydia wanted the interest to go to Jane.[31]

Lydia's gifts to Jane and her children suggest she was fairly close to them during her years in Lancaster and Washington, but we have no letters or other documents attesting to that. Circumstantial evidence might shed some light on the question. Recall that Lancaster ticket agent W. F. Hambright testified that Mrs. Smith often bought a ticket to Baltimore for herself as she sent Thad Jr. on his way back to Caledonia after his latest alcohol-saturated episode. Perhaps she stopped to visit her sister on her way home to DC.

We meet other members of Lydia's family for the first time in her will. She had a cousin named Matilda Erb living in Springfield, Massachusetts, in 1877. Lydia bequeathed Matilda and her two daughters, Emma Queen and Julia Erb, $200 each. To Jane Gordon, daughter of Charles White (Springville, Mass.) and Julia Jones (Palmer, Mass.), Lydia also left $200, but she didn't spell out her relationship to the two women in her will.

She remembered Eliza Toop of Harrisburg and her daughter, Matilda, with $100 legacies, and she directed her executors to invest $200 each for Sadie and Annie Queen, daughters of Emma Queen, the daughter of Lydia's cousin Matilda Erb. Lydia wanted the interest and principal on those $200 investments to be given to Sadie and Annie when they turned twenty-one. Lydia also remembered her good friends (and family) in Lancaster. Her cousin Anna Sulkey Martin received a $100 legacy. She left $50 to Salome Burrowes; Salome and her husband, Dr. Thomas H. Burrowes, had been close friends. Of course, Lydia remembered Dr. Carpenter's daughters, who were all grown up and married by 1884. She left each of them, "Mary, Katie, and Sally," $100, and she left Harry Miller, son of Dr. Carpenter's second wife, Laura Miller Carpenter, $100 as well. To Eliza Kerfoot, who along with her husband, Dr. George B. Kerfoot, shared many social functions with Stevens and Mrs. Smith, she gave $50.

The will Lydia Hamilton Smith wrote in 1877 included gifts for all three members of the West family, long part of the Stevens-Smith household. The entry reads: "Louis [*sic*] West (now residing with me but formerly of Lancaster), and Harriet, wife of Louis West, and Charles Sumner West, son of Louis and Harriet West, the $100 for Charles Sumner West to be invested, the principal and interest to be paid to him upon his arrival at majority."[32]

CHAPTER 19

THOSE LEFT BEHIND

After Mrs. Smith died, Mary Primm, the young woman from Caledonia Furnace who claimed to be the widow of Thaddeus Stevens's nephew Alanson, showed up in Lancaster for the fourth time. She first visited Stevens and Mrs. Smith shortly after Alanson died at Chickamauga during the Civil War. She tried to claim the $2,400 promissory note Stevens wrote to Alanson, the note Thad Jr. found in Alanson's trunk when he tried (and failed) to retrieve his brother's body from the battlefield. Mary was turned away. On her second visit, Mrs. Smith interceded for her, unsuccessfully as it turned out, when she came seeking to enroll Alanson's daughter, Alanson Jane, in a local school. We've already heard Mary testify that she traveled to Lancaster a third time, shortly before Thaddeus Stevens died. On that visit, Stevens directed her to Thad Jr., who refused to help her. On her fourth visit, in 1887, she brought an attorney.

Mary still sought the $2,400 promissory note and still claimed to be the legal widow of Alanson Stevens. She told the court she decided to renew her claim after John Sweeney, manager of Stevens's ironworks when she and Alanson "kept house" together there, visited her in Harrisburg in May 1884. Mary testified that Sweeney told her she had a claim against Thaddeus Stevens's estate and ought to press it. Mary said she asked Sweeney what claim she had and he replied, "Alanson's widow, how else?" Mary said, "I told him I could not push it, and he told me he would assist me all he could. He also told me to go to Mr. Roberts [Stevens's executor], who lived in Lancaster." We've already heard Sweeney flip-flop in his testimony on whether Mary and Alanson were legally married. Why he now encouraged Mary and yet weakly defended her claim is not clear. When asked if he urged Mary to pursue the claim, Sweeney admitted, "I may have told her that if she had a just claim the estate was able to pay it." It's not clear what Sweeney hoped to get out of this. He testified later that the attorneys for Stevens's estate had enlisted him to round up witnesses who would impeach Mary's character and help them reject her claim. Sweeney identified Edward McPherson as the executor who "hired" him. McPherson was the only original executor still alive as Mary Primm's case was heard. A. E. Roberts had followed O. J. Dickey to the grave on January 23, 1885.[1]

Mary Primm's lawyer, J. M. Wiestling, identified in court documents as the "attorney for Mrs. Alanson Stevens," battled the executors' lawyer, Charles Kline, for several years. During that time, the court heard from witnesses who supported Mary's claim and from those who impugned her character and denied that she was ever married to Alanson Stevens. John Sweeney testified that Mary showed him a "six or seven inch" scrap of paper, shortly after Alanson left for his three-year military service, on which Alanson had written, "I here acknowledge Mary Primm to be my lawful wife, as I go forth to battle. Signed A. J. Stevens." But by the time Mary brought her claim to court, she had lost the scrap of paper.[2]

The promissory note, missing since Thad Jr.'s death, surfaced during the proceedings, but Mary Primm was not to receive it. On January 11, 1894, the court issued its decision. In April of the preceding year, the auditors had reported that Mary (now Mrs. John W. Clason) "alleges she was the wife of Alanson J. Stevens, and that he left her surviving him as his widow, and one child, a daughter, Alanson Jane Stevens, who died on 22nd Day of August 1873 after the death of Thaddeus Stevens." The auditors said their examination of the estate showed "the heirs of Thaddeus Stevens, living at the time of his death, would be: Dr. Thaddeus M. Stevens [his nephew in Indiana], Mrs. Cauffman [Stevens's niece], Thaddeus Stevens, Jr., and, if Alanson J. Stevens and Mary J. Primm were lawfully married, Alanson Jane Stevens."[3] But Mary Primm was unable to prove, no matter how many witnesses she called, that she was ever legally married to Alanson. Her claim was disallowed; Mary departed, never to return.

Executor Edward McPherson denied another claim on Stevens's estate in 1886. In his will, Stevens had given instructions for what to do with his money if Thad Jr. failed to embrace sobriety, and those instructions involved, as we've already seen, Stevens's dream of starting a school for indigent children. If his nephew missed his chance to claim the entire estate, Stevens wrote, "I dispose of whatever may remain, as follows: If the aggregate sum shall amount to fifty thousand dollars, without which no further disposition thereof can be made, I give it all to my trustees to erect, establish and endow a house of refuge for the relief of homeless indigent orphans. Those shall be deemed orphans who shall have lost either parent." Stevens had a very specific site in mind for the orphans' home: "I wish the building to be erected in the city of Lancaster, south of East King Street, provided sufficient ground, not less than two acres, shall be donated therefore, if not, then on the west side of said street, on the same condition. If sufficient should not be gratuitously offered then I desire it to be built in Columbia."[4]

On January 5, 1886, an organization known as the Home for Friendless Children donated two acres of land for erecting the school Stevens envisioned and petitioned the executors to give them Stevens's $50,000 to build it. On April 3, Judge J. B. Livingston upheld McPherson's decision to deny the Home for Friendless Children's claim. In the record, McPherson explained that the Home for Friendless Children had been rejected for several reasons. He said the Home had filed its claim after researching how much land Stevens's estate had sold and how much it still owned without court approval, had submitted an inappropriate description of the land involved, and simply was not named in Stevens's will. Later documents would add that the Home for Friendless Children was turned down because "it was held the time had not arrived for the establishment of said home." The executors did not elaborate on why that was the case.

There appears to have been more to it than that. The *Lancaster Intelligencer* noted in 1876 that Thaddeus Stevens never contributed to the Home for Friendless Children "on the sole ground that it showed some preferences, or distinction at least, among its inmates on account of color." McPherson would have known Stevens's views on the subject. A Philadelphia paper reported, in 1881, that the Home for Friendless Children "rescinded their regulation forbidding the taking of colored children, in the hope, as many believe, that at least a portion of Mr. Stevens' money will be donated to them." Obviously, that didn't sway the executor.[5]

There the matter stood until March 11, 1899, when the Court of Common Pleas granted a charter to a group organized under the name The Stevens Orphans Home of Lancaster City. The new committee was tasked with "erecting, establishing and endowing a house of refuge for homeless indigent orphans." In 1901, the Lancaster Trust Company, which had been holding the remaining cash from Stevens's estate, was ordered to turn over the money, with accrued interest. It amounted to $70,653.90.[6] *Smull's Legislative Hand Book and Manual of the State of Pennsylvania*, published in 1913, picks up the story from there.

Apparently, $70,000 wasn't enough to build a school in 1901. But all was not lost. The *Hand Book*'s account suggests the school committee had friends in Harrisburg. In May 1905, the Pennsylvania legislature appropriated an additional $50,000 to buy land and begin construction. The state added another $100,000 in 1907. Smull's handbook reported that "the ground upon which the buildings are located contains about twenty acres and was purchased for a nominal consideration from the Directors of the Poor and House of Employment of Lancaster County."[7] That land was located on the south side of East King Street, exactly where Stevens wanted the school to be.

The state legislature changed the school's name from The Stevens Orphans Home to the Thaddeus Stevens Industrial School of Pennsylvania. The first students arrived around October 1, 1909. By 1913, enrollment had reached fifty-five. The governor of Pennsylvania appointed a board of trustees, and Charles I. Landis served as its first president.[8] Landis was the Lancaster County judge who later would defend Stevens and Mrs. Smith against the vicious portrayals of them in Thomas Dixon's novel *The Clansman* and D. W. Griffith's Klan-extolling film *The Birth of a Nation*. The school went on to win praise for its training of disadvantaged young people of all races.

In 2011, the *Stevens Tech Newsletter* announced plans to renovate the auditorium in the school's Old Main, also known as the Mellor Building, into the Lydia Hamilton Smith Gallery, to honor her work with Thaddeus Stevens. The newsletter told readers, "Turning this small auditorium with the anchoring beauty of its little balcony back to the era of antiquity will require the highest refining craftsmanship by our students . . . it is our desire to capture the strength and character of this outstanding lady as an African-American mother, housekeeper, business woman, etc., through pictorial displays and historical narratives with an illustrative overview of the twenty-four year working relationship between Lydia and Thaddeus Stevens. . . . We want to highlight the successful entrepreneurship of Lydia Hamilton Smith in the midst of a very dark time in our nation when slavery, segregation and oppression were rampant throughout the land."[9] The project was "shuffled to the side" in 2011, according to Stevens Tech librarian Timothy Creamer in 2019, but not canceled. Creamer said a Lydia Hamilton Smith Gallery is "still possible."

Thaddeus Stevens would, no doubt, have been gratified to see his dream become reality. His executor A. E. Roberts, had he lived to see it, might have been less excited. Recall his words to Mrs. Smith the night before he testified in her claim against Stevens's estate. He told the court, "I went a little further and said that I was quite as willing to pay her all she was entitled to for wages as to create a big fund for building the asylum." Regardless of his personal feelings, he, O. J. Dickey, and Edward McPherson carried out what they understood to be Stevens's wishes for establishing the orphans' school. Roberts's comment to Lydia suggests that, although he went along with it, he wasn't totally on board with Dickey's plan to deny Lydia's claim for wages to maximize the "residue" of the estate for use in building an orphans' school.[10]

As we've already seen, Isaac's widow, Sarah, and her son, David, were not in line for any inheritance when their husband and father died in 1884. The course of Sarah's life after Isaac died suggests that she never recovered from the loss of her husband. In 1886, she was still living at 327 North Street, the house where she had lived with Isaac and a house Lydia once owned, but the city directory for that year indicated that she was now a boarder. She may have been truly hard up by that time. In August, the grand jury charged Sarah and a young woman named Ida Ulmer with larceny. John A. Shober, operator of a rag and paper warehouse on Market Street, alleged that on May 1, "with force and arms, etc, [Sarah and Ida] stole one half-bin of coal, value $2.50." Shober was the only witness to the crime.[11] We don't know the outcome of the case.

In 1887, Dr. Henry Carpenter, dear friend and physician of both Lydia Hamilton Smith and Thaddeus Stevens, died, rather unexpectedly. Genealogical notes compiled by his descendants include an obituary that reported Dr. Carpenter "was stricken with paralysis early in April, but was then only slightly affected and had so far recovered in the latter part of May that he was able to appear on the streets in his carriage. Just as he seemed to be on the fair road to complete recovery, however, a second stroke paralyzed his left side. On Saturday evening last, he had so far recovered that he was discussing the advisability of going down stairs, but on Sunday morning he received a third and most severe stroke of all, which resulted fatally."[12] Dr. Carpenter was widely respected, in his day, as one of the finest physicians in Pennsylvania. He trained his son-in-law, Dr. Robert Bolenius, who treated Mrs. Smith when her health was failing. But Dr. Carpenter's most significant contribution may have been the care he provided, in tandem with Lydia Hamilton Smith, for Thaddeus Stevens. That care kept Stevens alive long enough to play his critical part in ending slavery and putting people of color on the road to the civil rights they had been denied for so very long.

In 1900, Sarah Smith was no longer living on North Street. She was a "patient" in the Lancaster County Almshouse and Insane Asylum, just across the field from where Stevens Tech would be built a few years later. Sarah didn't provide census taker Samuel W. Miller with as much information as other residents of the institution that year. The spaces for her age and occupation were not filled in. We can, however, compute her age from the fact that she was thirty in 1870, which made her sixty at the turn of the century. She was listed as a "housekeeper" while she lived with Isaac, but we don't know what work she might have done after he died.[13]

Sarah told Miller she was married and had three living children. That may be a sign of her deteriorating mental condition. We know, with near certainty, that Sarah and Isaac's daughter, Clara, and their son Isaac Alonzo died in childhood. David may have survived. There was a David Smith renting a house at 538 North Street in 1900; he's listed as twenty-three years old and married. Isaac's son David would have been around twenty-five in 1900. If David Smith on North Street was Isaac's son, we know nothing of his life in the years after his father's death. Sarah answered only three more questions for census taker Samuel Miller. She affirmed that she could speak English. And she answered "yes" when he read the words "cannot read" and "cannot write."[14]

The next record of Sarah Fillkill Smith was posted on August 10, 1904. The Register of Deaths at the Poor House entered her age as sixty-five. The official cause of death was tuberculosis. Sarah Smith apparently died without anyone, family members or friends, to notice and pay their respects. Under "Disposition of body," the record indicates: Anatomical Society. Sarah's last contribution to the world was as a specimen for medical research.[15]

CHAPTER 20

A LIFE WELL LIVED

Lydia Hamilton Smith was born twelve miles north of the Mason-Dixon Line. Originally surveyed by astronomers Charles Mason and Jeremiah Dixon to resolve a boundary dispute between the British colonies of Pennsylvania and Maryland, it had become, by the time of Lydia's birth in 1813, the dividing line between Americans who countenanced the enslavement of people of color and those who did not. The specter of slavery and its twin post–Civil War offspring—virulent racism and white supremacy—stalked every moment of Lydia's life.

Lydia was born free, the child of a sexual encounter, consensual or otherwise, between her mother, a Black woman, and a white man from Ireland. Lydia's America kept lists of "bastard" children, and most white people of her time believed that Black people belonged to an inferior race. As a person of color and a woman, Lydia faced challenging social obstacles, but she was not cowed by them. As this account illustrates, she exhibited an inspiring strength of character and profound resilience, even in the most trying of times.

The year after Lydia was born, Captains Meriwether Lewis and William Clark reported on their expedition from St. Louis to the Pacific Ocean. They noted the flora and fauna along the way, but their primary mission, given to them by President Thomas Jefferson, was to search for "the most direct and practicable water communication across the continent, for purposes of commerce."[1] A young and vigorous nation, caught up in the industrial revolution, had things to sell. Technological innovations arrived in a rush. Railroads connected the cities; the telegraph shattered time and space, allowing instant communication between far-flung corners of the country; the oil industry started pumping crude in Titusville, Pennsylvania, signaling the beginning of the end for steam power; Alexander Graham Bell shouted, "Mr. Watson—come here—I want to see you" into a mouthpiece and launched the telephone; the horse-drawn omnibus introduced inner-city mass transportation—and Mrs. Smith embraced them all. She was her century's equivalent of today's frequent fliers. She sent telegrams, rode the omnibus, and traveled by train so frequently that the ticket agents in Lancaster (and most likely Baltimore, Washington, and Philadelphia) knew her by name.

The humble circumstances of Lydia Hamilton Smith's birth denied her a formal education, but she applied her keen intelligence and became literate by the time she arrived in Lancaster to manage Thaddeus Stevens's household. Once there, with Stevens as her mentor, she set to work building, for herself and her sons, the financial security her single mother and her estranged husband had not. She invested—a little in railroad stocks (a good bet in the nineteenth century) and a lot more in real estate. In a time when women—Black or white—were considered incapable of handling business matters, Mrs. Smith owned as many as eight houses in Lancaster and two boardinghouses, one in Washington, DC, the other in Philadelphia. And we can't forget the horses and carriages she rented out in Washington. When her friends and neighbors testified, during her claim for back wages from Stevens's estate, that she had many responsibilities to look after, these are the things, in addition to managing Stevens's households in Lancaster and Washington, to which they referred. And her load grew heavier as Stevens's health declined and she was called upon to manage his affairs as well as hers.

Some of Mrs. Smith's contemporaries apparently thought she was a little too interested in making money. That seems to have been on O. J. Dickey's mind when he hatched his plan to cut off her access to Stevens's estate. Even Stevens acknowledged Lydia's "acquisitiveness" in one of his last conversations with his friend and colleague Simon Stevens. But, as you may recall, Thaddeus Stevens hastened to add, "No matter what her love of money is, she has never neglected me or my household—whether we were in health or in sickness." These words not only reveal Thaddeus Stevens's feelings about his "union" with Mrs. Smith but also testify to the generosity she exhibited in all aspects of her life.[2] In this account, we've looked on as she cared for those inside her "family" circle—writing encouraging letters to Stevens's nephews Alanson and Thad Jr., when their behavior threatened to alienate them from their Uncle Thaddeus; sitting by her son William as his life ebbed away after he shot himself; nursing Thad Jr. as he slowly drank himself to death; and making every provision she could think of to support her son Isaac when she was gone.

Historians at Lancaster's Bethel A.M.E. Church, testifying to their congregation's brave efforts to aid runaway slaves on the Underground Railroad, affirmed Stevens and Mrs. Smith as partners in the risky business of guiding fugitives to freedom. Discoveries at the tavern Stevens owned next door to their house on South Queen Street provide concrete evidence of their involvement. Mrs. Smith's self-financed relief mission to field hospitals for both Union and Confederate soldiers, after the Battle of Gettysburg, demonstrated that her generosity was unbounded by partisanship. And then there were the legacies in her will. Most of the sums were modest, but the list was long and universal. Lydia gave money from the estate she worked so hard to build to family and friends, Black and white, male and female.

As so often happens to those who attain a certain "celebrity" in their own time, Lydia Hamilton Smith's story—her accomplishments and her generosity—faded from memory soon after she was gone. Thomas Dixon resurrected her name, briefly, in his disgustingly racist novel *The Clansman* in 1905, but only to vilify her along with Thaddeus Stevens. Stevens's considerable contributions to the nation were likewise largely overlooked until the 1930s, when biographers rediscovered his legacy. Some of those biographers noticed Mrs. Smith standing at Stevens's side; some did not.

Those who include her in chronicling Stevens's life and work split into two camps on the question of their relationship. Most extol her beauty, intelligence, and domestic skills, but some refuse to entertain the possibility that a devoutly religious woman of color would have indulged in a sexual liaison with a white man, no matter how much he believed in the equality of all races. A few scholars report there is too little evidence to reach a definitive conclusion. But some, after reading Stevens's papers, newspaper accounts, and biographies written by his contemporaries are convinced that Lydia Hamilton Smith and Thaddeus Stevens were, indeed, a couple, united in every way except in the eyes of church and state. The debate continues today, even among those who celebrate Stevens and Mrs. Smith as exemplars of human rights and justice. The intent of this account, with regard to the question of Mrs. Smith's relationship to Thaddeus Stevens, has been to gather the available evidence and present it to readers for consideration. And readers are welcome to come down wherever they choose. But, after reviewing that information, I am inclined to believe that Lydia Hamilton Smith and Thaddeus Stevens enjoyed a committed relationship, not unlike that experienced by couples whose unions are sanctified by the church and certified by the state. It is not important to me—indeed, I'm not sure it is even appropriate for us to know—whether there was a sexual dimension to their shared life.

I would trace the arc of their relationship this way. They met and came to know each other in Gettysburg; their friendship continued through the years of Lydia's unfortunate marriage to Jacob Smith and was finally "consummated," in whatever way they chose to do so, when Lydia left Jacob and moved to Lancaster to be with Stevens. Self-righteous individuals repeatedly accused them of living in sin, but the only sin I see here was committed by a benighted society that refused to recognize that this white man and this Black woman loved each other as deeply as any white or Black couple anywhere.

It is a testimony to the personal strength of Lydia Hamilton Smith and Thaddeus Stevens that they endured the prohibitions and intolerance that confronted them throughout their life together and still went on to make valuable contributions to American society. In the end, what went on behind closed doors at 45 South Queen Street is not the most important thing to know about Mrs. Smith. Rather, it is the fact that she was truly an uncommon woman in turbulent times who should be recognized when historians chronicle America's dynamic and dangerous nineteenth century. My hope is that this book will help raise awareness of her to such a level that when history students of the future watch the final scene of the movie *Lincoln*, they will already know the name Lydia Hamilton Smith.

Notes

Details of United States census records derive from the FamilySearch database. Links to records can be found at "United States Census Online Genealogy Records," FamilySearch, https://www.familysearch.org/en/wiki/United_States_Census_Online_Genealogy_Records, and additional information is available at "Beginning Research in United States Census Records," FamilySearch, https://www.familysearch.org/en/wiki/United_States_Census. References to the census below include the year of the census and specific information about the city and ward number as applicable.

Introduction

1. Reynolds, *Mightier than the Sword*, 213.
2. Cook, *Thomas Dixon*, 51.
3. See "The Jezebel Stereotype," Ferris State University Museum, The Jim Crow Museum, https://www.ferris.edu/HTMLS/news/jimcrow/jezebel/index.htm.
4. Dixon, *Clansman*, 25.
5. Smith, "My Books Are Hard Reading," 51.
6. Franklin, "'Birth of a Nation,'" 419.
7. Landis, "Refutation." By "within her station," Landis likely means as a house-keeper. Judge Landis's article began as a letter to the Lancaster *New Era* newspaper in 1916 in response to what he (and many others) considered the slanderous portrayal of both Thaddeus Stevens and Lydia Hamilton Smith in Dixon's *Clansman*, which inspired *The Birth of a Nation* in 1915. Judge Landis wrote that he wanted to offer "some facts in detail, chiefly gleaned from records, and, therefore, not open to dispute." The only deviation from fact that I detect in Landis's contribution is his insistence that Lydia's son Isaac was so dark-skinned that he could "not [have] the slightest trace of Caucasian blood in his veins." Isaac's mother and grandmother were mixed-race women.
8. Levine, *Thaddeus Stevens*, 8–9. Levine erroneously states that Smith began working for Stevens in 1848 rather than 1844.
9. Baldwin's *Blues for Mr. Charlie* is a fictional treatment based on the 1955 murder of a Black fourteen-year-old, Emmett Till, in Money, Mississippi. Till was accused of getting "fresh" with the white wife of a store owner. In the play, the store owner, after murdering Emmett for his perceived indiscretion, acknowledges his fondness for a Black girl named Willa Mae and casually confesses that he initiated the relationship by raping her: "Yet and still, the first time I took Willa Mae, I had to fight her. I swear I did. Maybe she was frightened. But I never had to fight her again. No. It was good, boy, let me tell you, and she liked it as much as me." See Baldwin, *Blues for Mr. Charlie*, 67–68.
10. For the Lancaster newspaper story, see Pratt, "Statue Honors Once-Enslaved Woman," 6. For the full story of Elizabeth Freeman's successful quest for freedom, see the Massachusetts Court System, "Freedom Suits of the Pre-Constitutional Era: The Mum Bett Case," https://www.mass.gov/guides/massachusetts-constitution-and-the-abolition-of-slavery#-conclusion.

Chapter 1

1. Hadden, *Slave Patrols*. Hadden reports that Southern states considered militias so essential for keeping slaves in line that they were reluctant to send them to fight against the British and, after the war, they were adamant about maintaining the right of slave states to arm those militias. In Virginia, militias had become de facto slave patrols by the mid-1750s, and they needed guns to carry out their duties: militia commanders "could order all men to go to church armed with weapons, and appoint patrols to visit 'all negro quarters, and other places suspected of entertaining unlawful assemblies of slaves, servants, or other disorderly persons.'" (Hadden cites "An act, for the better Regulation of the Militia" in Hening, *Statutes at Large*, 19.) "Moreover, patrollers could take up slaves 'strolling about' between plantations without passes and take them to a justice of the peace, who could order them to be whipped" (Hadden, *Slave Patrols*, 31). See also Bogus, "Was Slavery a Factor." Bogus makes three points about what Virginians were thinking about militias as they met to consider ratifying the Bill of Rights, including the Second Amendment: (1) the *majority* (my emphasis) population in eastern Virginia was composed of enslaved Black people, (2) the principal instrument for slave control was the militia, and (3) previously, the militias were creatures of state government. Bogus suggests that Virginia congressman James Madison inserted the phrase "a free State" to make sure that states would retain "the power to arm their militias if Congress did not." In the context of the Supreme Court's 2008 decision making the right to bear arms universal, Bogus asks: "Would we think differently about the amendment if we realized that its genesis was, at least in part, a concern with preserving a form of governmental tyranny [i.e., slave patrols]?"

2. Joseph J. Ellis, "Thomas Jefferson," Britannica.com, https://www.britannica.com/biography/Thomas-Jefferson.

3. Wikipedia, s.v. "Valentine's Day," https://en.wikipedia.org/wiki/Valentine%27s_Day.

4. See Adams County Office of Planning and Development, "Connecting Adams: A History of Transportation in Adams County," https://storymaps.arcgis.com/stories/9c9f74754dc64c41950d036aa305a335.

5. See the Joshua Russell family tree in Glatfelter, Bolin, and Smith, "Sources Relating to Lydia Hamilton Smith," at the Adams County Historical Society. The Joshua Russell family tree is one of the documents supplied to the Historical Society by Edward R. (Ned) Brownley of Gettysburg in 2011. Brownley was then the owner of the Russell Tavern building.

6. "This and That," *Lancaster Inquirer*, October 6, 1883, reprinted with other articles by Randolph Harris in *Underground Railroad Origins in Pennsylvania* (blog), http://undergroundrroriginspa.org/wp-content/uploads/2016/03/Inquirer-news-clips-handout-4-6-12.pdf.

7. Joshua Russell family tree included in the documents donated to the Adams County Historical Society by Ned Brownley (see note 5 above). Brownley also points out that if Enoch Hamilton was Lydia's father, then his daughter with Jane McClure, Harriet Hamilton, would have been Lydia's half sister. No record has surfaced, so far, of Lydia acknowledging or claiming Harriet as her sister.

8. Landis, "Refutation."

9. Woodley, *Great Leveler*, 148.

10. For more, see Wikipedia, s.v. "Creole Peoples," https://en.wikipedia.org/wiki/Creole_peoples.

11. Brodie, *Thaddeus Stevens*, 57.

12. Sandburg, *Abraham Lincoln*, 274.

13. "Death Certificate, Lydia H. Smith, District of Columbia, 2/14/1884, Permit #40890," in Lydia Hamilton Smith Family File, LancasterHistory Library, Lancaster, PA. For Mrs. Smith's birth date, see also Glatfelter, Bolin, and Smith, "Sources Relating to Lydia Hamilton Smith," Adams County Historical Society.

14. "Death Certificate, Lydia H. Smith."

15. The Wikipedia entry for "Lydia Hamilton Smith" tracks her beginnings to Russell Tavern and suggests that her mother was "a free mulatto woman of European and African descent"; see https://en.wikipedia.org/wiki/Lydia_Hamilton_Smith.

16. Brodie, *Thaddeus Stevens*, 23–24.

17. Hoch, *Thaddeus Stevens in Gettysburg*, 13; Hall, *Reminiscences and Sketches*, 3.

18. Scovel, "Thaddeus Stevens," 545.

19. Hensel, "Early Letter," 398.

Chapter 2

1. Reprinting another newspaper's content was common in nineteenth-century America. That appears to be the explanation for two of the obituaries published for Lydia Hamilton Smith. On page 2 of the *Lancaster Intelligencer* for February 15, 1884, we learn that Mrs. O'Neill "removed from her country home to Gettysburg while Lydia was but a child, and remained there several years." Four days later, on February 19, 1884, the *Gettysburg Republican Compiler* reported (without attribution) that "Mrs. O'Neill, her mother, removed from her country home to Gettysburg while Lydia was but a child, and remained there several years." Both newspapers were very critical of Thaddeus Stevens and his political activities. They were unstintingly demeaning in their comments about the relationship between Stevens and Mrs. Smith.

2. "Thaddeus Stevens' Housekeeper Dead," *Lancaster Inquirer*, February 16, 1884, 3.

3. "Will of Lydia Smith of Lancaster," dated December 21, 1877, Will Book F, vol. 2, pp. 204–8, Lancaster County Archives, Lancaster, PA.

4. Ibid. For the Alex Reiman family and Jane Williams, see the United States Census Bureau, 1850 census, Ward 18, Baltimore, MD.

5. This fact was shared with the author by Dr. Faith Mitchell, who provided an important critique of the original manuscript. Mitchell, who holds a doctorate in medical anthropology from the University of California, Berkeley, has written about her own family's experiences in antebellum Pennsylvania. See Mitchell, "Growing Up."

6. Webster, "History of Black Girls."

7. National Register of Historic Places, "Reiman Block," Baltimore, MD, https://npgallery.nps.gov/AssetDetail/NRIS/84001350. For Alex Reiman, see the United States Census Bureau, 1870 census, District 01, Baltimore, MD.

8. United States Census Bureau, 1850 census and 1870 census.

9. "Will of Lydia Smith of Lancaster." Alex Reiman family and Jane Williams: United States Census Bureau, 1850 census. Jane Cooper is included in the household of Joseph Cooper in Baltimore in 1850: see United States Census Bureau, 1850 census, Ward 1, Baltimore, MD.

10. Jane Cooper in Baltimore in 1850: United States Census Bureau, 1850 census. Jane Cooper and Joseph Cooper in 1860: United States Census Bureau, 1860 census, Ward 1, Baltimore, MD.

11. Jane Cooper, widow, 1870: United States Census Bureau, 1870 census, Ward 11, Baltimore, MD. Jane Cooper, widow, 1880: United States Census Bureau, 1880 census, ED 95, Baltimore, MD.

12. "An Act for the Gradual Abolition of Slavery, March 1, 1780," Pennsylvania Historical and Museum Commission, http://www.phmc.state.pa.us/portal /communities/documents/1776-1865/abolition-slavery.html.

13. Hoch, *Thaddeus Stevens in Gettysburg*, 228.

14. Ibid., 229.

15. Ibid., 230–31. Hoch cites "Where Stevens Lived," *New York Times*, October 6, 1883, as the original source of the story. The story was also published in the *Lancaster Inquirer* on the same date. A hostelry is an inn or hotel; a James *McCreary* was licensed to keep a tavern on Gettysburg lot 21, near today's 20 Baltimore Street, from 1814 to 1819 and sold the property in 1823. In some versions of the story, Ephraim's surname is spelled "Ulrich."

16. Brodie, *Thaddeus Stevens*, 52.

17. Elsie Singmaster published *I Speak for Thaddeus Stevens* in 1947. Her research notes and various clippings related to Lydia Smith and Thaddeus Stevens are part of the Elsie Singmaster Collection: Research and Pamphlets, 6499, File Box 2, Binder 8, Adams County Historical Society, Gettysburg, PA. A handwritten page at the start of the section reads: "Lydia, in Gettysburg, Lancaster—Washington." Following up on speculation about Enoch Hamilton and Mrs. O'Neill, Singmaster spent considerable time tracking down "Hamiltons" in Adams County's Straban Township, which borders the town of Gettysburg and was the location of Russell Tavern, where Lydia was born. Singmaster points out that a blacksmith named Robert Hamilton was living near Russell Tavern in 1816, as well as other Hamiltons, and she concludes, "There were Hamiltons in Straban [Township], and it seems quite possible . . . Lydia took her name from this family."

18. "History: An Overview," Gettysburg Borough website, www.gettysburgpa .gov/history.

19. Darby, *Darby's Edition of Brookes' Universal Gazetteer*, 17.

20. Hoch, *Thaddeus Stevens in Gettysburg*, 5–6. Hoch's thorough review of the Hunter case and his description of Stevens's brilliance as a lawyer are well worth reading.

21. The newspaper account is part of Robert L. Bloom's excellent history of Adams County. Both Bloom and the *Centinel* are referenced in Hoch, *Thaddeus Stevens in Gettysburg*, 5. Bloom, *History of Adams County*, 138. The *Centinel* later became the *Adams Sentinel*.

22. Hoch, *Thaddeus Stevens in Gettysburg*, 5.

23. Hood, "Stevens, Thaddeus," 576.

24. The muckraking journalist Ray Stannard Baker gives a devastating account of a lynching in Springfield, Ohio, in *McClure's Magazine* in February 1905. He titled it "What Is a Lynching?" His reporting serves as a scathing indictment of the "upstanding citizens" of any community who are still capable of indulging their morbid curiosity at such horrific events.

25. Harris, *Review of the Political Conflict*, 19.

26. Ibid.

27. Ibid.

28. Hoch, *Thaddeus Stevens in Gettysburg*, 230–31.

29. Harris, *Review of the Political Conflict*, 67.

30. Hoch, *Thaddeus Stevens in Gettysburg*, 22.
31. Ibid., 61.
32. Brodie, *Thaddeus Stevens*, 35ff. Brodie considers the possibility that Stevens might actually have slain Dinah to prevent the child he had given her from being born. Brodie doesn't embrace that as the likely truth of the matter, however. (There was some disagreement on the exact date of Peter Stewart's death: on August 19, 1833, Gettysburg's *Adams Sentinel* reported that Stewart died on Friday night, August 16.)
33. Robertson, "Idealist as Opportunist," 51.

Chapter 3

1. Hoch, *Thaddeus Stevens in Gettysburg*, 44.
2. Ibid., 41.
3. Scovel, "Thaddeus Stevens," 546.
4. Hall, *Reminiscences and Sketches*, 21.
5. Morgan, *Annals*, 180–81.
6. Wikipedia, s.v. "penal treadmill," https://en.wikipedia.org/wiki/Penal _treadmill. The first American prison treadmill was erected in New York City in 1822.
7. Smedley, *History of the Underground Railroad*, originally published in 1883. Smedley was a physician in West Chester, Pennsylvania. He was a white man and a Quaker. He had no training as a historian or writer, and some scholars fault his book, noting that he gives the impression that white Quakers constituted almost all of the agents on the Underground Railroad (he rarely mentions Black agents or agents from other Christian denominations). Still, Smedley's "amateur" efforts yielded a wealth of details about the Underground Railroad and a virtual oral history of the Railroad directly from fugitives as well as Underground Railroad stationmasters and their families.
8. Hoch, *Thaddeus Stevens in Gettysburg*, 244.
9. Hood, "Stevens, Thaddeus," 576.
10. Brodie, *Thaddeus Stevens*, 31. Brodie's description of Thaddeus Stevens as he appeared during his first decade or so in Gettysburg draws on the description provided by Alexander Hood, his law student and friend. Hood, "Stevens, Thaddeus," 596.
11. Hoch, *Thaddeus Stevens in Gettysburg*, 58.
12. Ibid., 576.
13. Trefousse, *Thaddeus Stevens*, 27, 31.
14. Hood, "Stevens, Thaddeus," 576.
15. Hoch, *Thaddeus Stevens in Gettysburg*, 73.
16. Elsie Singmaster Collection: Research, 6499, File Box 1, Binder 3, Adams County Historical Society, Gettysburg, PA. This section includes notes from local newspapers, some related to Thaddeus Stevens and Lydia Hamilton Smith. The bulk of her entries range from 1831 to 1835. Singmaster was looking for information she could weave into her historical novel, *I Speak for Thaddeus Stevens*.
17. Hoch, *Thaddeus Stevens in Gettysburg*, 74.
18. Morgan, *Annals*, 194–95.
19. Ibid.
20. Hoch, *Thaddeus Stevens in Gettysburg*, 74.

Chapter 4

1. Palmer and Ochoa, *Selected Papers*, 1:18.
2. Elsie Singmaster, research notes for her novel *I Speak for Thaddeus Stevens*,

"Lydia, in Gettysburg, Lancaster—Washington," Elsie Singmaster Collection: Research and Pamphlets, 6499, File Box 2, Binder 8, Adams County Historical Society, Gettysburg, PA.

3.   "Lydia Smith Dead: Thad. Stevens Old Housekeeper," *Lancaster Intelligencer*, February 15, 1884, 2.

4.   "A Noted Woman Gone: Sudden Death of Mrs. Lydia Smith," *Lancaster Weekly Examiner and Express*, February 20, 1884, 6.

5.   Landis, "Refutation," 49.

6.   Notes from Miller, *Thaddeus Stevens*, found in Glatfelter, Bolin, and Smith, "Notes from Alphonse B. Miller's book, *Thaddeus Stevens* (New York: Harper & Brothers, 1939)," in "Sources Relating to Lydia Hamilton Smith," Section K, Adams County Historical Society.

7.   Brodie, *Thaddeus Stevens*, 87.

8.   Elsie Singmaster, research notes for her novel *I Speak for Thaddeus Stevens*, Elsie Singmaster Collection: Research and Pamphlets, 6499, File Box 1, Binder 3, Adams County Historical Society, Gettysburg, PA. Notes from local newspapers.

9.   Brian Johnson, "Calm Before the Storm: Gettysburg's African-American Community Before the Battle," *Gettysburg Compiler* (Civil War Institute, Gettysburg College), October 18, 2013, https://gettysburgcompiler.org/2013/10/18 /calm-before-the-storm-gettysburgs-african-american-community-before-the-battle/.

10.   This data combines the efforts of Elsie Singmaster and Dr. Charles Glatfelter's team at the Adams County Historical Society. Singmaster made note of Jacob Smith's name in the 1829 tax rolls. Glatfelter, Bolin, and Smith included their review of Gettysburg tax records in Section D of their "Sources Relating to Lydia Hamilton Smith." See note 6 above.

11.   Wikipedia, s.v. "Married Women's Property Acts in the United States," https://en.wikipedia.org/wiki/Married_Women%27s_Property_Acts_in_the_United _States#Pennsylvania.

12.   The information card for the lot Lydia Hamilton Smith purchased at St. Mary's Cemetery in Lancaster (Lot 609) lists William's date of birth as 1835. The simple stone at the head of the grave William shares with his brother, Isaac, does not list his birth date. In his "Refutation," Judge Landis transcribed the inscription on Lydia's sons' monument as: "Isaac / Died Apr. 7, 1884 / In the 37th year of his age / William / Died May 10, 1860 / In the 25th year of his age / Sons of / Jacob & Lydia H. Smith." As we'll see in a later chapter of this book, published accounts contemporary with William's death place it in 1861.

13.   The information card for Lydia's lot at St. Mary's Cemetery lists Isaac's birth date as 1847. The inscription on the monument he shares with his brother, William, indicates that he died on April 7, 1884, "In the 37th year of his age." Other records dispute that. When Isaac enlisted in Company E of the 6th US Colored Infantry on July 7, 1863, he was, according to the military record, twenty-six years old. Simple arithmetic reveals that he was born in 1837, not 1847, as the monument by his grave indicates. He would have been forty-seven when he died, not thirty-seven, as the monument is inscribed.

14.   John Sergeant was a prominent lawyer from Philadelphia, Pennsylvania. Hall doesn't tell us where Stevens met Sergeant's daughter. Wikipedia, s.v. "John Sergeant (politician)," https://en.wikipedia.org/wiki/John_Sergeant_(politician); Hall, *Reminiscences and Sketches*, 16.

15. Wikipedia, s.v. "Harrisburg, Pennsylvania," https://en.wikipedia.org/wiki/Harrisburg,_Pennsylvania#Pre-industry:_1800%E2%80%931850, and Eggert, *Harrisburg Industrializes*, 58.

16. The arsenal was for storing military materiel. Elsie Singmaster, research notes for her novel *I Speak for Thaddeus Stevens*, Elsie Singmaster Collection: Research and Pamphlets, 6499, File Box 1, Binder 3, Adams County Historical Society, Gettysburg, PA. Singmaster gleaned information about Harrisburg from Morgan, *Annals*. She did not preserve the numbers of the pages where the information was located.

17. Glatfelter, Bolin, and Smith, "Sources Relating to Lydia Hamilton Smith," Section C, 1840 Dauphin Co. Census, Adams County Historical Society.

18. Ibid., section D, review of Gettysburg tax records.

19. Ibid., section D.2.

20. Barker, *Map of Dauphin County, Pennsylvania*.

21. Singmaster, *I Speak for Thaddeus Stevens*, 206–7.

22. Hall, *Reminiscences and Sketches*, 16.

23. Brodie, *Thaddeus Stevens*, 88.

24. Hensel, "Jacob Eichholtz, Painter" (1913), 62; see also Hensel, "Jacob Eichholtz, Painter" (1912), 22, 37.

25. The Frick Art Reference Library (FARL) in New York first photographed the portrait in 1943. The photographer was Ira W. Martin; the record number for the photo is 35328. See Frick Digital Collections, https://library.frick.org/permalink/01NYA_INST/d73c5u/alma991005293909707141. Mrs. James (Rebecca) Beal, an amateur watercolor artist, art collector, and art scholar from Pittsburgh, was Jacob Eichholtz's granddaughter. See Karakatsanis, "Enduring Legacy." Mrs. Katharine McCook Knox, a native of Washington, DC, was an American art historian best known for her history of the Frick Art Reference Library and for curatorial work on presidential portraits. Wikipedia, s.v. "Katharine McCook Knox," https://en.wikipedia.org/wiki/Katharine_McCook_Knox.

26. As of 2006, the portrait was hanging in the Lyceum of Pennsylvania Hall on the campus of Gettysburg College in Gettysburg, Pennsylvania. A color photo reproduction of the painting is posted on the college website in a section called "The Cupola: Scholarship at Gettysburg College." The photo is accompanied by an informative student paper about the portrait and Stevens, written by Axel T. Kaegler, as part of the college's "Hidden Papers" project. See https://cupola.gettysburg.edu/hiddenimages/6/.

27. Palmer and Ochoa, *Selected Papers*, 1:xxix.

28. Ryan, *Worlds of Jacob Eichholtz*, 20. Ryan reported that this information was drawn from "Index to Letters from Jacob Eichholtz to his Son-in-law Robert Lindsay, September 7, 1832, to April 4, 1842," which is held in a private collection. Ryan found a photocopy of the index in the Archives and Special Collections section of Franklin & Marshall College's Shadek-Fackenthal Library in Lancaster, PA. Thomas H. Burrowes, Stevens's future neighbor in Lancaster, was the Pennsylvania secretary of state who commissioned the portraits.

29. Milley, "Jacob Eichholtz," 128.

30. Beal, *Jacob Eichholtz*, xxx. Beal was Jacob Eichholtz's granddaughter; see note 25 above. Rail service between Harrisburg and Lancaster began in 1838.

31. Ryan, *Worlds of Jacob Eichholtz*, 141.

32. Hoch, *Thaddeus Stevens in Gettysburg*, 230–31.

33. Trefousse, *Thaddeus Stevens*, 68. Alexander Harris reports that after two years in Lancaster, Stevens was earning $12,000 to $15,000 a year, and it remained at that level for many years. Harris, *Review of the Political Conflict*, 19.

34. Landis, "Refutation."

35. Timothy Smith kindly explained this process to me at the Adams County Historical Society in Gettysburg. He said that Stevens employed this approach at many of the properties he purchased at sheriff's sale.

36. For the price Stevens paid for what would be his final home in Lancaster, see Hoch, *Thaddeus Stevens in Gettysburg*, 49. For details about the property, see Delle and Levine, "Excavations." For occupants of Stevens's new properties, see also Delle and Levine, "Equality of Man Before His Creator," 132.

37. "Noted Woman Gone," 6.

38. "Thaddeus Stevens' Housekeeper Dead," *Lancaster Inquirer*, February 16, 1884, 3.

39. Death notice for Jacob Smith, *Gettysburg Republican Compiler*, January 3, 1853, 3.

40. In a report of the June 26, 2018, meeting of the Baltimore Civil War Roundtable, we are told that Darlene Colon was the guest speaker, and that on the subject of Lydia and Jacob's separation, Ms. Colon explained that Jacob "was away much of the time." See Baltimore Civil War Roundtable meeting, June 26, 2018, https://bcwrt.nalweb.net/previous2018.htm.

41. Brodie, *Thaddeus Stevens*, 86. Brodie quotes from an article originally published in the *Albany (NY) Evening Journal and Georgetown Courier*, August 8, 1868.

42. Glatfelter, Bolin, and Smith, "Sources Relating to Lydia Hamilton Smith," Section D-3, Dauphin Co. deeds 1841 & 1844, Adams County Historical Society. See also note 6 above.

43. Landis, "Refutation," 49–52.

44. "Noted Woman Gone," 6.

45. Landis, "Refutation," 49. Records indicate Jacob Smith was still very much alive in 1844.

46. Korngold, *Thaddeus Stevens*, 72.

47. Landis, "Refutation," 49. The house was on the east side of South Queen Street.

48. Death notice for Jacob Smith, *Gettysburg Star and Banner*, December 31, 1852, 2. This report was attributed to the *Harrisburg Telegraph*.

49. "Inauguration of Gov. Bigler," *Bloomsburg (PA) Star of the North*, December 18, 1851, 2.

50. Death notice for Jacob Smith, *Gettysburg Republican Compiler*.

51. "Mrs. Lydia Smith, Housekeeper for Thaddeus Stevens, Dies in Washington," *Lancaster New Era*, February 15, 1884, 4.

Chapter 5

1. "A Noted Woman Gone: Sudden Death of Mrs. Lydia Smith," *Lancaster Weekly Examiner and Express*, February 20, 1884, 6.

2. Woodley, *Great Leveler*, 3.

3. "Mrs. Lydia Smith, Housekeeper for Thaddeus Stevens, Dies in Washington," *Lancaster New Era*, February 15, 1884.

4. Harris, *Review of the Political Conflict*, 85.

5. Hensel, "Thaddeus Stevens as a Country Lawyer," 264.

6. Woodley, *Great Leveler*, 147.

7. Hood, "Stevens, Thaddeus," 582.

8. Current, *Old Thad Stevens*, 78.

9. Palmer and Ochoa, *Selected Papers*, 1:82.

10. Smedley, *History of the Underground Railroad*, 36. Smedley says that the group passed through in 1842. For an assessment of Smedley's contribution to Underground Railroad history, see chapter 3, note 7.

11. Portions of Gilbert's unpublished manuscript, included in an application to the National Park Service (prepared by consulting historian Randolph Harris), were instrumental in the park service's decision to add Thaddeus Stevens's house on South Queen Street to the National Underground Railroad Network to Freedom. At the time of this writing, LancasterHistory was engaged in developing the Thaddeus Stevens and Lydia Hamilton Smith Center for History and Democracy at that site. The full application seeking Network to Freedom status, with excerpts from Gilbert's manuscript, can be seen here: http://undergroundrroriginspa.org/wp-content/uploads/2016/10/StevensHouseOfficeNPSFinal1-2011.pdf.

12. Ibid.

13. Palmer and Ochoa, *Selected Papers*, 1:65. Palmer and Ochoa explain that Stevens was writing to Samuel Webb, a member of the executive council of the Pennsylvania Anti-Slavery Society. Webb and the committee had invited Stevens to join them for the opening of Pennsylvania Hall, a new building in Philadelphia dedicated to the abolition of slavery. The new edifice provides a handy gauge for measuring the pro-slavery sentiment in Pennsylvania in 1838. Pennsylvania Hall was dedicated on May 14, 1838. A mob burned it down three days later.

14. Ellis and Evans, *History of Lancaster County*, 240.

15. Harris, *Review of the Political Conflict*, 96.

16. Palmer and Ochoa, *Selected Papers*, 1:147.

17. For more on the Goodridge family and their involvement in the Underground Railroad, see McClure, "Glenalvin Goodridge." Also see Wikipedia, s.v. "William C. Goodridge," https://en.wikipedia.org/wiki/William_C._Goodridge#Biography.

18. "Our Local Church History," Bethel African Methodist Episcopal Church, Lancaster, PA, https://bethelamelancaster.com/our-local-church-history.

19. Trefousse, *Thaddeus Stevens*, 73. Trefousse found Stevens's letter to Jeremiah Brown in Charles D. Spotts, "The Pilgrim's Pathway: The Underground Railroad in Lancaster County," *Community History* 5, no. 6 (1966). Spotts, however, does not cite the source of Stevens's letter. Lancaster newspaperman Ellwood Griest claimed to be the first to publish the letter when he included it in his "This and That" column in the *Lancaster Inquirer* in October 1883. Griest also failed to reveal the source of the letter. Lancaster County historian Randolph Harris believes that Lydia Hamilton Smith may have given Griest the letter when he interviewed her shortly before she died.

20. Knowles, "African American Heritage Walking Tour."

21. Cornelius, "Speakers at Highland Presbyterian's Sr. Life Institute." Elsie Singmaster gathered the details of Lancaster's Underground Railroad network during her research for her historical novel, *I Speak for Thaddeus Stevens*. "Lydia, in Gettysburg, Lancaster—Washington," Elsie Singmaster Collection: Research and Pamphlets, 6499, File Box 2, Binder 8, Adams County Historical Society, Gettysburg, PA.

22. Harris, *Review of the Political Conflict*, 96.

23. Hood, "Stevens, Thaddeus," 589. See also Harris, *Review of the Political Conflict*, 97–98.

24. Brodie, *Thaddeus Stevens*, 93.

25. Hall, *Reminiscences and Sketches*, 26.

26. Meltzer, *Thaddeus Stevens*, 82.

27. Jolly, "Historical Reputation," 58.

28. Landis, "Refutation," 6.

29. Robbins and Roberts, "Early Feminists."

30. Brodie, *Thaddeus Stevens*, 95.

31. Woodley, *Great Leveler*, 156.

Chapter 6

1. For public education for Black children, see "Public Schools," *Adams Sentinel*, December 29, 1834. For Black children attending local schools in 1824, see Weaver, "Black Influence." Dr. Leroy Hopkins, whose scholarship includes the study of African American history in Pennsylvania, suggested to me, in personal correspondence, that "being Catholic Lydia may very well have benefitted from an extensive catechism class that would also have developed her literacy." Gettysburg's oldest Catholic church, St. Francis Xavier Church, wasn't completed until 1830, but priests were saying mass in private homes before 1827. Lydia might have received her catechetical instruction under those conditions. For the history of St. Francis Xavier Church, see St. Francis Xavier Catholic Parish, "Complete Timeline of Our Parish's History," https://drive.google.com/file/d/1gtk8IW-wdbGrUwi-8Ils6MVKteneJEFe/view.

2. Letter from John A. Coyle to Father George Brown, dated November 22, 1937, in "Lydia, in Gettysburg, Lancaster—Washington," Elsie Singmaster Collection: Research and Pamphlets, 6499, File Box 2, Binder 8, Adams County Historical Society, Gettysburg, PA.

3. "Mrs. Lydia Smith, Housekeeper for Thaddeus Stevens, Dies in Washington," *Lancaster New Era*, February 15, 1884, 4. This obituary identified the professions of her sons, William and Isaac.

4. Landis, "Refutation."

5. Brodie, *Thaddeus Stevens*, 99–100.

6. Eby, "John Beck," 19. Today, the Ladies Seminary is the Linden Hall School for Girls.

7. For Thaddeus Stevens Jr.'s dwelling, see United States Census Bureau, 1850 census, Warwick Township, Lancaster County, PA.

8. Eby, "John Beck," 1.

9. Hensel, "Thaddeus Stevens as a Country Lawyer," 269.

10. Wikipedia, s.v. "Missouri Compromise," https://en.wikipedia.org/wiki/Missouri_Compromise.

11. Wikipedia, s.v. "Henry Clay," https://en.wikipedia.org/wiki/Henry_Clay.

12. Atlee, "Thaddeus Stevens and Slavery."

13. Ibid.

14. Brodie, *Thaddeus Stevens*, 115.

15. Trefousse, *Thaddeus Stevens*, 84.

16. Nye, *Fettered Freedom*, 209.

17. Delle and Levine, "Excavations."

18. Bordewich, "Digging into a Historic Rivalry."

19. Still, *Underground Railroad*, 608–9.

20. Hensel, "Thaddeus Stevens as a Country Lawyer," 270.

21. Ibid.

22. Wikipedia, s.v. "John Merriman Reynolds," https://en.wikipedia.org/wiki /John_Merriman_Reynolds#House_of_Representatives.

23. Brodie, *Thaddeus Stevens*, 116–17. Brodie draws many of her details from William Parker's "Freedman's Story," his first-person account of the happenings at Christiana published in the February–March 1866 issue of *Atlantic Monthly* and republished by the magazine in 2012.

24. Brodie, *Thaddeus Stevens*, 117.

25. Hensel, "Thaddeus Stevens as a Country Lawyer," 274.

26. Ibid., 273–74.

27. Ibid., 275.

28. Wikipedia, s.v. "Anthony Ellmaker Roberts," https://en.wikipedia.org/wiki /Anthony_Ellmaker_Roberts.

Chapter 7

1. Trefousse, *Thaddeus Stevens*, 83.

2. Milton, *Age of Hate*, 264. Milton may not have actually visited the gambling parlors of Washington. He drew most of his details from a book by John B. Ellis, *Sights and Secrets of the National Capitol* (New York, 1869), 400.

3. Milton, *Age of Hate*, 264.

4. Ibid.

5. The record cited was provided to me by Timothy Smith, Historian and Collections Manager at the Adams County Historical Society, Gettysburg, PA. It bears the title: "Research on Gettysburg Town Lots, by Timothy H. Smith, Randy Miller and Andrew Dalton, Adams County Historical Society." The property in question is identified as Lot T-A: Adam Shoemaker Residence.

6. "Our Local Church History," Bethel African Methodist Episcopal Church, Lancaster, PA, https://bethelamelancaster.com/our-local-church-history.

7. Shiffler Fire Company Records, 1854–1886, MG-524, LancasterHistory archives, Lancaster, PA. This collection includes records of the Conestoga Hose Company and Shiffler Fire Company.

8. Ellis and Evans, *History of Lancaster County*, 391.

9. "Death of George Shifler [*sic*]," print held at the National Museum of American History, Smithsonian Institution, https://americanhistory.si.edu/collections /searchhttps:/objecthttps:/nmah_324746.

10. Ellis and Evans, *History of Lancaster County*, 391.

11. "Notes from Alphonse B. Miller's book, *Thaddeus Stevens* (New York: Harper & Brothers, 1939)," in Glatfelter, Bolin, and Smith, "Sources Relating to Lydia Hamilton Smith," Section D.4, Adams County Historical Society.

12. Glatfelter, Bolin, and Smith, "Sources Relating to Lydia Hamilton Smith," Adams County Historical Society.

13. Ibid.

14. Robertson, "Idealist as Opportunist," 63; Trefousse, *Thaddeus Stevens*, 84.

15. Trefousse, *Thaddeus Stevens*, 84.

16. Palmer and Ochoa, *Selected Papers*, 1:147.

17. Ibid.

18. Letter from Thaddeus Stevens Jr. to Mrs. [Lydia Hamilton] Smith, from Littleton, NH, March 26 [1854?], http//hdl.loc.gov/loc.mss/mso10266.mss41442.0008. Thad Jr.'s grandmother was living in Peacham.

19. Ibid.
20. Ibid.
21. Ibid.

Chapter 8

1. John Jones, Indictment, Furnishing liquor to a minor, RG 02–00 0933, NOV 1854 F002, LancasterHistory archives, Lancaster, PA.

2. *J. H. Bryson's Lancaster Directory for 1843*, "Jones, William, tavern, Mulberry corner at Walnut st.," 11. John Jones in 1857: *Lancaster City Directory . . . 1857*, "Jones, John, segarmaker, h Manor & W King," 53. For the statute Lydia used against John Jones, see note 1.

3. Isaac Smith, Quarter Sessions Papers, Misdemeanor, RG 02–00 0417, APR 1854 F059 QS, LancasterHistory archives, Lancaster, PA.

4. Trefousse, *Thaddeus Stevens*, 91.

5. Brodie, *Thaddeus Stevens*, 51.

6. Hood, "Stevens, Thaddeus," 582.

7. For more on the Know-Nothings, see Library of Congress, "Examiner's questions for admittance to the American (or Know-Nothing) Party, July 1854," https://www.loc.gov/item/mcc.062/.

8. Robertson, "Idealist as Opportunist," 62–64.

9. Hoelscher, "Thaddeus Stevens as a Lancaster Politician," 178.

10. Wikipedia, s.v. "A. E. Roberts," under the "late political career" heading, https://en.wikipedia.org/wiki/Anthony_Ellmaker_Roberts#Late_political_career.

11. Robertson, "Idealist as Opportunist," 65.

12. Depositions—June 24, 1887, Thaddeus Stevens Estate File 1867–1901, RG3-10.1, Lancaster County Archives, Lancaster, PA.

13. Drawn from "Underground Railroad, the Sole Surviving Captain Tells an Interesting Story, of the System of Taking Care of Fugitive Slaves Before the War," *Gettysburg Republican Compiler*, April 12, 1911, 11.

14. Hoch, *Thaddeus Stevens in Gettysburg*, 244.

15. Ibid.

16. Landis, "Refutation."

17. Delle and Levine, "Excavations."

18. Current, *Old Thad Stevens*, 114. Current's criticism of the house doesn't quite square with what we know about Lydia as a housekeeper and follower of fashion.

19. Woodley, *Great Leveler*, 149.

20. Current, *Old Thad Stevens*, 116.

21. Landis, "Refutation."

22. Letter from John A. Coyle to Father George Brown, November 22, 1937, in "Lydia, in Gettysburg, Lancaster—Washington," Elsie Singmaster Collection: Research and Pamphlets, 6499, File Box 2, Binder 8, Adams County Historical Society, Gettysburg, PA.

23. Ibid.

24. Gorrecht, "Charity of Thaddeus Stevens," 21.

25. Ibid., 30.

26. Ibid.

27. Ibid.

28. Ibid., 31. Dice could have given information to Mrs. Smith, too, if Stevens were away on business.

29. Ellis and Evans, *History of Lancaster County*, 391.

30. Ibid., 240.

31. "Story of Keziah," in Elsie Singmaster Collection: Research, 6499, File Box 1, Binder #2, Adams County Historical Society, Gettysburg, PA. See also "Columbus-America Discovery Group and the *SS Central America*," http://www.columbia.edu/~dj114/SS_Central_America.pdf.

Chapter 9

1. Trefousse, *Thaddeus Stevens*, 96.

2. Robertson, "Idealist as Opportunist," 49.

3. Palmer and Ochoa, *Selected Papers*, 1:176. Palmer and Ochoa discuss Mrs. Smith's role in Stevens's life, which they argue was more than simply a housekeeper—at least "a highly regarded friend."

4. Landis, "Refutation," 7.

5. Current, *Old Thad Stevens*, 194.

6. Letter from John A. Coyle to Father George Brown, November 22, 1937, "Lydia, in Gettysburg, Lancaster—Washington," Elsie Singmaster Collection: Research and Pamphlets, 6499, File Box 2, Binder 8, Adams County Historical Society, Gettysburg, PA.

7. Current, *Old Thad Stevens*, 194.

8. Palmer and Ochoa, *Selected Papers*, 1:147.

9. Depositions, Auditor's Report, Estate of Lydia Smith, September 25, 1886, Lydia Hamilton Smith Family File, LancasterHistory Library, Lancaster, PA.

10. Ibid.

11. Death notice, [William] Smith, *Lancaster Examiner and Herald*, April 10, 1861, 2; Brubaker, "Lydia Smith's Son Shot Himself."

12. Auditor's Report, Estate of Lydia Smith.

13. Ibid.

14. Ibid.

15. Ibid.

16. Brubaker, "Lydia Smith's Son Shot Himself"; "Our Local Church History," Bethel African Methodist Episcopal Church, Lancaster, PA, https://bethelamelancaster.com/our-local-church-history.

17. "Lydia Smith Dead, Thad. Stevens' Old Housekeeper," *Lancaster Intelligencer*, February 15, 1884, 2.

18. Wikipedia, s.v. "Religious Views on Suicide," https://en.wikipedia.org/wiki/Religious_views_on_suicide#Christianity. For Pius X on suicide, see Apostolic Apologetics, "Catechism of Saint Pius X," on the Fifth Commandment: https://sites.google.com/site/apostolicapologetics/library/catechism-of-saint-pius-x/on-the-commandments-of-god-and-of-the-church/the-fifth-commandment.

19. Depositions—June 24, 1887, Thaddeus Stevens Estate File 1867–1901, RG3-10.1, fourth folder, Lancaster County Archives, Lancaster, PA. Unless otherwise noted, all quotes in this section are drawn from depositions filed in connection with Mary J. Primm's claim, as Alanson J. Stevens's widow, on Thaddeus Stevens's estate.

20. Depositions, Thaddeus Stevens Estate File.

21. Ibid.

22. Ibid.

23. Ibid.

24. Ibid.

25. Ibid.

26. Ibid.

27. Military Genealogy Trails, "Franklin County PA Civil War Three Months' Service Soldiers," transcribed by Tammy Clark from Samuel P. Bates, *History of Pennsylvania Volunteers, 1861–1865,* vol. 1, http://genealogytrails.com/penn/franklin /military/3monthmen.htm. For Thaddeus Jr.: PA-Roots, "1st Regiment, Pennsylvania Volunteers, Company F., Recruited in Lancaster, Lancaster County for Three-Months Service, Mustered in April 20, 1861," http://www.pa-roots.com/pacw /infantry/1st/1stcof.html.

Chapter 10

1. Sandburg, *Abraham Lincoln,* 274.

2. Landis, "Refutation."

3. Invitation, Thaddeus Stevens to Mr. & Mrs. Wright, August 21, 1860, George Steinman Collection, MG-184, Box 1, Folder 20, LancasterHistory, Lancaster, PA.

4. United States Census Bureau, 1860 census, Lancaster, PA, SE Ward.

5. Glatfelter, Bolin, and Smith, "Sources Relating to Lydia Hamilton Smith," Section K, Adams County Historical Society. The public alley was probably South Christian Street.

6. Delle and Levine, "Equality of Man Before His Creator," 128.

7. Supreme Court Appeal Papers, resubmission of Simon Stevens deposition [in New York], December 12, 1873, Thaddeus Stevens Estate File 1867–1901, RG3-10.1, Lancaster County Archives, Lancaster, PA.

8. Delle and Levine, "Equality of Man Before His Creator," 128.

9. McMurry and Van Dolsen, *Architecture and Landscape,* 144. As this book was being written, LancasterHistory was at work on a Stevens and Smith historical museum comprising Lydia's house on East Vine Street (now known as the Lydia Hamilton Smith house), the former Kleiss Tavern on the northeast corner of South Queen and East Vine streets, and the Thaddeus Stevens House and Law Office at 45–47 South Queen Street.

10. Palmer and Ochoa, *Selected Papers,* 1:209.

11. Wikipedia, s.v. "First Battle of Bull Run," https://en.wikipedia.org/wiki /First_Battle_of_Bull_Run.

12. Thaddeus Stevens, "To Lydia Hamilton Smith. Washington July 24, 1861," quoted in Palmer and Ochoa, *Selected Papers,* 1:219.

13. "Thaddeus Stevens Jr.," Find a Grave, Memorials, https://www.findagrave .com/memorial/176549486/thaddeus-stevens.

14. Letter from Lydia Hamilton Smith to Thaddeus Stevens Jr., December 23, 1861, Lydia Hamilton Smith Family File, LancasterHistory Library, Lancaster, PA. The transcription is mine. I have not seen a photocopy or transcription of this letter published in any text or article related to Lydia Hamilton Smith.

15. Appointment of Auditors (1874), Thaddeus Stevens Estate File 1867–1901, RG3-10.1, Lancaster County Archives, Lancaster, PA.

16. Distribution Notes of Audit, Thaddeus Stevens Estate File 1867–1901, RG3-10.1, Lancaster County Archives, Lancaster, PA.

17. Bates, *History of Pennsylvania Volunteers*, 861. See also Palmer and Ochoa, *Selected Papers*, 1:329n1, after Stevens's letter to Alanson dated November 19, 1862.

18. Deposition—June 24, 1887, testimony of Martha Primm Myers and John Sweeney, Thaddeus Stevens Estate File 1867–1901, RG3-10.1, Lancaster County Archives, Lancaster, PA.

19. Ibid.

20. Palmer and Ochoa, *Selected Papers*, 1:328–29.

21. Ibid., 396.

22. Letter dated June 1, 1862: ibid., 397. Mary Primm's comments about her letter of December 4, 1862: Distribution Notes of Audit, Thaddeus Stevens Estate File 1867–1901, RG3-10.1, Lancaster County Archives, Lancaster, PA.

23. Tillman Tolbert's testimony, Distribution Notes of Audit, Thaddeus Stevens Estate File 1867–1901, RG3-10.1, Lancaster County Archives, Lancaster, PA.

24. Walter Crawford's testimony, Distribution Notes of Audit, Thaddeus Stevens Estate File 1867–1901, Folder 7, RG3-10.1, Lancaster County Archives, Lancaster, PA.

25. James Taylor's testimony, Distribution Notes of Audit, Thaddeus Stevens Estate File 1867–1901, Folder 7, RG3-10.1, Lancaster County Archives, Lancaster, PA.

26. Isaac Smith and Jacob Woods, Habeas Corpus papers, Guilty of drunken and disorderly conduct, 1862, RG 01–00 2313, Habeas 1862 F026, LancasterHistory archives, Lancaster, PA.

27. Ibid.

28. Palmer and Ochoa, *Selected Papers*, 1:330.

29. "Thaddeus Stevens, Jr.," FindAGrave, Memorials, https://www.findagrave.com/memorial/176549486/thaddeus-stevens.

30. Palmer and Ochoa, *Selected Papers*, 1:397.

31. Ibid.

32. Wikipedia, s.v. "Enrollment Act," https://en.wikipedia.org/wiki/Enrollment_Act. For Stevens's efforts on behalf of his pacifist constituents: Ellis and Evans, *History of Lancaster County*, 240. See also Harris, *Review of the Political Conflict*, 336, and Hoch, *Thaddeus Stevens in Gettysburg*, 192. For the reception and "egging" in Lancaster: Trefousse, *Thaddeus Stevens*, 132–33.

33. Palmer and Ochoa, *Selected Papers*, 1:403–4.

34. Isaac Smith and John Buckley, Indictment, Hawking and Peddling, RG 02–00 0933, APR 1863 F014, LancasterHistory archives, Lancaster, PA. For Pennsylvania law on "Peddlers" in 1863: Pepper and Lewis, *Digest of the Laws of Pennsylvania*, 3413–14.

35. Gopsill, *Gopsill's Directory*, 108.

36. Isaac Smith—Jan. 20, 1868, Prison Description Docket, vol. 1, 1851–1887, p. 120, RG 08–11 [0402] 005, LancasterHistory archives, Lancaster, PA.

37. Landis, "Refutation."

38. "Our Local Church History," Bethel African Methodist Episcopal Church, Lancaster, PA, https://bethelamelancaster.com/our-local-church-history. For the United States Colored Troops: Wikipedia, s.v. "United States Colored Troops," https://en.wikipedia.org/wiki/United_States_Colored_Troops.

39. "Generosity," *Star and Banner*, (Gettysburg, PA) August 6, 1863, 2. See also Glatfelter, Bolin, and Smith, "Sources Relating to Lydia Hamilton Smith," Section G.4, Adams County Historical Society.

40. See note 5 above. Dr. Glatfelter added his comment to Section G.4.

41. For the extent of Stevens's losses: Trefousse, *Thaddeus Stevens*, 134–35. "Thaddeus Stevens' Policy," *Lancaster Intelligencer*, July 7, 1863, 2. For the *Lancaster Examiner and Herald* comments, published March 3, 1863: Trefousse, *Thaddeus Stevens*, 133.

42. Gorrecht, "Charity of Thaddeus Stevens," 27.

43. For a description of the fighting: Bates, *History of Pennsylvania Volunteers*, 859. For Thad Jr.'s letter from Stevenson, Alabama: Palmer and Ochoa, *Selected Papers*, 1:413n1, after Stevens's letter to John Sweeney, dated October 5, 1863.

44. Powell, *Chickamauga Campaign*, 345n37.

45. Trefousse, *Thaddeus Stevens*, 136.

46. Depositions—June 24, 1887, Thaddeus Stevens Estate File 1867–1901, RG3-10.1, Lancaster County Archives, Lancaster, PA.

47. For John Cole's testimony, see ibid.

48. For Simon Stevens's testimony, see Distribution Notes of Audit, Thaddeus Stevens Estate File 1867–1901, RG3-10.1, Lancaster County Archives, Lancaster, PA.

Chapter 11

1. Ellis and Evans, *History of Lancaster County*, 250.

2. Gorrecht, "Charity of Thaddeus Stevens," 28.

3. Supreme Court Appeal Papers, Thaddeus Stevens Estate File 1867–1901, RG3-10.1, Lancaster County Archives, Lancaster, PA. Simon Stevens was deposed in New York City on December 12, 1873.

4. Appointment of Auditors (1874), Thaddeus Stevens Estate File 1867–1901, RG3-10.1, Lancaster County Archives, Lancaster, PA. Dr. Carpenter was deposed March 19, 1874. Depositions from Hetty Franciscus and Jacob Keneagy were submitted April 7, 1875.

5. Current, *Old Thad Stevens*, 193.

6. Gorrecht, "Charity of Thaddeus Stevens," 24.

7. Blakemore, "James Buchanan."

8. Wikipedia, s.v. "Carl Schurz," https://en.wikipedia.org/wiki/Carl_Schurz.

9. Schurz, *Reminiscences*, 214–15.

10. Ibid.

11. Ibid.

12. Palmer and Ochoa, *Selected Papers*, 1:177. Stevens addressed the Union League on April 4, 1863.

13. Hoch, *Thaddeus Stevens in Gettysburg*, 246.

14. Appointment of Auditors (1874), Thaddeus Stevens Estate File 1867–1901, RG3-10.1, Lancaster County Archives, Lancaster, PA. See note 4 above.

15. Ibid.

16. Ibid.

17. Ibid.

18. Ibid.

19. Ibid.

20. I am indebted to historian Tim Talbott for uncovering Isaac's unusual military history. You can read his work and review documents he found at his blog, *Random Thoughts on History*, http://randomthoughtsonhistory.blogspot.com/2018/06/the-curious-case-of-pvt-isaac-smith-6th.html. Isaac's military records are posted at

fold3.com: https://www.fold3.com/image/219041042. Fold3 utilizes records made available by the National Archives and Records Administration (NARA).

21. Talbott, *Random Thoughts.*

22. Ibid.

23. Crook, *Through Five Administrations*, 28–29.

24. "Assassination of President Lincoln," *New York Herald*, April 15, 1865, 1, Sally E. Nungesser Papers, MG-839, LancasterHistory archives, Lancaster, PA. Mrs. Nungesser was the great-great-great-granddaughter of Joshua Stevens, Thaddeus Stevens's older brother. Her collection includes the original copy of Lydia Hamilton Smith's letter to Thaddeus Stevens Jr. from December 23, 1861. It also contains a copy of the "Reparations Bill For African Slaves in the United States—1st session 40th Congress Mar. 11, 1867, [introduced by] Thaddeus Stevens of PA H. R. 29."

25. Trefousse, *Thaddeus Stevens*, 159.

26. Ibid., 101, 159.

27. Woodley, *Great Leveler*, 148.

28. Milton, *Age of Hate*, 17.

29. McClellan, *Historic Dress in America*, 285.

30. Milton, *Age of Hate*, 17.

31. Greenhow, *My Imprisonment*, 201–2.

32. "Mrs. Thad. Stevens," *Idaho Semi-Weekly World* (Idaho City, Idaho Territory), June 17, 1868, 4, https://chroniclingamerica.loc.gov/lccn/sn89055027/1868-06-17/ed-1/seq-4/.

33. Ibid.

34. Editorial, *Bolivar Bulletin* (Hardeman County, Tennessee), September 8, 1866, 1, https://chroniclingamerica.loc.gov/lccn/sn85033306/1866-09-08/ed-1.

Chapter 12

1. Trefousse, *Thaddeus Stevens*, 165.

2. Wikipedia, s.v. "Civil Rights Act of 1866," https://en.wikipedia.org/wiki/Civil_Rights_Act_of_1866.

3. Federal Judicial Center, "Civil Rights Act of 1866," https://www.fjc.gov/history/timeline/civil-rights-act-1866.

4. White, *Life of Lyman Trumbull*, 272–73. White quoted from a letter from Washington published in the April 12, 1866, issue of *The Nation*, https://archive.org/details/lifelyman00whitrich/page/272.

5. "African American Heritage: Freedmen's Bureau," US National Archives and Records Administration, https://www.archives.gov/research/african-americans/freedmens-bureau. List of Reconstruction measures: "Civil War Reconstruction, 1861–1877: Reconstruction and Rights," Library of Congress, http://www.loc.gov/teachers/classroommaterials/presentationsandactivities/presentations/timeline/civilwar/recontwo/.

6. *Memphis Argus* quote: Fordney, *George Stoneman*, 124.

7. *Memphis Avalanche* quotes: Tosh, *Life and Times of Benjamin Helm Bristow.*

8. Ibid.

9. Brodie, *Thaddeus Stevens*, 101. Brodie reports (101n17) finding Lydia's letter in the Thaddeus Stevens Papers in the Library of Congress, Washington, DC.

10. Depositions—June 24, 1887, Thaddeus Stevens Estate File 1867–1901, RG3-10.1, Lancaster County Archives, Lancaster, PA.

11. "Thaddeus Stevens Papers: General Correspondence, 1829–1869; 1866, June–July," Library of Congress, https://www.loc.gov/item/mss414420032/.

12. Hood, "Stevens, Thaddeus," 587. Hood was referring to the second session of the 39th Congress. Those who knew of Stevens's condition included Hood himself as well as Lydia, Dr. Carpenter, O. J. Dickey, and others.

13. Lizzie Stevens's 1865 letter: "Thaddeus Stevens Papers: General Correspondence, 1829–1869; 1866, June–July," Library of Congress, https://www.loc.gov/item/mss414420032/.

14. Lizzie Stevens's January 1866 letter: Palmer and Ochoa, *Selected Papers*, 2:68.

15. Ibid.

16. Ibid.

17. Keagy's letter, dated January 21, 1867: Hall, *Reminiscences and Sketches*, 17.

18. Palmer and Ochoa, *Selected Papers*, 2:243 (Stevens's response is presented in its entirety).

19. Hall, *Reminiscences and Sketches*, 17.

20. Brodie, *Thaddeus Stevens*, 89.

21. Ibid., 89–90. Brodie found Stevens's letter to W. B. Melius in the Thaddeus Stevens Papers in the Library of Congress, Washington, DC.

22. Ibid.

23. Ibid. By "fellows living within sight of my door," Stevens is probably referring to the *Lancaster Intelligencer*.

24. Ibid., 91–92.

25. Ibid.

26. For the *Intelligencer* piece about Mrs. Smith's visit to the paper, see "A Distinguished Visitor—Yesterday," *Intelligencer Journal*, February 3, 1866, 2, https://www.newspapers.com/clip/87417210/mrs-smith-distinguished-visitor/. Lancaster journalist Jack Brubaker provided me with important background on Lydia's confrontation with the *Intelligencer* staff. You can find his article "Students Raising Funds to Restore Lydia Smith's Gravestone" in the *Lancaster New Era*, February 13, 2007, 10.

27. Daniels, "Reparations for Slavery."

28. "Thaddeus Stevens, His Remains Lying in State in the Capitol—His Last Sickness—Incidents of His Life," *New York Times*, August 14, 1868, 5.

29. Palmer and Ochoa, *Selected Papers*, 1:82.

30. Blanchard, "Thaddeus Stevens—His Religion."

31. Jonathan Blanchard, editorial correspondence ("Thaddeus Stevens—His Sin"), *Christian Cynosure*, November 17, 1868.

32. Remini, "Henry Clay and the Historian," 483–84.

33. Langguth, *After Lincoln*, 199.

34. "Daniel Sickles," HistoryNet.com, https://www.historynet.com/daniel-sickles.

35. Campbell, *Lives of Lord Lyndhurst and Lord Brougham*, 209.

36. Wilkinson, *Daniel Webster*, 123, 126, 127.

37. Meltzer, *Thaddeus Stevens*, 74–75.

38. Blanchard, "Thaddeus Stevens—His Religion."

39. Ibid.

40. Ibid.

41. Coulter, *South During Reconstruction*, 119. Coulter's book is part of a ten-volume set, *A History of the South*, edited by Coulter and others.

42. Gorrecht, "Charity of Thaddeus Stevens," 25–26.

43. Hood, "Stevens, Thaddeus," 575.

44. Wikipedia, s.v. "Omni Bedford Springs Resort," https://en.wikipedia.org /wiki/Omni_Bedford_Springs_Resort.

45. Deposition of Dr. Henry Carpenter, Appointment of Auditors (1874), Thaddeus Stevens Estate File 1867–1901, RG3-10.1, Lancaster County Archives, Lancaster, PA.

46. Isaac Smith, Habeas Corpus papers, Drunk and disorderly conduct, 1867, RG 01–00 2313, Habeas 1867 F020, LancasterHistory archives, Lancaster, PA.

47. Brodie, *Thaddeus Stevens*, 383n17. Brodie reports finding a copy of Stevens's letter to Isaac in the Thaddeus Stevens Papers in the Library of Congress, Washington, DC.

48. Current, *Old Thad Stevens*, 267.

49. Ibid., 289.

50. Ibid.

51. Isaac Smith, Indictment, Armed and malicious disruption of church worship service, RG 02–00 0933, JAN 1868 F002, LancasterHistory archives, Lancaster, PA.

52. "Isaac Smith—Jan. 20, 1868," Prison Description Docket, vol. 1, 1851–1887, p. 120, RG 08–11 [0402] 005, LancasterHistory archives, Lancaster, PA.

53. "Will of Thaddeus Stevens," Thaddeus Stevens Estate File 1867–1901, RG3-10.1, Lancaster County Archives, Lancaster, PA.

54. Ibid.

55. Ibid.

56. Ibid.

57. Palmer and Ochoa, *Selected Papers*, 2:339.

58. For Stevens's March 19, 1867 speech, see "Speech of Hon. T. Stevens, of Pennsylvania, Delivered in the House of Representatives, March 19, 1867," https://ia800302 .us.archive.org/8/items/speechofhontstev01stev/speechofhontstev01stev.pdf.

59. Palmer and Ochoa, *Selected Papers*, 2:339.

Chapter 13

1. "Thaddeus Stevens, His Remains Lying in State in the Capitol—His Last Sickness—Incidents of His Life," *New York Times*, August 14, 1868, 5.

2. All of this testimony is found in depositions filed in Lydia Hamilton Smith's claim against the Thaddeus Stevens Estate. See Appointment of Auditors (1874), Thaddeus Stevens Estate File 1867–1901, RG3-10.1, Lancaster County Archives, Lancaster, PA.

3. Woodley, *Great Leveler*, 409.

4. Current, *Old Thad Stevens*, 301.

5. For the impetus that led to articles of impeachment against President Andrew Johnson, see History.com, *This Day in History*, "President Johnson Impeached," https://www.history.com/this-day-in-history/president-andrew-johnson-impeached.

6. Milton, *Age of Hate*, 576.

7. Ibid., 627.

8. Hood, "Stevens, Thaddeus," 588.

9. Isaac Smith, Indictment, Larceny, RG 02–00 0933, APR 1868 F052, LancasterHistory archives, Lancaster, PA.

10. "Marriages, McKinney–Mathiot," *Lancaster Intelligencer Journal*, May 1, 1868, 2.

11. Census records indicate Dr. Isaac McKinney and his first wife, Susan, were living in Jersey Shore, PA, in 1860. They had three children: Mary W., who was five years old; Rose S., three; and William, two. United States Census Bureau, 1860 census, Jersey Shore Borough, PA. In 1870, Catherine M. McKinney appears as Isaac McKinney's spouse. Catherine and Dr. McKinney lived in Jersey Shore for many years. When Dr. McKinney died, Catherine returned to Lancaster and resided there until her death in 1902. See "Obituary. Death of Mrs. Catherine M. McKinney at an Advanced Age—A Life Full of Good Deeds," *Lancaster Semi-Weekly New Era*, August 2, 1902, 2.

12. Letter from Lydia Hamilton Smith letter to Mrs. McKeny [McKinney], May 3, 1868, Washington, DC, MG-0115, F016 It02, LancasterHistory Archives, Lancaster, PA. This is one of two letters in Mrs. Smith's hand held by LancasterHistory.

13. United States Census Bureau, 1870 census, Lancaster, Ward 4.

14. Lydia Hamilton Smith letter, May 3, 1868. The women were all part of the Stevens-Smith social circle.

15. Ibid.

16. Ibid.

17. Ibid. Lizzie, Thaddeus Morrill Stevens's wife, had died in January 1867.

18. Brodie, *Thaddeus Stevens*, 365.

19. Quoted in Current, *Old Thad Stevens*, 300.

20. Ibid.

21. Quoted in Woodburn, *Life of Thaddeus Stevens*, 602.

22. Jonathan Blanchard, editorial correspondence ("Thaddeus Stevens—His Sin"), *Christian Cynosure*, November 17, 1868.

23. Ibid.

24. Ibid.

25. "Thaddeus Stevens, His Remains."

26. Ibid.

27. Woodley, *Great Leveler*, 144.

28. Woodburn, *Life of Thaddeus Stevens*, 585. The $30,000 Stevens secured for the Sisters of Charity was earmarked for completion of hospital construction. The sisters, already widely respected for the creation of St. Vincent's Orphanage and School in Washington, DC, first operated Providence out of rented quarters at Second and D Streets in the city. Providence initially served both the wealthiest and the poorest residents of Washington. Especially in its early days, it attracted the finest physicians and surgeons in the city. See also Caulfield, "History of Providence Hospital, 1861–1961."

29. "Thaddeus Stevens, His Remains."

30. Ibid.

31. For individuals Stevens spoke with on the day he died, see Trefousse, *Thaddeus Stevens*, 240.

32. Woodley, *Great Leveler*, 409.

33. Gorrecht, "Charity of Thaddeus Stevens," 21.

34. Current, *Old Thad Stevens*, 317–18.

35. For Lydia's comments, see "Thaddeus Stevens, His Remains"; for the assurances offered by the A.M.E. ministers, see Trefousse, *Thaddeus Stevens*, 240.

36. "Thaddeus Stevens, His Remains."

37. "Where Stevens Lived: The Old Lancaster Residence and Some of Its Interesting Reminiscences," *Philadelphia Times*, October 13, 1883, 4.

38. Woodburn, *Life of Thaddeus Stevens*, 586; for Mrs. Smith's and Thad's reactions to Stevens's death, see Trefousse, *Thaddeus Stevens*, 240.

39. Woodley, *Great Leveler*, 410.

Chapter 14

1. This section is a composite of several descriptions of Stevens's funeral preparations. Jolly, "Historical Reputation," 60–61; Woodley, *Great Leveler*, illustration opposite 411; "Thaddeus Stevens, His Remains Lying in State in the Capitol—His Last Sickness—Incidents of His Life," *New York Times*, August 14, 1868, 5; "Thaddeus Stevens," *Harper's Weekly*, 549.

2. "Thaddeus Stevens, His Remains," 5.

3. Ibid.

4. Ibid.

5. Jolly, "Historical Reputation." Minute guns were commonly used in a military funeral ceremony.

6. "Hon. Thaddeus Stevens," *Philadelphia Inquirer*, August 18, 1868, 1.

7. Ibid.

8. Ibid.

9. Brodie, *Thaddeus Stevens*, 366.

10. "Thaddeus Stevens; A Large Number of Distinguished Persons Present. The Remains Viewed by Hundreds of His Friends. Imposing Funeral Ceremonies Yesterday," *New York Times*, August 18, 1868, 1.

11. Woodley, *Great Leveler*, 412.

12. "Hon. Thaddeus Stevens," 1.

13. Woodley, *Great Leveler*, 411.

14. "Hon. Thaddeus Stevens," 1.

15. Jolly, "Historical Reputation."

16. "Thaddeus Stevens; A Large Number of Distinguished Persons Present."

17. Woodburn, *Life of Thaddeus Stevens*, 585.

18. "Thaddeus Stevens," *Harper's Weekly*, 549.

19. Woodley, *Great Leveler*, 413.

20. Unless otherwise noted, details about Stevens's funeral are taken from "Hon. Thaddeus Stevens," 1.

21. In this and the following paragraphs, see, for O. J. Dickey details: Ellis and Evans, *History of Lancaster County*, 240; for A. E. Roberts details: Wikipedia, s.v. "A. E. Roberts," https://en.wikipedia.org/wiki/Anthony_Ellmaker_Roberts; and for Edward McPherson details: Wikipedia, s.v. "Edward McPherson," https://en.wikipedia.org/wiki/Edward_McPherson.

22. Depositions, Thaddeus Stevens Estate File 1867–1901, RG3-10.1, Lancaster County Archives, Lancaster, PA. The following paragraphs all contain quotations from these depositions.

23. Will of Thaddeus Stevens, Thaddeus Stevens Estate File 1867–1901, RG3-10.1, Lancaster County Archives, Lancaster, PA.

24. Depositions, Thaddeus Stevens Estate File 1867–1901, RG3-10.1, Lancaster County Archives, Lancaster, PA. Lydia's claim only covered the last six years of Stevens's life.

25. Jonathan Blanchard, editorial correspondence ("Thaddeus Stevens—His Sin"), *Christian Cynosure*, November 17, 1868.

26. Bishop Daniel Payne's biographical information is taken from Kayomi Wadi, "Daniel Alexander Payne (1811–1893)," Black Past, November 19, 2008, https://www.blackpast.org/african-american-history/payne-daniel-alexander-1811-1893/.

27. Blanchard, editorial correspondence.

28. Ibid.

29. See Blanchard, "Marriage of Frederick Douglass," 8.

30. Blanchard, editorial correspondence.

Chapter 15

1. Will of Thaddeus Stevens, Thaddeus Stevens Estate File 1867–1901, RG3-10.1, Lancaster County Archives, Lancaster, PA.

2. Ibid.

3. Ibid.

4. Ibid.

5. Ibid.

6. See "Thaddeus Stevens School," *DC Historic Sites*, https://historicsites.dcpreservation.org/items/show/573.

7. "Monument to Thaddeus Stevens," *The Elevator,* January 1, 1869, Center for Bibliographical Research, California Digital Newspaper Collection, https://cdnc.ucr.edu/?a=d&d=ELI18690101.2.4&e=-------en--20--1--txt-txIN--------1.

8. Auditor Report, Thaddeus Stevens Estate File 1867–1901, RG3-10.1, Lancaster County Archives, Lancaster, PA.

9. United States Census Bureau, 1870 census, Washington, DC.

10. See "Discover Our History" on the Willard InterContinental Hotel website, https://washington.intercontinental.com/history/.

11. "Mrs. Lydia Smith's Effects—Sale of a Portrait of Thaddeus Stevens for $12," *Lancaster New Era*, April 14, 1884, 1.

12. United States Census Bureau, 1870 census, District of Columbia.

13. *Directory of Lancaster County 1869–70*, "Smith, Isaac, (col'd) barber, h North [St.]," 83, PowerLibrary, PA Photos and Documents, LancasterHistory—City Directories 1843–1900, http://digitalcollections.powerlibrary.org/cdm/compoundobject/collection/slchs-cd01/id/1466/rec/11.

14. United States Census Bureau, 1870 census, Lancaster, Ward 7.

15. United States Census Bureau, 1870 census, Borough of Mercersburg.

16. "Compiled Military Service Records of Volunteer Union Soldiers Belonging to the 41st through 46th Infantry Units Organized for Service with the United States Colored Troops (USCT)," NARA publication number M1994, National Archives and Records Administration, https://www.fold3.com.

17. Wheeler, "Hunt On."

18. "United States General Index to Pension Files, 1861–1934," Sarah Fillkill in entry for David Fillkill, 1866, The index is searchable at https://www.familysearch.org/search/collection/1919699.

19. Moyer, "Remarkable Radical."

20. "Our Local Church History," Bethel African Methodist Episcopal Church, Lancaster, PA, https://bethelamelancaster.com/our-local-church-history. James Wickersham founded the teacher's college in Millersville, five miles southwest of Lancaster. He was a major figure in Pennsylvania public education for many years. See Wikipedia, s.v. "James P. Wickersham," https://en.wikipedia.org/wiki/James_P._Wickersham.

21. Auditors Reports, Thaddeus Stevens Estate File 1867–1901, RG3-10.1, Lancaster County Archives, Lancaster, PA.

22. Lydia Smith, grantee, Deed C-10-274, July 8, 1871, Lancaster County Recorder of Deeds, https://www.lancasterdeeds.com.

23. *Directory of Lancaster City 1871*, "Smith, Isaac H.," 98, PowerLibrary, PA Photos and Documents, LancasterHistory—City Directories 1843–1900, http://digitalcollections.powerlibrary.org/cdm/ref/collection/slchs-cd01/id/496.

24. Glatfelter, Bolin, and Smith, "Sources Relating to Lydia Hamilton Smith," Adams County Historical Society.

25. Letter from Lydia Smith to Mrs. McKeney [McKinney], Washington, May [no year specified], Thaddeus Stevens Collection, Part 1, MG-115, F016 It 01. It is one of two original letters in Lydia's hand held by LancasterHistory and transcribed by Martha Abel, Library/Archives Assistant at LancasterHistory. LancasterHistory archives, Lancaster, PA.

26. Ibid.

27. Ibid.

28. Ibid.

29. Lydia Smith, grantee, Deed I-10-534, April 8, 1873, Lancaster County Recorder of Deeds website, https://www.lancasterdeeds.com.

30. Executor's Accounts, Thaddeus Stevens Estate File 1867–1901, 1, RG3-10.1, Lancaster County archives, Lancaster, PA.

31. "A Noted Woman Gone: Sudden Death of Mrs. Lydia Smith," *Lancaster Weekly Examiner and Express*, February 20, 1884, 6.

Chapter 16

1. Appointment of Auditors, Thaddeus Stevens Estate File 1867–1901, RG3-10.1, Lancaster County Archives, Lancaster, PA.

2. Opinion, Thaddeus Stevens Estate File 1867–1901, RG3-10.1, Lancaster County Archives, Lancaster, PA. Roberts and Dickey were likely prepared to produce the deceitful receipt to prove that Mrs. Smith's claims against the estate had been paid.

3. Ibid.

4. Ibid., my emphasis.

5. Ibid.

6. Ibid.

7. Supreme Court Appeal Papers, resubmitted deposition of Simon Stevens, January 30, 1874, Thaddeus Stevens Estate File 1867–1901, RG3-10.1, Lancaster County Archives, Lancaster, PA.

8. Landis, "Refutation," 49.

9. Deposition of Elizabeth Alwine, May 5, 1892, Distribution Notes of Audit, Thaddeus Stevens Estate File 1867–1901, RG3-10.1, Lancaster County Archives, Lancaster, PA.

10. Ibid.

11. Isaac Smith, Indictment, Larceny, 1873, RG 02–00 0933, AUG 1873 F073, LancasterHistory archives, Lancaster, PA.

12. Will of Thaddeus Stevens, Thaddeus Stevens Estate File 1867–1901, RG3-10.1, Lancaster County Archives, Lancaster, PA.

13. Auditor's Reports, Thaddeus Stevens Estate File 1867–1901, RG3-10.1, Lancaster County Archives, Lancaster, PA.

14. Examiner's Report, Depositions taken February 22, 1879, Thaddeus Stevens Estate File 1867–1901, RG3-10.1, Lancaster County Archives, Lancaster, PA.

15. Ibid.

16. Ibid.

17. Ibid.

18. Ibid.

19. Ibid.

20. Appointment of Auditors (1874), Thaddeus Stevens Estate File 1867–1901, RG3-10.1, Lancaster County Archives, Lancaster, PA.

21. The report appeared a Gettysburg newspaper and was reprinted in a historical feature. My copy of the story was acquired from that edition. "100 Years Later," *Gettysburg Times*, June 17, 1975, 4.

22. Examiner's Report, dated Apr. 26, 1879, and Auditors Reports, dated Dec. 21, 1876, Thaddeus Stevens Estate File 1867–1901, RG3-10.1, Lancaster County Archives, Lancaster, PA.

23. The only other reference to Lydia Hamilton Smith's claim against Thaddeus Stevens's estate that I found in my research was in an article by W. U. Hensel published around 1912: see Hensel, "Jacob Eichholtz, Painter" (1912–14), 169. Hensel was writing about the portrait of Lydia Smith that had been discovered around 1912 in Lancaster. Hensel provided a brief description of Lydia. "Its subject," he wrote, "is well remembered by our older citizens as the housekeeper, nurse, and business manager of Mr. Stevens, from at least as early as January 1, 1845, until he died in 1868. At that time, she was not without the vigor to prosecute a claim against his estate."

24. "Death of O. J. Dickey," *Lebanon Daily News*, April 22, 1876, 1.

25. Lydia Smith, grantee, Deed W-10-104, January 14, 1876, Lancaster County Recorder of Deeds, https://www.lancasterdeeds.com. Dr. Carpenter included his loan to Lydia in a memorandum filed with the auditors of Lydia's estate. It was part of an itemized list of "monies" Carpenter paid for Lydia between 1875 and 1884. A copy of the Auditor's Report for Lydia's estate is in the Lydia Hamilton Smith Family File at LancasterHistory, Lancaster, Pennsylvania.

26. "Lydia Smith Dead," *Lancaster Intelligencer*, February 20, 1884, 5.

27. Auditors Reports, dated December 21, 1876, Thaddeus Stevens Estate File 1867–1901, RG3-10.1, Lancaster County Archives, Lancaster, PA.

28. Supreme Court Appeal Papers, dated January 22, 1877 and May 7, 1877, Thaddeus Stevens Estate File 1867–1901, RG3-10.1, Lancaster County Archives, Lancaster, PA.

29. Ibid.

Chapter 17

1. The ages of Sarah Boardman's children were calculated from census records. United States Census Bureau, 1880 census, Lancaster, PA, ED152. See also Dr. H. B. Stedman, "Henry Carpenter, M.D.," in Ellis and Evans, *History of Lancaster County*, 250–51.

2. Deposition of George Heiss, Auditor's Report, Estate of Lydia Smith, September 25, 1886, Lydia Hamilton Smith Family File, LancasterHistory Library, Lancaster, PA. The porch repair was on the house Lydia occupied when she first came to Lancaster.

3. Lydia Smith, grantee, Deed E-Mis.-170, September 26, 1879, Lancaster County Recorder of Deeds, https://www.lancasterdeeds.com. The Lancaster city directory listed Mrs. Harriet West at 414 S. Water St., which suggests that was the house Lydia sold to her husband. *Barnes' Annual Lancaster City Directory for 1886*, "West, Harriet, Mrs., h 414 S Water [St.]," 314. Lewis West does not appear in census records for Lancaster or Washington, DC, after 1870.

4. "Our Local Church History," Bethel African Methodist Episcopal Church, https://bethelamelancaster.com/our-local-church-history.

5. *Directory of Lancaster City 1879–80*, "Smith, Isaac (col'd) shaving saloon, 47 S. Queen, h 327 North [St.]," 194, PowerLibrary, PA Photos and Documents, LancasterHistory—City Directories 1843–1900, http://digitalcollections.powerlibrary.org /cdm/compoundobject/collection/slchs-cd01/id/3478/rec/12.

6. Ages and occupations based on United States Census Bureau, 1880 census, Lancaster, PA, Ward 7. Mary Taylor in entry for Polly Williams, 1880.

7. Ibid.

8. Isaac Smith, Indictment, Assault and battery, 1880, RG 02–00 0933, JAN 1880 F063, LancasterHistory archives, Lancaster, PA.

9. Lydia Smith, grantee, Deed Book C-10-274, July 8, 1871, Lancaster County Recorder of Deeds, https://www.lancasterdeeds.com.

10. "Society at the National Capital. Colored Teachers, Dinners, Parties, and Weddings," *Weekly Louisianian*, February 21, 1880, 1.

11. Expenses submitted included, Auditor's Report, Lydia Hamilton Smith Family File, LancasterHistory, Lancaster, PA.

12. Ibid.

13. Ibid.

14. "Where Stevens Lived: The Old Lancaster Residence and Some of Its Interesting Reminiscences," *Philadelphia Times*, October 13, 1883, and "Thaddeus Stevens, Some New and Exceedingly Interesting Anecdotes of the Great Commoner," *Philadelphia Times*, September 4, 1881, 3. The tobacco shop was George Heiss's; the barbershop was Isaac's workplace.

15. "Chat By The Way," *Reading (PA) Daily Times and Dispatch*, October 20, 1883.

16. United States Census Bureau, 1880 census, Washington, DC. Lewis West is listed in the household of William L. Hodgkins, Washington, DC.

17. Ibid.

18. Ibid.

19. *Barnes' Annual Lancaster City Directory for 1886*, "West, Harriet, Mrs., h 414 S. Water [St.]," 314.

20. United States Census Bureau, 1880 census, Washington, DC.

21. Lydia Smith, Administrator's Account, 1886, RG 04–00 0150, AdAcct 1886 F031 S, LancasterHistory archives, Lancaster, PA. Dr. Robert M. Bolenius submitted his bill to Lydia's executors after her death.

22. Lydia's last visit to Lancaster in September, 1883: "Thaddeus Stevens' Housekeeper Dead," *Lancaster Inquirer*, February 16, 1884, 3. *Lancaster Inquirer*, "This and That," October 6, 1883, reprinted with other articles by Randolph Harris in *Underground Railroad Origins in Pennsylvania* (blog), http://undergroundrroriginspa.org /wp-content/uploads/2016/03/Inquirer-news-clips-handout-4-6-12.pdf. Lydia's purchase of coal: Estate of Lydia Smith, Auditor's Report, Sept. 25, 1886, Lydia Hamilton Smith Family File at LancasterHistory Library, Lancaster, PA.

23. The quote from the February 15, 1884, *Washington Star* was included in "A Noted Woman Gone: Sudden Death of Mrs. Lydia Smith," *Lancaster Weekly Examiner and Express*, February 20, 1884, 6.

24. "Lydia Smith Dead," *Lancaster Intelligencer*, February 20, 1884, 5.

25. "Death Certificate, Lydia H. Smith, District of Columbia, 2/14/1884, Permit #40890," in Lydia Hamilton Smith Family File, LancasterHistory Library, Lancaster, PA.

Chapter 18

1. "A Noted Woman Gone: Sudden Death of Mrs. Lydia Smith," *Lancaster Weekly Examiner and Express*, February 20, 1884, 6.

2. Ibid. Burgdorf's name appears on the death certificate.

3. Deposition of George Heiss, Auditor's Report, Estate of Lydia Smith, Sept. 25, 1886, Lydia Hamilton Smith Family File, LancasterHistory Library, Lancaster, PA.

4. For mention of Isaac Smith accompanying his mother's body to Lancaster, see "Mrs. Lydia Smith, Housekeeper for Thaddeus Stevens, Dies in Washington," *Lancaster New Era*, February 15, 1884, 4.

5. For theft of the crepe from Lydia's doorway, see "A Sacrilegious Thief," *Lancaster New Era*, February 18, 1884, 4.

6. Deposition of George Heiss. Heiss made and sold cigars in the house.

7. Ibid.

8. "Noted Woman Gone," 6.

9. "Lydia Smith Dead: Thad. Stevens Old Housekeeper," *Lancaster Intelligencer*, February 15, 1884, 2.

10. "Funeral of Mrs. Lydia Smith," *Lancaster New Era*, February 18, 1884, 4.

11. Lydia Smith, will dated December 21, 1877, Will Book F, vol. 2, pp. 204–8, Lancaster County Archives, Lancaster, PA. For the inscription on Lydia's tombstone, see Landis, "Refutation."

12. "Noted Woman Gone," 6.

13. "Lydia Smith Dead," 2.

14. "Mrs. Lydia Smith, Housekeeper for Thaddeus Stevens," 4.

15. Both newspaper articles were posted on *Civil War Quilts* (blog), "Lydia Hamilton Smith and a Movie Quilt," May 12, 2018, http://civilwarquilts.blogspot.com/2018/05/lydia-hamilton-smith-and-movie-quilt.html.

16. Ibid.

17. Auditor's Report, Estate of Lydia Smith, Sept. 25, 1886, Lydia Hamilton Smith Family File, LancasterHistory Library, Lancaster, PA.

18. Lydia Smith, will dated December 21, 1877.

19. Ibid.

20. Ibid.

21. "Deaths," *Lancaster Daily Intelligencer*, April 7, 1884, 3.

22. "Death of 'Little Ike' Smith," *Lancaster Daily Intelligencer*, April 8, 1884, 3.

23. "Death of Isaac Smith," *Lancaster New Era*, April 8, 1884, 4.

24. "Death of a Well-Known Character," *Harrisburg State Journal*, April 12, 1884, 4.

25. Auditor's Report, Estate of Lydia Smith, September 25, 1886, Lydia Hamilton Smith Family File, LancasterHistory Library, Lancaster, PA.

26. *Ferris Bros.' Lancaster City and County Directory 1884*, 50. "Where Stevens Lived: The Old Lancaster Residence and Some of Its Interesting Reminiscences,"

Philadelphia Times, October 13, 1883, 4; "Thaddeus Stevens, Some New and Exceedingly Interesting Anecdotes of the Great Commoner," *Philadelphia Times*, September
4, 1881, 3. "Chat By the Way," *Reading (PA) Daily Times and Dispatch*, October 20,
1883, 2.

27. "Mrs. Lydia Smith's Effects—Sale of a Portrait of Thaddeus Stevens for $12,"
Lancaster New Era, April 14, 1884, 1. Auditor's Report, Estate of Lydia Smith, September 25, 1886, Lydia Hamilton Smith Family File, LancasterHistory Library, Lancaster, PA.

28. Auditor's Report, Estate of Lydia Smith.

29. Ibid.

30. United States Census Bureau, 1880 census, Baltimore, MD.

31. Lydia Smith, will dated December 21, 1877.

32. Ibid.

Chapter 19

1. Distribution Notes of Audit and Examiners Report, Thaddeus Stevens Estate
File 1867–1901, RG3-10.1, Lancaster County Archives, Lancaster, PA.

2. Thaddeus Stevens Estate File 1867–1901, RG3-10.1, Lancaster County Archives,
Lancaster, PA.

3. Ibid.

4. Will of Thaddeus Stevens, Thaddeus Stevens Estate File 1867–1901, RG3-10.1,
Lancaster County Archives, Lancaster, PA.

5. Opinion, Jan. 11, 1894, and Petition of Stevens Orphans Home of Lancaster
City, Thaddeus Stevens Estate File 1867–1901, RG3-10.1, Lancaster County Archives,
Lancaster, PA. *Lancaster Intelligencer* observation on Stevens and the Home for Friend-
less Children: "The Stevens Estate," *Lancaster Intelligencer*, April 26, 1876, 2. For the
Philadelphia newspaper's report that the Home changed its policy to accommodate
Stevens's's views: "Thaddeus Stevens, Some New and Exceedingly Interesting Anec-
dotes of the Great Commoner," *Philadelphia Times*, September 4, 1881, 3.

6. See note 5.

7. Smull, Smull, Cochran, and Baker, *Hand Book*, 181c–181d.

8. Ibid.

9. "Lydia Hamilton Smith Gallery," *The Tower*, Summer 2011, Sally E. Nungesser Papers, MG-839, LancasterHistory archives, Lancaster, PA.

10. Appointment of Auditors, 1874, Thaddeus Stevens Estate File 1867–1901,
RG3-10.1, Folder 6, Lancaster County Archives, Lancaster, PA.

11. *Barnes' Annual Lancaster City Directory for 1886*, "Smith, Sarah, widow Isaac,
bds 327 North.," 281. Ida Ulmer does not appear in the city directory for 1886. John
Shober is listed on 274. For court record of the theft, Ida Ulmer, Sarah Smith et
al., Indictment, Larceny, 1886, RG 02–00 0933, AUG 1886 F030, LancasterHistory
archives, Lancaster, PA.

12. Carpenter, *Genealogical Notes*, 209.

13. Sarah Smith: United States Census Bureau, 1900 census, Lancaster County
Almshouse and Insane Asylum. David Smith in 1900: United States Census Bureau,
1900 census, Lancaster City, Ward 7.

14. Ibid.

15. Register of Deaths at the Lancaster County Poor and House of Employment,
1902–1982. "#294 Sarah Smith, B [Black], F [female], d. 8-10-1904 (b. ca. 1839)–d.

At 65 (?), Disease: tuberculosis, Disposition of body: Anatomical Society," MG-277, Book 30, LancasterHistory archives, Lancaster, PA.

Chapter 20

1. World Digital Library, Library of Congress, "Timeline: United States History," https://www.wdl.org/en/sets/us-history/timeline/#8.

2. Supreme Court Appeal Papers, resubmission of Simon Stevens deposition [in New York], December 12, 1873, Thaddeus Stevens Estate File 1867–1901, RG3-10.1, Lancaster County Archives, Lancaster, PA.

BIBLIOGRAPHY

Archival Sources, Government Documents, and Unpublished Documents

Adams County Historical Society, Gettysburg, PA

Brownley, Edward R. (Ned). "The Joshua Russell Family Tree." Section B.6 of "Sources Relating to Lydia Hamilton Smith: Died February 14, 1884," compiled by Dr. Charles H. Glatfelter, Larry C. Bolin, and Timothy Smith.

Glatfelter, Charles H., Larry C. Bolin, and Timothy Smith, comps. "Sources Relating to Lydia Hamilton Smith: Died February 14, 1884." [These documents are contained in an 11 × 17 inch manila folder with "Smith, Lydia Hamilton" printed in large letters, in pencil, on the top left tab. The Adams County Historical Society has a second folder, virtually identical to this one, but Lydia's name is written on the upper left tab in felt-tip pen. The work of Glatfelter, Bolin, and Smith is not in that folder.]

Elsie Singmaster Collection: Research and Pamphlets, 6499. Research notes for *I Speak for Thaddeus Stevens* (1947).

Lancaster County Archives, Lancaster, PA

Thaddeus Stevens Estate File 1867–1901. One document box, alphabetical by estate proceeding, WPA: #309, RG3–10.1.

"Will of Lydia Smith of Lancaster." Will Book F, vol. 2, 204–8, Lancaster County Archives.

LancasterHistory Archives, Lancaster, PA
Habeas Corpus Papers

Isaac Smith—Drunk and Disorderly Conduct, 1867. Object ID: Habeas 1867 F020.

Isaac Smith and Jacob Woods, Guilty of Drunken and Disorderly Conduct, 1862. Object ID: Habeas 1862 F026.

Indictments

John Jones, Furnishing Liquor to a Minor, 1854. Object ID: NOV 1854 F002.

Isaac Smith, Assault and Battery. Object ID: JAN 1880 F063.

Isaac Smith, Larceny. Object ID: AUG 1873 F073.

Isaac Smith and John Buckley, Hawking and Peddling, 1863. Object ID: APR 1863 F014.

Ida Ulmer, Sarah Smith et al., Larceny, August 17, 1886. Object ID: AUG 1886 F030.

Quarter Sessions: Name: Isaac Smith, African American, Additional Notes: Misdemeanor, 1854. APR 1854 F059 QS.

Lydia Hamilton Smith Family File

"Estate of Lydia Smith, Auditor's Report, Sept. 25, 1886, Presented read and confirmed, Attest: Mr. B. Keller, Clerk of Court." (Photocopy.)

Last Will and Testament of Thaddeus Stevens of Lancaster, Penna.

Sally Nungesser Collection.

"Prison Description Docket 1, 1851–1887: Isaac Smith—Jan. 20, 1868."

Register of Deaths at the Lancaster County Poor and House of Employment. Collections of LancasterHistory, MG-277, Book 30.

Shiffler Fire Company Records, 1854–1886. Includes records of the Conestoga Hose Company and Shiffler Fire Company for 1854–1886. Call number: MG-524. George Steinman Collection. Ephemera, Box 1, Folder 20.

Library of Congress, Washington, DC
Thaddeus Stevens Papers: General Correspondence, 1829–1869; 1866, June–July 1866. Manuscript/Mixed Material. https://www.loc.gov/item/mss414420032/.

Newspapers and Magazines
Adams Sentinel (Gettysburg, PA)
Baltimore Sun
Bloomsburg (PA) Star of the North
Bolivar (TN) Bulletin
Christian Cynosure
Gettysburg Republican Compiler
Gettysburg Star and Banner
Gettysburg Times
Harper's Weekly
Harrisburg State Journal
Idaho Semi-Weekly World
LaCrosse (WI) Democrat
Lancaster Daily Intelligencer
Lancaster Examiner and Herald
Lancaster Inquirer
Lancaster Journal
Lancaster New Era
Lebanon Daily News
Memphis (TN) Argus
Memphis (TN) Avalanche
New York Herald
New York Times
Philadelphia Inquirer
Times of Philadelphia
The Tower (Thaddeus Stevens College of Technology newsletter)
Washington Post
Washington Star
Weekly Louisianian

Other Published Sources
Atlee, Benjamin Champneys. "Thaddeus Stevens and Slavery." *Papers Read Before the Lancaster County Historical Society (The Journal of Lancaster County's Historical Society)* 15, no. 6 (1911): 167–86. https://www.lancasterhistory.org/images/stories/JournalArticles/vol15no6pp167_186_538252.pdf.
Baker, Ray Stannard. "What Is a Lynching?" *McClure's Magazine*, February 1905. http://www.digitalhistory.uh.edu/active_learning/explorations/lynching/baker1.cfm.
Baldwin, James. *Blues for Mr. Charlie*. New York: Vintage Books, 1964.
Barker, W. J. *Map of Dauphin County, Pennsylvania: From Actual Surveys*. Philadelphia: Published by Wm. J. Barker, 1858. https://www.loc.gov/resource/g3823d.la000735/?r=0.052,-0.021,1.153,0.525,0.

Barnes' Annual Lancaster City Directory for 1886. Lancaster, PA: Jno. H. Barnes, 1886. https://digitalarchives.powerlibrary.org/papd/islandora/object /papd%3Aslchs-cd01_9568.

Bates, Samuel P. *History of Pennsylvania Volunteers, 1861–1865: Prepared in Compliance with Acts of the Legislature.* Vol. 5. Harrisburg: B. Singerly, state printer, 1869–71.

Beal, Rebecca J. *Jacob Eichholtz, 1776–1842: Portrait Painter of Pennsylvania.* Philadelphia: Historical Society of Pennsylvania, 1969.

Blakemore, Erin. "James Buchanan Bought and Freed Slaves— But Not for the Reason You Might Think." History.com, July 26, 2017, updated September 1, 2018. https://www.history.com/news/james-buchanan -bought-and-freed-slaves-but-not-for-the-reason-you-might-think.

Blanchard, Jonathan. "Marriage of Frederick Douglass." *Christian Cynosure,* February 7, 1884.

———. "Thaddeus Stevens—His Religion." *Christian Cynosure,* November 3, 1868.

Bloom, Robert L. *A History of Adams County, Pennsylvania, 1700–1990.* Gettysburg: Adams County Historical Society, 1992.

Bogus, Carl T. "Was Slavery a Factor in the Second Amendment?" *New York Times,* May 24, 2018. www.nytimes.com/2018/05/24/opinion/second-amendment -slavery-james-madison.html.

Bordewich, Fergus M. "Digging into a Historic Rivalry." *Smithsonian Magazine,* February 2004. https://www.smithsonianmag.com/history /digging-into-a-historic-rivalry-106194163/.

Brodie, Fawn M. *Thaddeus Stevens: Scourge of the South.* New York: W. W. Norton, 1959.

Brubaker, Jack. "Lydia Smith's Son Shot Himself." *Lancaster New Era,* March 15, 2013. https://lancasteronline.com/opinion/columnists/lydia-smith-s-son-shot -himself/article_ cb991c86-3856-5ae0-a268-a7ffa9844d7a.html.

Campbell, John C. *Lives of Lord Lyndhurst and Lord Brougham.* London: John Murray, 1869. https://archive.org/details/livesoflordlyndh08camp/.

Carpenter, Seymour D. *Genealogical Notes of the Carpenter Family.* Springfield, IL: Edwin Sawyer Walker, 1907. https://archive.org/details/genealogicalnote1907carp/.

Caulfield, Philip A. "History of Providence Hospital, 1861–1961." In *Records of the Columbian Historical Society, Washington, D.C., 1960–62,* edited by Francis Coleman Rosenberger, 231–49. https://jstor.org/stable/i40002889.

Cook, Raymond A. *Thomas Dixon.* New York: Twayne, 1974.

Cornelius, Earl. "Speakers at Highland Presbyterian's Sr. Life Institute Will Discuss Lancaster County's Unique Place on the Underground Railroad." *LancasterOnline-LNP,* March 25, 2017. https://lancasteronline.com/features/faith_values /speakers-at-highland-presbyterian-s-sr-life-institute-will-discuss/article _f9347c9e-1162-11e7-b518-434446f6c928.html.

Coulter, E. Merton. *The South During Reconstruction, 1865–1877.* Vol. 7. Baton Rouge: Louisiana State University Press, 1947.

Crook, William Henry. *Through Five Administrations: Reminiscences of Colonel William H. Crook, Body Guard to President Lincoln.* New York: Harper & Brothers, 1910. https://archive.org/details/throughfiveadmin06croo/.

Current, Richard Nelson. *Old Thad Stevens: A Story of Ambition.* Madison: University of Wisconsin Press, 1942.

Daniels, Ron. "Reparations for Slavery." *Baltimore Sun,* August 22, 1994. https://www .baltimoresun.com/news/bs-xpm-1994-08-22-1994234149-story.html.

Darby, W. *Darby's Edition of Brookes' Universal Gazetteer; or, a New Geographical Dictionary . . . Illustrated by a . . . Map of the United States, The Third American Edition, with Ample Additions and Improvements.* Philadelphia: Bennett & Walton, 1823.

Delle, James A., and Mary Ann Levine. "Equality of Man Before His Creator: Thaddeus Stevens and the Struggle Against Slavery." In *The Limits of Tyranny: Archaeological Perspectives on the Struggle Against New World Slavery,* edited by James A. Delle, 121–46. Knoxville: University of Tennessee Press, 2015.

———. "Excavations at the Thaddeus Stevens and Lydia Hamilton Smith Site, Lancaster, Pennsylvania: Archaeological Evidence for the Underground Railroad." *Northeast Historical Archaeology* 33, no. 1, article 10 (2004). http://digitalcommons.buffalostate.edu/neha/vol33/iss1/10.

Dixon, Thomas. *The Clansman: An Historical Romance of the Ku Klux Klan.* New York: Doubleday, Page, 1905.

Eby, Simon P. "John Beck: The Eminent Teacher." *Papers Read Before the Lancaster County Historical Society (The Journal of Lancaster County's Historical Society)* 2, no. 5 (1898). https://www.lancasterhistory.org/images/stories/JournalArticles/vol2no5pp111_139_811735.pdf.

Eggert, Gerald G. *Harrisburg Industrializes: The Coming of Factories to an American Community.* University Park: Penn State University Press, 1993.

Ellis, Franklin, and Samuel Evans. *History of Lancaster County, Pennsylvania: With Biographical Sketches of Its Pioneers and Prominent Men.* Vol. 1. Lancaster County, PA: Everts & Peck, 1883.

Ferris Bros.' Lancaster City and County Directory 1884. Retrieved from LancasterHistory.org-City Directories 1843–1900 at https://digitalarchives.powerlibrary.org/papd/islandora/object/papd%3Aslchs-cd01_11850.

Fordney, Ben Fuller. *George Stoneman: A Biography of the Union General.* Jefferson, NC: McFarland, 2008.

Franklin, John Hope. "'Birth of a Nation': Propaganda as History." *Massachusetts Review* 20, no. 3 (1979). https://www.jstor.org/stable/25088973?seq=1.

Gopsill's Directory of Lancaster, Harrisburg, Lebanon and York. Jersey City: James Gopsill, 1863. https://digitalarchives.powerlibrary.org/papd/islandora/object/papd%3Aslchs-cd01_1901.

Gorrecht, W. Frank. "The Charity of Thaddeus Stevens." *Papers Read Before the Lancaster County Historical Society (The Journal of Lancaster County's Historical Society)* 37, no. 2 (1933).

Greenhow, Rose O'Neal. *My Imprisonment and the First Year of Abolition Rule at Washington.* London: Richard Bentley, 1863.

Hadden, Sally E. *Slave Patrols: Law and Violence in Virginia and the Carolinas.* Cambridge, MA: Harvard University Press, 2001.

Hall, William M. *Reminiscences and Sketches, Historical and Biographical.* Harrisburg, PA: Meyers Printing House, 1890. https://www.google.com/books/edition/Reminiscences_and_Sketches_Historical_an/N4zTjalx43sC.

Harper's Weekly. "Thaddeus Stevens." August 29, 1868, 59. https://www.google.com/books/edition/Harper_s_Weekly/_OWm9L6sQr0C.

Hening, William Waller, ed. *The Statutes at Large: Being a Collection of All the Laws of Virginia.* Vol. 5. Richmond, VA: Franklin Press, 1819. https://babel.hathitrust.org/cgi/pt?id=mdp.35112104867819.

Hensel, W. U. "An Early Letter by Thaddeus Stevens." *Papers Read Before the Lancaster County Historical Society (The Journal of Lancaster County's Historical Society)* 10, no. 10 (1906), 396–401.

———. "Jacob Eichholtz, Painter." *Papers Read Before the Lancaster County Historical Society (The Journal of the Lancaster County Historical Society)*, suppl., 16, no. 10 (1912): 3–39.

———. "Jacob Eichholtz, Painter." *Penn Germania: A Popular Journal of German History and Ideals in the United States* (Cleona, PA) 2, no. 3 (1912–14): 89–96.

———. "Jacob Eichholtz, Painter." *Pennsylvania Magazine of History and Biography* 37 (1913): 48–75.

———. "Thaddeus Stevens as a Country Lawyer." *Papers Read Before the Lancaster County Historical Society (The Journal of Lancaster County's Historical Society)* 10, no. 7 (1905–6): 247–90.

Harris, Alexander, ed. *A Biographical History of Lancaster County.* Lancaster, PA: E. Barr, 1872. https://archive.org/details/biographicalhist00harr.

———. *A Review of the Political Conflict in America; also Resume of the Career of Thaddeus Stevens.* New York: T. H. Pollock, 1876. https://archive.org/details/areviewpolitica00harrgoog.

Hoch, Bradley R. *Thaddeus Stevens in Gettysburg: The Making of an Abolitionist.* Gettysburg: Adams County Historical Society, 2005.

Hoelscher, Robert T. "Thaddeus Stevens as a Lancaster Politician, 1842–1868." *Journal of the Lancaster County Historical Society* 78, no. 4 (1974): 157–213.

Hood, Alexander H. "Stevens, Thaddeus." In *A Biographical History of Lancaster County*, edited by Alexander Harris, 568–98. Lancaster, PA: E. Barr, 1872. https://archive.org/details/biographicalhist00harr.

J. H. Bryson's Lancaster Directory, for 1843. Lancaster, 1843. Reprint, Laughlintown, PA: Southwest Pennsylvania Genealogical Services. https://digitalarchives.powerlibrary.org/papd/islandora/object/papd%3Aslchs-cd01_24.

Jolly, James A. "The Historical Reputation of Thaddeus Stevens." *Journal of the Lancaster County Historical Society* 74, no. 2 (1970): 33–71.

Karakatsanis, Costas G. "The Enduring Legacy of the James and Rebecca Beal Collection." *Storyboard* (Carnegie Museum of Art), August 11, 2015. https://storyboard.cmoa.org/2015/08/the-enduring-legacy-of-the-james-and-rebecca-beal-collection/.

Knowles, Laura. "African American Heritage Walking Tour Explores Little Known History in Lancaster." *LancasterOnline-LNP*, June 12, 2016. https://lancasteronline.com/features/entertainment/african-american-heritage-walking-tour-explores-little-known-history-in/article_2bcc054e-2f52-11e6-9181-23054ad06238.html.

Korngold, Ralph. *Thaddeus Stevens: A Being Darkly Wise and Rudely Great.* New York: Harcourt, Brace, 1955.

The Lancaster City Directory . . . 1857. Lancaster, PA: Sprenger & Westhaeffer and Murray, Young, 1857. https://digitalarchives.powerlibrary.org/papd/islandora/object/papd%3Aslchs-cd01_895.

Landis, C. I. "A Refutation of the Slanderous Stories Against the Name of Thaddeus Stevens Placed Before the Public by Thomas Dixon." *Papers Read Before the Lancaster County Historical Society (The Journal of the Lancaster County Historical Society)* 28, no. 3 (1924): 49–52.

————. *Thaddeus Stevens: A Letter Written to the Daily New Era, Lancaster, Pa., By Hon. Charles I. Landis, President Judge of the Second Judicial District of Pennsylvania.* Lancaster, PA: Press of The New Era Printing Company, 1916.

Langguth, A. J. *After Lincoln: How the North Won the Civil War and Lost the Peace.* New York: Simon & Schuster, 2014.

Levine, Bruce. *Thaddeus Stevens: Civil War Revolutionary, Fighter for Racial Justice.* New York: Simon & Schuster, 2021.

McClellan, Elisabeth. *Historic Dress in America, 1800–1870.* Philadelphia: George W. Jacobs, 1910. https://archive.org/details/historicdressina00mccl.

McClure, Jim. "Glenalvin Goodridge: 7 Things to Know About This Pioneering African-American Photographer." *York Daily Record,* October 12, 2018. https://www.ydr.com/story/news/history/blogs/york-town-square/2018/10/12/glenalvin-goodridge-early-american-york-county-pa-photo-studio/1551470002/.

McMurry, Sally, and Nancy Van Dolsen, eds. *Architecture and Landscape of the Pennsylvania Germans, 1720–1920.* Philadelphia: University of Pennsylvania Press, 2011.

Meltzer, Milton. *Thaddeus Stevens and the Fight for Negro Rights.* New York: Thomas Y. Crowell, 1967.

Miller, Alphonse Bertram. *Thaddeus Stevens.* New York: Harper & Brothers, 1939.

Milley, J. C. "Jacob Eichholtz 1776–1842: Pennsylvania Portraitist." Master's thesis, University of Delaware, 1960. (Copy held at LancasterHistory in Lancaster, PA.)

Milton, George Fort. *The Age of Hate: Andrew Johnson and the Radicals.* New York: Coward-McCann, 1930.

Mitchell, Faith. "Growing Up Free and Black in Mid-Nineteenth Century Lancaster County." *Journal of Lancaster County's Historical Society* 113, no. 2/3 (2011): 102–13.

Morgan, George Hallenbrooke. *Annals, Comprising Memoirs, Incidents and Statistics of Harrisburg: From the Period of Its First Settlement; For the Past, the Present and the Future.* Harrisburg, PA: Geo. A. Brooks, 1858.

Moyer, Steve. "Remarkable Radical: Thaddeus Stevens." *Humanities* 33, no. 6 (2012). https://www.neh.gov/humanities/2012/novemberdecember/feature/remarkable-radical-thaddeus-stevens.

Nye, Russel B. *Fettered Freedom: Civil Liberties and the Slavery Controversy, 1830–1860.* East Lansing: Michigan State College Press, 1949.

Palmer, Beverly Wilson, and Holly Byers Ochoa, eds. *The Selected Papers of Thaddeus Stevens.* Vol. 1, *January 1814–March 1865.* Vol. 2, *April 1865–August 1868.* Pittsburgh: University of Pittsburgh Press, 1997.

Parker, William. "The Freedman's Story: An Escaped Slave Recalls His Violent Showdown with Slave-Catchers." 1866. *Atlantic Monthly,* February 2012. https://www.theatlantic.com/magazine/archive/2012/02/the-freedmans-story/308793/.

Pepper, George Wharton, and William Draper Lewis. *A Digest of the Laws of Pennsylvania: From the Year One Thousand Seven Hundred to the Sixth Day of July, One Thousand Eight Hundred and Eighty-Three.* Vol. 2. Philadelphia: T. & J. W. Johnson, 1896.

Powell, David A. *The Chickamauga Campaign—Glory or the Grave: The Breakthrough, the Union Collapse, and the Retreat to Chattanooga.* El Dorado Hills, CA: Savas Beatie, 2015.

Pratt, Mark. "Statue Honors Once-Enslaved Woman Who Won Freedom in Court." *LNP/LancasterOnline,* August 22, 2022.

Remini, Robert V. "Henry Clay and the Historian: A One Hundred-Year Perspective: Review of Henry Clay, Statesman for the Union." *Florida Historical Quarterly* 71, no. 4 (1993). https://www.jstor.org/stable/30150394.

Reynolds, David S. *Mightier Than the Sword: Uncle Tom's Cabin and the Battle for America*. New York: W. W. Norton, 2011.

Robbins, Liz, and Sam Roberts. "Early Feminists Issued a Declaration of Independence. Where Is It Now?" *New York Times*, February 9, 2019. https://www.nytimes.com/interactive/2019/02/09/nyregion/declaration-of-sentiments-and-resolution-feminism.html.

Robertson, Andrew. "The Idealist as Opportunist: An Analysis of Thaddeus Stevens' Support in Lancaster County, 1834–1866." *Journal of the Lancaster County Historical Society* 84, no. 2 (1980).

Ryan, Thomas R., ed. *The Worlds of Jacob Eichholtz: Portrait Painter of the Early Republic*. Lancaster, PA: Lancaster County Historical Society, 2003.

Sandburg, Carl. *Abraham Lincoln: The Prairie Years and the War Years*. New York: Harcourt, 1954.

Schurz, Carl. *The Reminiscences of Carl Schurz, 1829–1906*. New York: McClure, 1907.

Scovel, James M. "Thaddeus Stevens." *Lippincott's Monthly Magazine* 61 (April 1898). https://www.google.com/books/edition/Lippincott_s_Monthly_Magazine/mt1EAQAAMAAJ.

Singmaster, Elsie. *I Speak for Thaddeus Stevens*. Boston: Houghton Mifflin, 1947.

Smedley, Robert Clemens. *History of the Underground Railroad in Chester and the Neighboring Counties of Pennsylvania*. Lancaster, PA: Office of the Journal, 1883. Reprint, Harrisburg, PA: Stackpole Books, 2005.

Smith, John David. "My Books Are Hard Reading for a Negro: Tom Dixon and His African American Critics, 1905–1939." In *Thomas Dixon Jr. and the Birth of Modern America*, edited by Michelle K. Gillespie and Randal L. Hall, 46–79. Baton Rouge: Louisiana State University Press, 2006.

Smull, John Augustus, William P. Smull, Thomas Baumgardner Cochran, and W. Harry Baker, eds. *Smull's Legislative Hand Book and Manual of the State of Pennsylvania*. Harrisburg: C. E. Aughinbaugh, printer to the State of Pennsylvania, 1913.

Stedman, H. B. "Henry Carpenter, M.D." In *History of Lancaster County, Pennsylvania: With Biographical Sketches of Its Pioneers and Prominent Men*, edited by Franklin Ellis and Samuel Evans, vol. 1, chap. 22. Lancaster County, PA: Everts & Peck, 1883.

Still, William. *The Underground Railroad: A Record of Facts, Authentic Narratives, Letters, etc.* Philadelphia: Porter & Coates, 1872.

Tosh, Ted Rockwell. *The Life and Times of Benjamin Helm Bristow*. New York: Page Publishing, 2016.

Trefousse, Hans L. *Thaddeus Stevens: Nineteenth-Century Egalitarian*. Mechanicsburg, PA: Stackpole Books, 2001.

Weaver, Jenine. "The Black Influence—Series 1: 1780–1850." *Gettysburg Connection*, March 2, 2021. https://gettysburgconnection.org/the-black-influence-series-1-1780-to-1850/.

Webster, Crystal Lynn. "The History of Black Girls and the Field of Black Girlhood Studies: At the Forefront of Academic Scholarship." *American Historian*, March 2020. https://www.oah.org/tah/issues/2020/the-history-of-girlhood/the-history-of-black-girls-and-the-field-of-black-girlhood-studies-at-the-forefront-of-academic/.

Wheeler, Linda. "Hunt On for Virginia's Long Lost Camp Casey." *Washington Post*, February 27, 2015. https://www.washingtonpost.com/news/house-divided /wp/2015/02/27/hunt-on-for-virginias-long-lost-camp-casey/.

White, Horace. *The Life of Lyman Trumbull*. Boston: Houghton Mifflin, 1913.

Wilkinson, William Cleaver. *Daniel Webster: A Vindication, with Other Historical Essays*. New York: Funk & Wagnalls, 1911.

Woodburn, James Albert. *The Life of Thaddeus Stevens: A Study in American Political History, Especially in the Period of the Civil War and Reconstruction*. New York: Bobbs-Merrill, 1913. https://archive.org/details/lifethaddeus00woodrich.

Woodley, Thomas Frederick. *Great Leveler: The Life of Thaddeus Stevens*. New York: Stackpole Sons, 1937.

INDEX